ARMIES AND WARFARE
IN THE
PIKE-AND-SHOT ERA

By the same author

All for a Shilling a Day
Captain Carey's Blunder
At Them With the Bayonet!
Colonial Small Wars 1837–1902
Conflict in Hampshire
The Bowmen of England
The Weapons and Equipment of the Victorian Soldier
Victoria's Enemies – 19th Century Colonial Wars
Victorian Military Campaigns in Africa
Victorian Military Campaigns in India
Khartoum; the Gordon Relief Expedition 1884/5
Tel-el-Kebir; the War with Egypt 1882
Omdurman: Kitchener's Dongola Campaign 1896/8
Campaigning with the Duke of Wellington;
the Peninsular War 1808/1814 (published in Chicago 1993)
Khaki and Red: N. W. Frontier India 19th Century
Redcoats for the Raj; 'Tales from a Victorian Barrackroom'
– an historical novel
Warriors and Warfare in Ancient and Medieval Times

Armies and Warfare in the Pike-and-Shot Era

Donald Featherstone

CONSTABLE · LONDON

First published in Great Britain 1998
by Constable and Company Limited
3 The Lanchesters, 162 Fulham Palace Road
London W6 9ER
Copyright © Donald Featherstone 1998
The right of Donald Featherstone to be identified
as the author of this work has been asserted by him
in accordance with the Copyright, Designs and Patents Act 1988
ISBN 0 09 478410 8
Set in Linotron Sabon 10½ pt by
SetSystems Ltd, Saffron Walden, Essex
Printed in Great Britain by
St Edmundsbury Press Ltd
Bury St Edmunds, Suffolk

A CIP catalogue record for this book
is available from the British Library

CONTENTS

CONTENTS

Introduction

THE 'PIKE-AND-SHOT' ERA lasted roughly from the mid-fifteenth to late-seventeenth centuries, when many forward steps in the art of warfare were brought about by the replacement of the bow and hand-hurled weapons by artillery and hand-held fire-arms. Its beginning heralded the conclusion of the Middle Ages and was marked by such notable military events as the fall of Constantinople, the end of the Hundred Years War, the Wars of the Roses and Charles VIII's invasion of Italy. These conflicts were all greatly influenced by gunpowder weapons, which so dominated the battlefield in the sixteenth century that body-armour was discarded, save for light 'Prestige' armour worn by the nobility and the pikeman's helmet and breastplate, also used by the heavy cavalry. The military social system was turned upside down by the English yeoman and the Swiss pikeman as they shook the dominance of the knight, who found himself superseded by the common handgunner and the artilleryman. Ironically, the knight's body armour became obsolescent at the same time as it reached its peak of development.

The late fifteenth century, a crucial epoch of change which marked the beginning of the Reformation and the inspirational forces leading to the Renaissance, saw the development of complex political patterns in Europe and a bitter religious struggle brought about a period of military uncertainty. There was blundering experimentation in the tactical and technical introduction of gunpowder, as artillery completed the discomfort and downfall of the heavy armoured cavalry-man, a process begun by the longbow and the pike, both of which were the forerunners of Western infantry, when the missile-throwing hand weapon combined in principle with the pike to become musket and bayonet. This, together with the remorseless advance of field artillery, laid the foundations of modern warfare.

The Mediaeval formation of three dense 'battles', or blocks of mounted men and infantry, lingered until the early years of the sixteenth century, although extremely vulnerable to fire-arms and artillery. Small-arms became more decisive than artillery and French supremacy in this arm, achieved at the end of the previous century, was rapidly reversed by improved handling of small-arms by Spanish infantry, who were consistently ahead of other nations in their development and employment. But towards the end of the period, the French became almost as accomplished, after a series of disas-trous defeats inflicted upon them by the Spaniards.

The period saw the progressive importance of fire-arms and, partly arising from this, the increased development of field fortifications or entrenchments, which made cavalry charges impracticable. Perhaps more significant was the appreciation of the value of the well-trained and disciplined foot-soldier, notably the Swiss pikeman and the German landsknecht who successfully defeated both cavalry and infantry. But, in a period of constant change, in time the fearful attacks of redoubtable formations such as these began to be held in check by the fire of arquebusiers, which led to far-seeing commanders employing missile-men and cavalry alongside their pikemen. The rapidly increasing effectiveness of gunpowder-weapons running par-allel to the resurgence of the infantryman laid the foundations of tactical combinations of cavalry/infantry/artillery for the four centur-ies that followed.

The manner of warfare itself began to change and it became slightly less creditable to win a pitched battle than to achieve success by manoeuvre, or by cutting the enemy's line of communication, by starving him out, or by distracting him through the sudden movement of hostile troops to an unguarded front. Generals who had not suffered disaster were equally esteemed with those who had won positive successes. The French and Dutch Wars of Religion in the late sixteenth century were notable for the manner in which generals

waited to see how the balance of forces might change, often neglect-
ing tactical advantages in the hope that a few more weeks of physical
and financial starvation would bankrupt their enemy and so make
battle unnecessary. Commanding-generals were thus placed in a
difficult position, never knowing when their armies were going to
melt away according to the vagaries of their mercenaries; if morale
was low and pay in arrears then commanders tended to manoeuvre
cautiously and avoid decisions.

Small-arms were very effective but musketeers were extremely
vulnerable when reloading, nor could the arquebuses be fired quickly
enough to protect their users from a) the dreaded 'push of pike', b)
the onslaught of cavalry or c) even the Spanish sword-and-buckler-
men, so that they had to be protected by pikemen whilst other
arquebusiers (crossbowmen in the French army) kept the enemy at a
distance. Thus was combined the effects of fire-power with offensive
shock-action – of great tactical importance during the slow and
painful process of forming-up a sixteenth-century army for battle.
Realising that the successful army was that which possessed the right
proportion of the various arms, commanders continually sought a
system that gave maximum benefit from fire-power. They blended
cavalry shock-action with small-arms attack, together with artillery
fire, pike assaults and field fortifications. The Spaniard Gonsalvo de
Córdoba successfully employed entrenched arquebusiers to hold and
defeat much larger French forces. Soon the increased effectiveness of
the fire-arms together with the growing strength of fortifications
forced generals to accept battle only when they were sure of being
successful. The Battle of Ceresole in 1544, the half-way point in the
century, confirmed that infantry (musketeers, Swiss and landsknecht
pikemen) could repulse a cavalry attack, other than in flank. In this
conflict, Swiss infantry and French cavalry almost completely wiped
out 7,000 landsknechts fighting for the Spanish. The expense and
unreliability of mercenaries made commanders reluctant to give
battle and was a primary factor in keeping armies small in size.
Although well disciplined and good fighters, mercenaries lacking
patriotic feeling were hard to handle, and frequently refused to fight
at the start of the battle unless paid a bonus, otherwise threatening
to join the enemy. Unable to afford to maintain a standing army, in
wartime rulers relied upon hired mercenaries to augment their rela-

tively small permanent army. The French permanent units were mostly cavalry reinforced by German reiters and their infantry were Swiss mercenaries or German landsknechts.

To sum up, early in the period massed phalanxes of pikemen, particularly the Swiss, were capable of sweeping both infantry and cavalry from the field; while in other armies, massed formations of pikemen countered the shock tactics of heavily armoured horsemen armed with the lance. Then the arquebus was superseded by the longer-range musket but musketeers still had to be protected by pikemen, although the effectiveness of massed formations of pikes was countered by tactics of fire and movement. Musketeers were grouped in combined formations with pikemen until the invention of the bayonet rendered the pikeman obsolete and the universal infantryman came on to the battlefields of the world. The lance of the cavalryman was replaced by the pistol and the sword, although the pistol was their prime weapon and they rarely charged home. Cavalry still used shot as their main weapon but the armoured horseman first fired his pistol into the closely packed ranks of the enemy to force a gap before charging.

Infantry moved on their own two feet from the very beginnings of warfare until the Second World War, not marching in cadenced step until the middle of the eighteenth century. The sixteenth century saw the resurgence of infantrymen, but even so they could no longer march on to the field of battle like the Swiss phalanx, because of the missile weapons arrayed against them. On the other hand, the cavalry did not ride down their own infantry in their chivalrous eagerness to get at the foe, as the French did at Crécy in 1346.

1

The Arrival of Gunpowder

THE DATE OF THE invention of gunpowder is veiled in mists of antiquity, although in 1249 the English friar Roger Bacon is reputed to have made a cryptic announcement which has been accepted as the first recognisable mention of the substance. The 'Greek Fire' employed by the defenders of Constantinople against the Saracens in 673 is thought to have been a form of gunpowder, and it has been said that the early Chinese had knowledge of a similar incendiary substance. However, the historian Sir Charles Oman was sceptical about any possibilities of Eastern origins:

> All attempts to prove that the credit of discovering gunpowder should be assigned to the Chinese, the Arabs or even the Hindus comes from misconceptions as to the meaning of certain words describing military devices . . . There would seem to be no doubt that the Chinese possessed incendiary compounds, as did the Byzantines, long before the tenth century of our era. But that they had explosive compounds is nowhere proven.

Similarly, the fourteenth-century claims of a German monk, Berthold Schwarz, have been dismissed as being too vague.

Resembling the common black powder of much later years, early gunpowder consisted of a mixture of saltpetre (potassium nitrate or nitre), charcoal and sulphur. Within a generation of these early examples of gunpowder, the explosive had become well-known, and within sixty years its powers were being used for the propulsion of missiles.

In past years the artefacts of war had been readily available and comparatively cheap, and bows, arrows, spears and the like could be hand-manufactured in large quantities, although armour was beyond the reach of the common man. The dawn of gunpowder gave rise to a small but flourishing munitions industry, foundries springing up throughout Europe to supply the growing need. But an economic factor was also created, bombards and handguns were costly and only wealthier communities and lords, barons and the like could afford them in any numbers.

Perhaps through lack of communication or simplicity of the mediaeval mind, this world-shaking innovation that was to revolutionise warfare and, with it, the history of the world, was accepted with a calmness that possibly explains the early obscurity surrounding the origin of fire-arms. Accepting that soldiers do not welcome change that clashes with acknowledged military tradition, it would seem that scholars of the day similarly showed little foresight when considering the role of gunpowder weapons in the future march of civilisation.

ARTILLERY

Gunpowder weapons appeared in the first quarter of the fourteenth century; it is known that 'guns with powder' were imported into England from Ghent in 1314 and bombards are mentioned in accounts of a siege of Metz in 1324, while the earliest pictorial proof is in the Millemete Manuscript of 1327 which depicts an armoured knight applying a linstock to a vase-shaped piece carrying a feathered bolt. This fits with the French naming their earliest gunpowder weapons *pots de fer*, crude, squat bell-mouthed pieces with very short ranges. These were the origin of the mortar, a wide-mouthed weapon capable of high-trajectory fire that could drop a cannon-ball over the ramparts of a besieged town or castle, and they were also the tactical ancestor of the modern howitzer. It is known that there were a few gunpowder weapons at the Battle of Crécy in 1346 but they did not have any influence on the result, just as at Agincourt in

1415 when French artillery pieces seemed to have been masked by their own troops. So far as the Hundred Years War is concerned it was not until the siege of Orléans in 1428–29 that recorded instances of the use of artillery can be found.

By the middle of the fourteenth century, artillery had ceased to be a novelty, and by the fifteenth century every European army fielded guns, and they had been introduced into Asia by the Turks. It is not unreasonable to say that, apart from their 'fear factor', they were probably only a little more effective than the ballistae, the onagri, the catapultra, and the carro-ballistae, competently handled by the Romans, among others, many centuries before. These Mediaeval artillery pieces were simple cast-iron or wrought-iron tubes, transported on ox-drawn sledges and needing emplacement on earthen mounds or log platforms, so that the bombard was unsuitable for field operations and used only for sieges. The situation was changed in the early years of the century, when the introduction of the culverin provided the first field-piece. Mounted on sledges at first, although by the middle of the century wheels were in use, the culverin had a bore of one to three inches. However, the development of artillery weapons at this time failed to keep in step with that of small-arms simply because of the difficulties of combining mobility with reliable long-range fire-power.

Mortars and bombards of large calibre outnumbered the culverins, for the best results of the current artillery were secured in siegecraft. Some guns were huge, to the extent that to this day they still attract exclamations of wonder from viewers – one such is 'Mons Meg', which can be seen in Edinburgh Castle, an early fifteenth-century wrought-iron bombard with a bore of twenty-inches which fired a stone ball weighing 300 pounds. There were even larger bores, on monsters with a range of but a few hundred yards.

Jan Ziska, in the Hussite Wars (1419–34), was the first soldier to use artillery with tactical intelligence in a manner 200 years ahead of his time, his wagon-forts being the first – and only – approach to the problem of field artillery in the early fifteenth century. His system was to emplace bombards in the intervals between his wagons so that they, in conjunction with infantry well-armed with handguns, successfully repulsed all attacking cavalry and infantry, allowing the inevitable fierce Hussite counterattack. The sole snag in this concept was that the enemy had to be the first to attack, because Ziska always emplaced his guns in the wagon-fort, on suitable ground, prior to the start of the battle.

It was in France that the greatest advances in gun-making and gunnery in general were made, notably by the Bureau Brothers, beginning in about 1440 and leading to a relatively sudden end to the Hundred Years War (1337–1453). The English system of men-at-arms fighting on foot supported by large flanking formations of archers had brought almost uninterrupted success from Crécy in 1346, through Poitiers in 1356 to Agincourt in 1415 and Verneuil in 1422, but its weaknesses were exposed at Formigny in 1450 and Castillon-on-the-Gironde in 1453, the last two battles the English fought in France during this war. At Formigny, French artillery fire forced a disastrous counter-attack, as it did at Castillon three years later, when the redoubtable Talbot made a hopelessly futile assault on artillery massed behind entrenchments, losing his life in the process. Before those battles the French, with amazing speed, besieged and captured English-held towns and castles, battering them into submission with their artillery.

By the end of the fifteenth century, artillery had made mediaeval fortifications obsolete. This was not entirely due to its wall-battering qualities but also because such fortifications had not solved the problem of emplacing large cannon suitable for counter-battery work.

Remaining pre-eminent among artillerists, in the last decade of the fifteenth century the French introduced true field-artillery, demonstrating its worth in a significant victory at Fornovo in 1495, when their new mobile field artillery – light cast-bronze cannon on two-wheeled horse-drawn carriages – rapidly unharnessed, unlimbered and went promptly into action from a march column. Some French cannon at Fornovo had trunnions, which facilitated both the mounting of cannon on permanent wheeled-carriages and reasonably accurate aiming and ranging – a great improvement on earlier methods of raising and lowering the weapon's bore. The French had evolved the principle of the limber, besides training drivers of lighter guns to move as rapidly as light cavalry, and could claim at this time to have cannon for every conceivable purpose of siege or battlefield. The French could parade a great train of artillery, including cannons, culverins and falcons, with the largest gun weighing 6,000 pounds

[8]

and mounted on wheels, the smallest firing shot no bigger than medical pills. In 1494 Charles VIII of France's expedition to Naples was the wonder of the age, with huge guns requiring twelve horses to draw their four-wheeled carriages, besides the already mentioned artillery.

However, nothing stands still in life, certainly not weapons of war, and it was not far into the sixteenth century when French artillery supremacy was overhauled and overshadowed by dramatic Spanish advances in infantry small-arms and their tactical employment. At about the same time, the French lost their superiority in artillery construction and techniques to the more imaginative German gun-makers, who in their turn were soon overshadowed by the Spanish in both artillery and almost every other aspect of military science for the rest of the century. As a result of all this neutralisation artillery tended to decline in importance during the sixteenth century, except in attack/defence of fortifications and in naval warfare. Although few major battles were fought without artillery, after the bloody Battle of Ravenna in 1512, small-arms became more decisive.

In the seventeenth century, that outstanding Swedish soldier Gustavus Adolphus revolutionised the employment of artillery by a series of brilliant innovations in tactical, technical and organisational fields, among them the four-pounder infantry-support field-pieces capable of being handled by four men and drawn by a single horse; each 1,000-strong infantry regiment had two guns and with them, using the first-ever artillery cartridge, eight rounds could be discharged while musketeers fired six volleys. The Swedish two-pounder swivel breech loaders could fire three times as quickly as comparable enemy artillery, and even the heavier brass cannon and howitzers were light enough to keep up with infantry and cavalry.

The English Civil War (1642–51) reveals a marked paucity of accurate information on artillery in the conflict, so that it is difficult to assess period-trends in that field, although in general artillery does seem to play a relatively insignificant part. Battle accounts tell of tactical success by small numbers of guns at 1st Newbury in 1643 in the area of Round Hill, and at Langport in 1645 while Prince Rupert lost all his guns at Marston Moor (his 'Galloping Guns' were a genuine form of horse artillery). There seems to have been a marked tendency for artillery to become lighter and more mobile and the Swedish 'battalion' gun was in constant use, as were James Wemyss's leather guns. Both Royalist and Parliamentary armies followed the Swedish practice of attaching two light field-pieces to each regiment of Foot. The amateur civilian armies of the Civil War knew of the excellent use of artillery in the Thirty Years War but rarely got around to attempting any emulation, seemingly regarding artillery as a branch of science not far removed from the occult!

Not only in the English Civil War but also in other wars of the period, and indeed for some future years, artillery commanders were soldiers, but some of the gunners, the transporters and drivers were civilians, often running away when battle commenced. This meant that the Fusilier companies, designated as artillery-guards, found themselves more often preventing their own men from running away than protecting them from the enemy, whose musketeers frequently picked off the gunners. Ammunition supply, made difficult by bad roads and poor communications, presented recurrent logistical problems, and there was a perpetual danger from explosions of gunpowder – at the siege of Reading in 1643 an officer, firing a cannon, 'by chance, fired the powder barrels', killing and wounding several men. The powder-charge was sometimes re-packed into cartridges, but mostly it was simply carried in a barrel, being transferred to the gun by a metal scoop; artillery drill-books of the time emphasised the importance of covering the powder barrel to prevent accidents.

During the days of the Covenanter Wars – and extending for more than 100 years, to the battles of the '45 – it was a distinct asset for armies facing Scottish Highlanders to be equipped with artillery, because the Scots detested artillery, and called guns 'the musket's mother', needing much persuasion before facing them. Scots armies were always short of ammunition for the few guns they possessed, often going into battle with only a single round per piece; more often than not, their armies were completely without guns.

Until comparatively modern times, solid shot was the standard projectile, and throughout the Middle Ages, for reasons of economy, stone-shot was preferred to that of iron and major towns maintained ammunition quarries. Red-hot shot and crude incendiary shells were used before 1470, and gunners of the fourteenth century are known to have experimented with hollow iron spheres whose two halves were filled with gunpowder and clamped or screwed together. Such projectiles were 'grenades' when round and 'bombs' when oblong and were detonated by a time-fuse which was affixed to them and lit before firing. Devised to cause widespread damage, stone or leaden balls were packed into a bag or container with a wooden base, and scattered when leaving the gun's mouth. Known as 'case-shot', it came into use about the middle of the fifteenth century. An early version consisted of ramming 'langridge' – loose fragments of iron and flint – into the bore of the gun, secured by a wad of moss before firing, and spreading lethally on leaving the barrel.

The fifteenth century saw most existing fortifications rendered obsolete by the frightening advance of field artillery. Perhaps the most dramatic demonstration of the effectiveness of the new gunpowder weapons in siegecraft was seen at the siege of Constantinople in 1453. This was a city with legendary massive walls and fortifications which had defied innumerable assaults for centuries; yet the devastating artillery of Mohammed II battered them down and ended the siege in a mere fifty-five days. This siege-success was also aided by mining operations by the besiegers, demonstrating another important use to which gunpowder could be put.

However, victory was not inevitable. In 1428, an English army, complete with siege-train of mortars and bombards drawn by oxen, appeared before the ancient city of Orléans on the Loire, which had prepared itself thoroughly for a major struggle by providing itself with a concentration of artillery, much borrowed from neighbouring towns, of seventy mortars, bombards and culverins, besides other war-engines. Manned by a strong garrison, the town walls were six feet thick and rose impressively to a height of thirty-three feet above the moat, with five gates and thirty-four towers completing a system of outer defences, topped by stone battlements and parapets. For seven months both besieged and besiegers fought an artillery duel of attrition, revealing that, as relatively late in the gunpowder period as 1428–29 while artillery could crush lesser strongholds, strong-walled cities still had a good chance of holding out. Orléans was relieved by a force led by Joan of Arc in May 1429.

Moving ahead 100 years, the situation had changed and it was apparent that city walls and mediaeval ramparts could no longer withstand the artillery of the day; hitherto invincible cities reluctantly replaced their centuries-old walls with elaborate enceintes, with bastions and glacis, horn works and covered-ways. New cities, like Hesdin, Vitry and Havre, were built with modern defences, and instead of stark high walls challenging the besieger's guns, the new

works of military architects encouraged digging-in and laying low –
the scientific engineer was once more prevailing over the artillerist.
Now, sweeping conquests of mediaeval fortresses, antiquated cities
and the like by pounding artillery was no longer possible, as scientific
fortifications became the vogue – owing much to Gonsalvo Fernández
de Córdoba at Cerignola, and to be seen at Ravenna and Bicocca,
both stages for fierce acts of warfare. Sieges began to last far longer
as wars went on, as at Ostend when an interminable siege straggled
its way through three summers, from 1600 to 1604. The Dutch-
Spanish Wars in the Netherlands was transformed into one long
series of field operations, lacking field-battles for long periods. Truly,
the spade had secured mastery over the cannon-ball.

Gunpowder, and the improved weapons it spawned, brought
about a revolution in tactics that did not impress dyed-in-the-wool
soldiers of the old school. During the War of the Roses (1455–85),
it is recorded that the Lancastrians regarded it as an atrocity that the
Yorkists were 'traitoriously ranged in bataille . . . their cartes with
gonnes set before their batailles'. Yet, within only a generation, a
score of years, everyone was using wheeled cannon.

2

Archer to Arquebusier –
The Decline of the English Longbow

AT THE TIME OF the expulsion of the English from their Continental possessions, no blame was laid at the door of the longbow, nor did there seem to be any permanent discrediting of its power. Nevertheless, as future events proved, in spite of the triple victories of Crécy, Poitiers and Agincourt, to say nothing of many lesser successes, archery was in decline as a weapon of war in the mid-fifteenth century. However, the bow still retained its supremacy as a missile weapon over the clumsy arbalest, with its complicated array of wheels and levers. In fact, the testimony of all Europe was given in favour of the longbow – Charles of Burgundy considered a corps of 3,000 English bowmen to be the flower of his infantry; thirty years before, Charles of France had made the archer the basis of his new militia in a vain attempt to naturalise the weapon of his enemies beyond the Channel. After a similar endeavour, James of Scotland had resigned himself to ill success and so made the archery of his subjects the object of ridicule. Before that, however, he had ordered a law to be passed by the Scottish Parliament in 1424:

That all men might busk thame to be archares, fra they be 12 years of age; and that at ilk ten pounds worth of land, thair be made bow makres, and specialle near paroche kirks, quhairn upon hailie days men may cum, and at the leist schute thrusye ab out, and have usye of archarie; and whassa usis not archarie, the laird of the land sall rais of him a wedder, and giff the laird raisis not the same pane, the kings shiref or his ministers sall rais it to the King.

In England Edward IV proclaimed that every Englishman and Irishman living in England must have a bow of his own height 'to be made of yew, wych, or hazel, ash or auborne or any other reasonable tree, according to their power'. The same law provided that buttes or mounds of earth for use as marks must be erected in every town and village, and listed a series of penalties for those who did not practise with the longbow. Richard III was one of the kings who recognised the value of the archer; Shakespeare makes him say, just prior to the Battle of Bosworth: 'Draw archers, draw your arrows to the head!' It is also recorded that Richard sent a body of 1,000 archers to France to aid the Duke of Brittany. Henry VII also provided anti-crossbow legislation and sent large levies of English archers to fight for the Duke of Brittany. During this entire period English longbowmen served in many parts of the then known world.

The introduction of gunpowder was the beginning of the end for the archer; although over 400 years were to pass before the bow and arrow were finally overcome by gunfire, the seeds were sown in the fourteenth century at Crécy and Sluys. The making of a skilful archer was a matter of years, but an adequate gunner could be produced in a few months – it was far too easy to attain a certain amount of proficiency with the new weapons for the bow to retain its popularity. At first the longbow was vastly superior to the newly invented handguns and arquebuses, which did not attain any great degree of efficiency before the end of the fifteenth century. When they did, the bow – the weapon par excellence of England – fell into disuse, although the archer could discharge twelve or fifteen arrows while the musketeer was going through the lengthy operation of loading his piece. The longbow could be aimed more accurately and its effective range of 200-240 yards was greater; the hitting-power of a war-arrow, weighing about two ounces, was far greater than that of a musket-ball, weighing from one-third to half an ounce. Archers could be lined up as many as ten deep and shoot together over each other's heads to put down an almost impassable barrage; and it was a terrifying barrage that could be seen descending. It is not unreasonable to claim that the musket used at Waterloo in 1815 was inferior

[14]

to the longbow used at Agincourt in 1415, both in range and accuracy.

Early fire-arms were reasonably good weapons of defence when they could be rested upon ramparts and their powder kept dry, otherwise they were far less deadly than the longbow in competent hands. In 1590 Sir John Smyth, a formidable military writer of the time, in his work *The Discourse* presented a wholesale condemnation of the new weapons, the 'mosquet', the caliver and the 'harquebus'. The book was hastily suppressed by English military authorities; the stern, lone voice, crying for a return to the older and more effective ways of the longbow, did not coincide with current military thinking. One also has to consider that the merit of early fire-arms lay in the prestige which they brought to the princes who armed their men with them.

In many of the battles of the War of the Roses, artillery was combined with archers, so that the enemy was put in a position where he had either to fall back or to charge in order to escape missile fire just as similar tactics had won the field of Hastings for William in 1066. At Edgecott Field spearmen made a renewed attempt to stand against a mixed force or archers and cavalry. Here the Yorkists were entirely destitute of light troops, their bowmen having been drawn off by their commander, Lord Stafford, in a fit of pique. This meant that Pembroke and his North Welsh troops were left unsupported. The natural result followed; in spite of the strong position of the King's son, the rebels, by force of archery fire, quickly caused them to descend from the hill into the valley, where they were ridden down by the Northern horse as they retreated in disorder.

During the period of this war, armour had possibly reached its elaborate peak, as an old description of a knight arming for the Battle of Tewkesbury indicated:

> . . . and arming was an elaborate process then, as the knight began with his feet, and clothed himself upwards. He put on first, his sabatynes or steel clogs; secondly, the greaves or shin-pieces; thirdly, the cuisses, or thigh-pieces; fourthly, the breech of mail; fifthly, the tuillettes; sixthly, the breastplate; seventhly, the vambraces or arm-covers; eighthly, the rerebraces, for covering the remaining part of the arm to the shoulder; ninthly, the gauntlets;

tenthly, the dagger was hung; eleventhly, the short sword; twelfthly, the surcoat was put on; thirteenthly, the helmet, fourteenthly, the long sword was assumed; and, fifteenthly, the pennoncel, which he carried in his left hand.

Notwithstanding the undoubted strength of this array, the archer still appeared to achieve sufficient penetration with his shafts to be considered a worthwhile part of the forces.

At Towton, on Palm Sunday, 29 March 1461, Lord Falconbridge, commanding part of the army of Edward IV, used his archers in an interesting tactical expedient which sufficed to decide the day when both armies were employing the same weapon. The snow, which was falling very heavily, was being blown by a strong wind from behind the Yorkists and into the faces of the Lancastrians; it rendered the opposing lines only partially visible to each other. Falconbridge ordered his archers to the front, to act more or less as skirmishers. It must be explained that two types of arrows were then in use – the flight arrow and the sheaf arrow. The former was lightly feathered, with a small head; the latter was high-feathered and shortly shafted with a large head. Flight arrows were shot at a great distance and, at proper elevation, could kill at 240 yards. Sheaf arrows were for closer fighting, requiring but a slight elevation, and were often shot at point-blank range.

The advancing archers had been carefully instructed to let fly a shower of sheaf arrows, with a greater elevation than usual, and then to fall back some paces and stand. Aided by the gale, the Yorkist arrows fell among the Lancastrian archers, who, perceiving that they were sheaf arrows and being misled by the blinding snow as to their opponents' exact distance from them, assumed that the enemy were within easy range. They commenced firing volley after volley into the snowstorm, all of which fell sixty yards short of the Yorkists until the snow bristled with the uselessly expended shafts like porcupine quills. When the Lancastrians had emptied their belts, the Yorkists moved forward and began firing in return, using not only their own shafts but also those so conveniently sticking out of the snow at their feet. Their shooting had great effect and men fell on all sides as the wind-assisted shafts came hissing into them; in a short time it was possible for the billmen and men-at-arms of Warwick and King Edward to advance comfortably forward without receiving any harassing fire from the Lancastrian archers. Needless to say, the Yorkist archers then laid aside their bows and went in with the more heavily armed infantry. It was a stratagem that won the battle, and was one that could only be used when the adversaries were perfectly conversant with each other's armaments and methods of war.

Even in the late fifteenth and early sixteenth centuries the longbow still retained its supremacy over the arquebus and had yet some famous fields to win, notably that of Flodden in 1513, where, as will be seen from the next chapter, the old manoeuvres of Falkirk were repeated by both parties, the pikemen of the lowlands once again being shot to pieces by the archers of Cheshire and Lancashire. As late as the reign of Edward VI we find Kett's Insurgents beating, by the rapidity of their archery fire, a corps of German hackbuteers whom the government had sent against them. Nor was the bow entirely extinct as a national weapon even in the days of Queen Elizabeth. It was in the reign of the Virgin Queen that the first really great archery writer appeared on the English scene. Roger Ascham, tutor to Elizabeth when she was a princess, was the author of the book *Toxophilus*, which remains the classic in the field. Allowing for certain minor differences, the phraseology and certain advances which have been made in equipment, Ascham's book is as valuable to the archer today as it was when it was written four centuries ago. His 'instructions' can be, and are, used today in teaching novice archers. Ascham's relation to the bow corresponds to that of Izaak Walton to the rod and reel.

3

Arrows versus Artillery –
The Last Battles of the
Hundred Years War

THE SECOND QUARTER of the fifteenth century found France, for the first time perhaps, facing up to the fact that the old, chivalrous methods of warfare paid no dividends; that some effective innovation had to be discovered to combat the English system. Through bitter necessity and hard experience, the professional officers of France – Xaintrailles, La Hire and Dunois, for example – stumbled upon a method of minimising the superiority of the English archers. It was so simple that it had probably been considered and discarded many times; in short, when the English were found drawn up in a good defensive position, the French refused to attack. For the first time the French acknowledged that there was little or no chance of beating an English army in such a position and that there was little point in sending forward large bodies of troops as a target to be riddled with English arrows. The French commanders knew that the longbow could keep more heavily armed men at a distance – therein lay its superiority. But once the cavalry or men-at-arms got among the archers and their supporting men-at-arms, weight of numbers might well decide the resulting *mêlée* and the French could usually put more men into the field.

With this enlightenment came some French victories; the usual tactical causes of the English defeats lay in the French attacking them when they were on the march, in camp or in towns where it was impossible quickly to form an order of battle on ground specifically chosen for its defensive qualities. The tendency towards a reversal in the almost monotonous run of English victories inevitably led to a noticeable shedding of the old confidence born of persistent success over men using futile tactics. There was a little more caution, initiative became stifled and plans could not be made with the former certainty of success. Both commanders and men in the English armies were too experienced and professional in their outlook for this new development to unduly undermine their morale, but they were per- turbed, almost indignant. Naturally, with success and the knowledge that the English were not quite so sure of themselves, French confi- dence flowered and they began to seek, and win, conflicts where they were able, in a sudden onslaught, to hit the English before they could form up defensively.

The English commanders, with the traditions of Crécy, Poitiers, Agincourt and a host of similar but smaller battles behind them, disliked taking the offensive. When the opposing commanders refused to attack them in their carefully chosen position, but instead held off until such time as they could assail when least expected, then the English began to lose battles. The Battle of Patay, fought on the 18 June 1429, is typical of the sort of conflict that now took place, with the English being liable to a sudden onslaught.

Patay occurred at a time when the French, inspired by Joan of Arc, had recently raised the siege of Orléans and were endeavouring to capture those Loire towns still in English hands. An English force under Lord John Talbot and Sir John Fastolf, numbering perhaps 3,000 men, was retreating towards Patay after an unsuccessful attack on the Loire bridge at Meung, eighteen miles south. Hot on their heels were the mounted vanguard of the Duke d'Alençon, moving considerably faster than the English, who were regulated by the speed of their baggage-train. In their attempts to make contact with the enemy, d'Alençon had patrols scouting in all directions; the English had similar groups in their rear to warn them of the arrival of the enemy. The word eventually came – the French advance-guard was close on their heels; at about the same moment the French discovered the whereabouts of the English, who revealed their position by characteristically raucous 'Halloos!' as a stag burst through their ranks!

Halting at a point where their track diverged from the old Roman road over which they had been marching, the English looked in a hurry for a good defensive position. The country was dotted with small clumps of trees and hedges, some of which bordered the road and were ideal for lining with archers; in a slight dip in the ground, Talbot stood with about 500 men. Fastolf deployed the main body on a ridge south-east of Patay, about 200 yards behind Talbot.

Topping the slight rise, the mounted French advance-guard saw the English drawn up in the dip in front of them; the archers were hammering their stakes into the ground and preparing their bows. Composed of specially selected men, well mounted and led by La Hire and Poton de Xaintrailles, two of the most experienced commanders in the French army, it was a force alight with fervour imparted to the whole army by the Maid of Orléans. Pausing only to take in the situation, the cavalry thundered down the slope in a wild torrent to burst upon the startled archers before a bow could be drawn upon them, hitting them frontally and in flank. The lightly armed infantry stood no chance whatsoever; they were overwhelmed in a matter of seconds and cut down where they stood, the few who did manage to scramble away only adding to the confusion and dismay that covered Fastolf's men on the ridge.

Well might they be dismayed; their deployment on the ridge had been slow and they were far from completing their formation. They were not a particularly well-trained or experienced bunch of men, besides being dispirited by the retreat from Meung. They were able to do practically nothing before the French were through Talbot's force and upon them. The situation was made even more grave by the rapid arrival of the French main body, right on the heels of their advance-guard. It was all over very quickly; Talbot and most of the other leaders were captured, but Fastolf managed to get away, leaving behind his baggage and guns. His escape was a little epic in itself, consisting of marching sixty miles in a day and a night, formed up in a stout body of archers who fought off every attack with arrows and then, when they were all gone, taking to the sword before reaching safety. But their weary steps were dogged with confusion and bewilderment – never before had they experienced anything like the French cavalry's headlong charge; they found it difficult to fathom this dramatic transition from the usual French prudence tinged with apprehension.

It was a bewilderment that was to grow. For more than 100 years the tactical employment of the English archer had brought success and each battle can be said to have favourably influenced the battle that followed. Crécy had been won because of the experience gained at Halidon Hill; Agincourt was, in its turn, influenced by Crécy and Poitiers. Now the wheel was turning. The side that had always won were prevented from continuing their victorious path because their opponents no longer played the game to the heavily loaded English rules. And the wheel turned in another inverse manner – just as the French had been continuously beaten through a slavish adherence to outmoded tactics, now came an anomalous turn. English commanders were being defeated by the improved military skill of the French because they persisted in slavishly applying the defensive tactics of Edward III and Henry V. For more than a century the French had been desperately trying to discover a method or a tactic that would minimise the deadly longbow; now it was the turn of the English to think hard. They had to come up with some new system as successful as the longbow to deal with the superior numbers of the French, otherwise the English were foredoomed to defeat by their numerical inferiority.

The running sore that was the Hundred Years War slithered into its century of years – having begun at Morlaix in 1337 – with a truce made in 1444, when Charles VII was on the throne of France. It was a time when the dragging conflict was slowly slipping away from England, as their hold on Normandy and Guienne remorselessly loosened. The French King seized the opportunity to execute a series of long meditated and much needed reforms in the French army, laying the foundation of the national standing army, as their military organisation, spurred by a century of disappointment and failure, took a gigantic leap ahead of England's. He established a national militia of fifteen companies of men-at-arms and archers, each 600-strong; organised town garrisons of trained men and improved equipment, discipline and regular payment. But most important of all, he formed the finest artillery park seen in the world up to that time.

The English made no similar efforts, and the conduct and morale of their irregularly paid troops on French soil was said to have been less than might have been expected of them. Inevitably, the now confident and well organised French broke the truce in 1449 by invading Normandy, an English dominion, capturing town after town until the province fell into their hands like a pack of cards. In 1450 reinforcements were scraped-up in an attempt to save Normandy, and on the 15 April of that year a major battle was fought at Formigny, not far from Omaha Beach of D-Day fame. An impressive monument commemorating the Battle of Formigny stands at the junction of a main thoroughfare and a lesser road leading inland from the beach, incongruously blending with the many smaller and less classical memorials of the major war fought almost 500 years later.

The English lost the Battle of Formigny because their commanders were still influenced by the tactics of Agincourt, while the French no longer made the blunders of past years. It was the penultimate battle of the Hundred Years War – a small-scale engagement, but one that decided the fate of all Normandy.

The prelude to the battle was the threat posed to the Duke of Somerset, commander of all the English armies in France, by an overwhelming French force, led by King Charles of France in person. In order to provide Somerset with reinforcements, an English army of about 4,000 men had been scraped together by stripping Norman fortresses of their garrisons and bringing some 2,500 reinforcements from England, under the command of Sir Thomas Kyriell. It was a force made up of a few hundred men-at-arms, about 1,500 archers and the remainder billmen.

At first the force had some successes and by mid-April they had come to the area around the village of Formigny, where they found themselves confronted by a French corps under the young Count of Clermont. It was one of several French divisions that had been sent out to arrest the progress of the English force, and consisted of about 3,000 men, thus being numerically inferior to the English. Nevertheless, true to form, Kyriell refused to assume the initiative; he grouped his force in the little valley containing the village, with their backs to a small brook lined with orchards and plantations well calculated to cover their rear. The veteran English commander, experienced in the defensive battles that had previously brought success, disregarded the need to push forward; he awaited Clermont's attack and prepared to defeat it when it came. His archers, with plenty of time at their disposal, planted their stakes and dug ditches and potholes in front of their line to impede the enemy cavalry – it was a throw-back of over a century. Kyriell formed his men up on a frontage of about 1,000 yards in a thin line of dismounted men-at-arms, with three groups of archers projecting forward in bastions; it was Henry V's formation at Agincourt thirty-five years before.

At about three o'clock in the afternoon, the French force came marching straight up the road; they deployed in three lines to the right and left so that they faced the English, who were about 500 yards away. There both sides stood, eyeing one another. The French noted with some apprehension that the English were still improving their already substantial defences. The French commanders went into conference – in the old days they would have rushed forward in a headlong attack, but the new-style French army did things differently. Although the young and inexperienced Clermont, burning with the impetuosity of youth, was all for the immediate attack he was sufficiently malleable to listen to his more experienced officers, who warned him, through long experience, to be wary of the English in a prepared position. Anyway, why hurry? Was not the Constable de Richemont near at hand with reinforcements?

So, for two or three hours some aimless skirmishing went on; it was a period of far more use to the French than to the English, for their reinforcements drew nearer by the minute. Some French attacks, on foot, were put in to feel out the flanks, but all were repulsed, as were some half-hearted mounted attacks also on the flanks. From their position behind stakes and potholes, the archers took a heavy toll of the enemy. De Richemont still had not arrived when Clermont recalled that he had brought guns with him; he ordered Giraud, Master of the Royal Ordnance, to drag up his two culverins. Under the eyes of the probably apprehensive English, the heavy guns were dragged to a spot outside bow range from which they could enfilade the English line.

After the usual fussy technical preparations beloved of gunners throughout the ages, they opened fire. It was a nagging bombardment, shots arriving in succession until the archers were so frustrated that they broke their ranks and rushed out from behind their stakes. Aided by a wing of the billmen, they charged headlong at the guns and a fierce but brief mêlée took place around them until the French were routed and reeled away, leaving the precious pieces silent and in the hands of the English.

The battle would have been won had Kyriell advanced his whole force at this crucial moment. The French, dispirited by their losses, were beginning to melt away from the field and the archers were triumphantly trying to drag the heavy guns back to their own lines, not knowing how to 'spike' them. But the English commander, obsessed by his defensive tactics, would not move an inch; he did not even send out aid to the archers who had seized the guns but were themselves now under great pressure, having been attacked by one of the flank 'battles' of French dismounted men-at-arms. A desperate struggle was taking place around the artillery pieces, archers and billmen battling to hold off their attackers whilst others strained and sweated in their efforts to get the guns away. It was an uneven struggle; the more lightly armed English were slowly but remorselessly pushed back by their heavier opponents, whilst their comrades looked on sullenly a few hundred yards away. Eventually the English infantry had to abandon the guns altogether as they fought for their very lives. The very resistance of the archers proved disastrous to the English in their strong position, because the French pushed them back before them in a slow and progressive advance towards the stakes, so that the archers were unable to use their bows to harass the enemy for fear of hitting their own men. Soon the fighting was taking place immediately in front of the stakes, and the rest of the French force, seeing the battle going their way, had moved forward en masse so that fierce fighting was taking place at all points. But just as the English superiority in numbers was beginning to tell, and the French were showing signs of wavering, de Richemont arrived on the skyline with his reinforcements. They came from a direction that immediately threatened the English left flank and rear.

Kyriell was now in dire straits; he had no reserve, so was forced to bend his line back into a right-angle, or rough semi-circle, to fight on the two fronts. The arrival of the new troops reinvigorated Clermont's weary men, and the fatigued and disheartened English began to crumple under the shock. Fighting hard, they gave ground until they were forced into several isolated groups, which fought on stubbornly and died hard with no quarter being given or asked. One party of 500 archers are said to have fought to the very last man, in the bloody, muddy ground of a garden by the brookside. A few hundred archers escaped, but Kyriell and his infantry were surrounded and annihilated, the commander himself being spared and captured. Four-fifths of the English force were killed in this major disaster to English arms. Had intelligent offensive tactics been used, the battle could have been won by the English before it even began, and failing that, there was another opportunity to win it halfway through its course.

So, Normandy was lost; Anjou and Maine had already been made-over to the father of Henry VI's Queen; Guienne and Gascony, which had been English since the reign of Henry II, alone remained, although Guienne was on the point of falling into French hands. However, Gascony was in no hurry to be rid of the English, telling them that, if an army could be sent to aid her, she would revolt against the French to rejoin her old mistress. Then, in 1452, Aquitaine revolted against the new French rule and England's King Henry VI sent a small army, under John Talbot, now seventy-one-year-old Earl of Shrewsbury, to Bordeaux. They were greeted with delight and, for a short time, Talbot performed wonders that might be expected from such a peerless paladin, sole surviving general of Agincourt, until in mid-summer, rather against his better judgement, he marched to the relief of the town of Castillon, besieged by the French. Talbot marched eastward, twenty-six miles up the Dordogne river, where he surprised a large force of French archers in their quarters in a dawn attack, putting many of them out of action and pursuing the survivors to the main French camp, three-quarters of a mile away. The French were strongly entrenched in a fully fortified camp, with numerous guns in position (contemporary accounts say from 100 to 300 pieces of artillery) backed by a large army.

Talbot decided to attack at once, despite being without his artillery train; it was said that he was deceived by reports of large numbers of horsemen leaving the camp giving the impression of it being abandoned, whereas they were riding out to make room for the archers who had been chased back there. Although in keeping with Talbot's fearless approach to war, it was a rash, impetuous and hopeless venture, it bore all the brave and chivalrous imprints of the age to which the English leader had brought an almost legendary colour. His army fought with the weapons that had brought countless victories for more than a century, and every man dismounted save John Talbot alone who, by virtue of his three score-years-and-ten, remained mounted on a little white cob. Unarmed, from the horse's back, he directed operations, wearing no armour and a cap of purple velvet, in accordance with his vow to the French king, on release from capture after Patay in 1429, thirty-four years earlier, that he would never again wear armour against France.

Led by the indomitable old man, the small English force hurled themselves on the French entrenchment, storming forward with such impetuosity that they almost carried the position. To the roaring of guns in the smoke-filled river-valley, the English, massed in a single column, persisted in charge after charge for a full hour, until riddled and slaughtered by the artillery fire, they fell back. Then the French sallied forth in a counterattack, to turn the defeat into a rout. Talbot's cob was brought down by a cannon-ball, throwing him heavily to the ground where, possibly unconscious, his skull was cleft by a French battleaxe as he lay, pinned under his dead horse. Scarcely a man of his 6,000-strong force escaped destruction, and young John Talbot – Lord Lisle – refused to leave his father and was killed by his side.

From that date – 17 July 1453 – the ancestral domains of seven generations of English kings passed from them for ever; with the destruction of the last invading army of the Hundred Years War, Agincourt became an anachronistic memory. The French, magnanimous in victory, subsequently erected a monument to John Talbot, Earl of Shrewsbury, at Castillon, on the spot where he died. Standing before it, the imaginative and knowledgeable historian will find it arouses a host of chauvinistic feelings!

4

The Armies

THE EARLY PART of the 'Pike-and-Shot Period' saw most monarchs backed by a number of permanent standing forces which provided a nucleus for armies raised at times of war, because national economies of the age precluded the cost of maintaining a large standing army in times of peace. When war occurred rulers relied upon temporarily hired mercenaries to supplement their relatively small permanent forces; the French, for example, backed-up their permanent cavalry units with Swiss mercenary pikemen, or landsknechts, German reiters, and sometimes Italian infantry and cavalry condottiere companies.

A country's nobility and its towns had an obligation of feudal origin to provide militia, levied when necessary, as in times of foreign invasion. In a low-key defensive role they could provide support to the professional forces, but in an offensive operation this undisciplined and poorly organised militia would have presented a liability that made them not worth paying or logistically supporting.

And yet, at the close of the fifteenth and beginning of the sixteenth centuries the infantry of Europe were rapidly growing in efficiency and importance. In France, the successful steps taken to expel the English from their soil had been steadily continued – Louis XI hired Swiss sergeants to drill his infantry, and Picardie, the senior regiment of the old French line, was already in potential existence. Italy's reputation as the birthplace of all arts included the new-born art of war, eagerly espoused by France, and it was said that few armies have caused greater wonder in Europe than that which marched with Charles VIII through Florence in 1496.

Only the Renaissance could have paraded such oddly-assorted armies where mercenaries combined with patriots, crossbows with arquebuses, and military savants mingled with the last exponents of chivalry.

The Battle of Fornovo in 1495 taught the Italians a great deal. After seeing the brutal directness of the French shatter their old *condottiere* system of scientific and bloodless warfare, they realised that their chessboard-manoeuvre battles were no longer practical, and that an army had to have infantry who, if humanly possible, could compete with the Swiss. Aware that there were no other pikemen capable of this, the Italians took a leaf out of the Spanish book and specialised in arquebusiers, sometimes massing as many as 3,000 of them, to form the celebrated 'Black Bands'. But they could only raise small forces of stradiots, light irregular horsemen, invaluable for desperate raids and surprise-attacks, but unable to withstand charges by gendarmerie or other heavy cavalry. Although Italian mercenaries gained a reputation of sorts in the wars of the period, they were usually casual and temporary formations assembled by some adventurer, disbanded when peace came.

Francis I of France in 1581 raised 'legions' of French infantry on the Spanish pattern, originally from Picardy, Champagne, Normandy and Languedoc, formed into groups of about 600 pikemen, 500 arquebusiers and 100 halberdiers. But the peasant-material and lack of training made them very dubious bodies and during the last twenty years of the great struggle between Valois and Hapsburg, French commanders much preferred to have Swiss or landsknechts infantry instead of their own native foot soldiers. The legions continued on a diminished scale during the Wars of Religion; those of Picardy and Champagne, after many reformations and reorganisations, persisted into the seventeenth century and may be considered ancestors of the similarly named regiments famous in later glorious days of French military achievement.

The Pike-and-Shot period extended into the seventeenth century, marking the beginning of the modern concept of warfare, as devised by Gustavus Adolphus, who was only thirty-six years of age when killed at Lützen in 1632. Successfully campaigning since the age of seventeen, the Swedish King became one of the greatest warriors ever to stride the pages of military history as the first great exponent of scientific warfare. Alone, he built up the first truly national army of modern times, which consistently defeated the conventional armies and mercenaries of the period. This was accomplished by an original method of warfare based on the Swedish brigade system, a tactical formation composed of 1,000–1,500 men. It combined small battle groups of musketeers and pikemen in a wedge-shaped formation, drawn up in three lines with three groups of pikemen (648 men) forming a protecting triangle and 864 musketeers in five groups behind them in the intervals and along the flanks. Based on fire-power and mobility, the Swedes increased the proportion of musketeers to pikemen and created small units known as companies. A company consisted of seventy-eight musketeers and fifty-four pikemen and there were four companies in a battalion, eight battalions in a regiment and two to four regiments in a brigade. Using their light and faster-loading musket with prepared charges carried in a slung bandolier, with fire-discipline and training these Swedish formations produced maximum fire-power. Each musketeer could fire thirty shots in an hour. Usually closing up to three ranks in the firing line with the front rank kneeling and the other two firing over their heads, a Swedish brigade had far greater fire-power than the square formation invariably adopted by the enemy.

In contrast to their plumed and colourfully uniformed opponents, the Swedish army were drab in their sleeveless peasant smocks, loose knee-breeches and woollen stockings, all of home-spun drab. Their regiments were distinguished by silk ensigns of white, blood-red, yellow and green colouring, solid-colour blue and black, with embroidered emblems and mottoes. Only pikemen and heavy cavalry wore the cuirass, making the Swedish army far more mobile than their opponents; they used the pike as an offensive weapon, its shaft shortened to eleven feet.

In the latter years of the Pike-and-Shot period, infantry were held in lower esteem than cavalry; the mounted arm was at the height of its fame and most well-equipped armies endeavoured to field sufficient cavalry to form at least half the number of the infantry arm. In England, the old heavy cavalry were becoming obsolete, being replaced by light dragoons or mounted infantry, armed with swords, pistols and carbines, whose role was to reconnoitre and cover troop movements. These cavalrymen wore light steel casques and cuirasses, or sometimes only a buff coat.

Cromwell's New Model Army marched at the slow rate of about thirteen miles a day, due to their heavy arms and equipment, particularly the armoured pikemen. The pikemen wore iron corselets and head pieces, carrying a pike and sword; they were heavy troops whose main role was to repel cavalry charges. Combinations of musketeers and pikemen required a high degree of efficiency, derived from stern discipline, since any ill-combined movements would be unlikely to beat back a cavalry-charge. An infantry regiment during the English Civil War consisted of two musketeers to each pikeman; in the Scottish army of 1644 the proportion was 3:2.

In the fifteenth century, it was said that the finest body-guards so far as valour and stature was concerned were the Scottish archers, but the army which performed so valiantly at Auldearn in 1645 were ill-dressed and poorly armed and equipped. Some of them carried ancient matchlocks, a few bore claymores, and there was a variety of pikes and cudgels. The bow-and-arrow was still most effectively employed by the Scots. During the Covenanter Campaigns, Scots cavalry were armed with four pistols, a carbine and a lance.

This period included the 'last of the Pike-and-Shot Wars' when conflicts between Austrians and Turks culminated in the Siege of Vienna in 1683. These were colourful campaigns that involved native levies drawn from all over the Ottoman Empire – Egyptians, Babylonians, Transylvanians, Wallachians and Albanians fighting as mounted and foot archers, heavily armoured cavalry, camel-borne artillery, spearmen and swordsmen and men armed in an almost mediaeval fashion with bows, spears, swords and bucklers. Usually enjoying a superiority in numbers, the Turks relied on a small nucleus of spahis and janissaries to do the hard fighting. Although trained by European renegades, the Turkish artillery was never as good as that of the Christians. Their tactics were less sophisticated and their leaders unequal to commanders of the calibre of Jan Sobieski of Poland, the Duke of Lorraine and later Eugène of Savoy.

5

The Mercenary Armies

AMONG THE PROBLEMS taxing the minds of commanders in the late fifteenth and early sixteenth centuries few ranked higher than that of countering or reproducing the combat-efficiency of the remorseless phalanxes of mercenary pikemen, whose avalanche-like advance struck terror into the hearts of opposing troops and crushed every army daring to stand in their way. This new breed of soldier, coming into being in the middle of the thirteenth century, was a professional who lived by the sword. Well-equipped and highly trained and bound by the highest standards of *esprit de corps*, companies of these men were available for hire by anyone who could pay their price. In due course, wartime rulers who were unable to afford to maintain standing armies, relied upon these hired mercenaries to supplement their relatively small permanent armies. Thus the ambitions of Europe's princes led to every sixteenth-century army becoming dependent upon mercenaries, whose loyalty was often governed by the lure of loot, so that their progress was marked by ruthlessness, untrustworthiness and greed. Coupled with the expense, this unreliability of mercenaries was a major factor in keeping armies small in size, and making commanders reluctant to give battle. Inevitably lacking patriotism, although well disciplined good fighters, mercenaries were hard to handle, often refusing to fight unless paid up to the hilt and not averse to walking off the field either before or even halfway through a battle, as at Pavia in 1525 when 6,000 Swiss absconded even though their pay was up to date.

Among the earliest types of professional soldiers were the *condottieri*, warrior-commanders of multi-nationality companies whose trade was war and temporarily loyal to those paying them the highest rates. They first became noted when fighting, for hire, for the rich Italian city-states in the thirteenth and fourteenth centuries. They were succeeded as mercenaries by Swiss pikemen, whose ascendancy began in the war between Switzerland and Burgundy in 1476–77 and lasted until more than halfway through the century that followed. Destined by nature, the rugged country from which they came, and forced by poverty to fight on their own feet rather than horseback, they were natural infantrymen and as such they developed their fighting system.

These redoubtable mercenaries were imitated and followed by similar formations of German landsknechts – who were equally capable of deserting to the enemy on the eve of battle. Mercenaries acted in this characteristic style right down to the Thirty Years War in the seventeenth century, when both Gustavus Adolphus and Wallenstein enlisted such deserters wholesale.

Until the middle of the seventeenth century, the French seemed to have little faith in their own native infantry, and the bulk of their footsoldiers were Swiss mercenaries, regarded by French commanders of the day as the dominant power in war. If they were not available, German landsknechts were hired as the best substitute; both these mercenary armies employed only the best men, and the 'doppelsoldner' – soldiers who fought in the front ranks for extra pay – were formidable veterans. Accepted military uniforms were uncommon so that soldiers wore strange versions of civilian clothes dictated by their immediate commanders. The landsknechts were noted for wearing the most outlandish and extravagant uniforms of the day.

Italian mercenaries, often lighthorsemen and arquebusiers, also served with the French, but were little trusted and rarely inspired sufficient confidence in their prowess to be sent into battle against the Swiss or landsknechts. Possibly they were employed by the French to make up the marked shortage of their own native soldiers skilled in the use of fire-arms.

When mercenaries met in battle they fought brilliantly but where possible avoided causing casualties. Because of the potential for ransom money, mercenaries preferred taking prisoners to taking lives.

During the seventeenth century national armies began to take the field and the professional hired companies began to go out of business, leaving behind them traditions of military skill, discipline, organisation and *esprit de corps* which were to influence the soldiers that followed them.

6

The Leaders

With the advent of the Pike-and-Shot Era, more than three centuries had passed since the invention of gunpowder, during which time generalship advanced little beyond the bow-and-arrow past, without a single nation or military leader dominating the world. There were some competent soldiers – Henry V of England, John Hunyadi of Hungary, and some Ottoman leaders – but one man towers above them all in the late Middle Ages – Jan Ziska, the Hussite leader, because he alone comprehended the possibilities of such gunpowder weapons as the handgun and the wheeled cannon. New techniques of siegecraft and fortification were devised for the Spanish invaders of Italy by Pedro Navarro, foremost engineer of his day; Fernado Devalos the Marquis of Pescara became famed for innovations and reforms to infantry which moulded the warfare of the fifteenth century; and the Duke of Ferrara aided the French to win victories by his improvements in artillery and artillery techniques. In the final years of the sixteenth century, Maurice of Nassau raised a regular army in the Netherlands which was professional, highly disciplined and inspired by the best military motives throughout their long-term enlistment. They were at least a match for the best Spanish troops and far superior to most of the mercenary forces they encountered.

Known as the 'Great Captain', the Spanish leader Gonzalo de Córdoba adapted Roman sword-and-buckler tactics to gunpowder weapons, whose potential he recognised and exploited in conjunction with field entrenchments as a defence against attack, particularly by cavalry. In his campaigns in the Naples area at the turn of the fifteenth century, de Córdoba held extensive frontages by arquebusiers behind entrenchments, allowing him to hold and outmanoeuvre much larger enemy forces. More than that, he solved the basic infantry problem – the need to protect arquebusiers in the open while they were reloading by using pikemen to steady and protect them, and to exploit handgun firepower by offensive shock-action – and, in so doing, governed infantry tactics for many years. At Pavia in 1525, when both sides were well entrenched, his Imperialists turned the French position by a night-march, and were victorious through their arquebusiers decimating the French cavalry.

Throughout the period, the Art of War progressively flowered, nurtured by enlightened commanders who, realising that successful armies required the right proportion of the various arms, constantly sought a system that would produce maximum benefit from firepower. They did this by blending shock action with the attack of small-arms troops, allied to artillery fire, assaults by pike and field fortifications. Such gifted leaders arose as Henri de La Tour d'Auvergne de Turenne, Johann Tilly of Germany, Count Wallenstein, France's Prince Louis of Conde, the Duke of Enghien (later known as Condé), the Duke of Luxembourg, Duke Henri II de Montmorency, the engineer Sebastien LePrestre de Vauban, Oliver Cromwell of England, Italy's Count Montecuccoli, and, above all, Gustavus Adolphus of Sweden. This last-named soldier was responsible for many of the changes that allowed the transition of the seventeenth century from Middle Ages to Modern Era, so far as military weaponry, tactics and military organisation were concerned. Gustavus Adolphus was the father of modern field artillery, devising the concept of massed and mobile artillery fire; he banished the columnar concepts of infantry combat by substituting linear tactics which survived until the First World War, although vestiges remain in modern infantry doctrine; he modified cavalry tactics, giving them both fire-power and shock capability. But his supreme tactical contribution to warfare was the concept of tactical teamwork among the three combat arms of infantry, artillery and cavalry.

Thus, as noted in Chapter Four, the Pike-and-Shot period extended into the seventeenth century, marked by the beginnings of the modern concept of warfare, greatly aided by the Swedish soldiers of the Thirty Years War who, while not mercenaries, were thoroughly professional in that they knew no other occupation than soldiering and warfare.

7

Tactics of the Armies

THE EARLY YEARS of the Pike-and-Shot era were an unsettled period of military history, as organisational and tactical methods were sought that would adapt new and improved types of gunpowder weapons to the combat styles of the period. Things began to take shape towards the end of the sixteenth century as the capabilities of small-arms and the growing effectiveness of field and permanent fortifications began to remedy the vulnerability of arquebusiers and musketeers striving to reload their weapons during the heat of battle. On a larger scale was the tentative experimentation in tactics based on shock-action by heavy cavalry and horsemen armed with hand-weapons; the most effective offensive and defensive tactics arising from artillery fire; and the problems of making and resisting massed pike assaults.

The tactical use of gunpowder weapons was in its infancy and the best was yet to come. Some countries, such as France and Italy, mistrusted the new styles and continued to use the old crossbow, but the Spaniards, Swiss and Germans employed arquebusiers, with the Spaniards consistently ahead of other nations in their development and employment of infantry small-arms. In fact, French supremacy in the use of artillery, achieved at the end of the fifteenth century, was superseded by the proficient handling of hand-held fire-arms by Spanish infantry.

The superiority of English infantry defensive tactics over French chivalry lasted well into the fifteen century, when Henry V and his brother John of Bedford continued to defeat the French through their fundamental technical superiority, involving heavily armoured pikemen and highly mobile archers in disciplined defensive formation against mediaeval cavalry and infantry. Although, in the end, the final successes were gained by the French, it substantiated what had gone before in the form of good defensive infantry supported by the Bureau Brothers' guns in place of the longbow. Later, well-trained and disciplined formations of Swiss pikemen and German landsknechts were protected in their irresistible charges by flanking arquebusiers, then came developments leading to combined arms-teams when cavalry – both heavy and light – were added. By the end of the fifteenth century, the French, leaders in this style of infantry/artillery/cavalry warfare, had set a pattern which was to dominate land warfare for the next four centuries. Two distinct tactical ploys, evident at the battles of Montlhery (1465), Granson (1476) and Morat (1476), provided the background to these developments, namely the revival of the use of heavy cavalry, and the use of massed Swiss pikemen moving in echelon. As noted in Chapter Three, after many years of attacking in the same old way and being defeated by the English in the same old way, the French had at last recognised that the English defensive system was only effective against an enemy who conveniently attacked an English army in a good defensive position, as at Agincourt and Verneuil in 1415 and 1424. In the last battles to decide the Hundred Years War – Formigny (1450) and Castillon (1453) – the French rejoiced in new tactics which they could see had uncovered the weaknesses of the English defensive system, although it was still used with some success at Bosworth in 1487 and Flodden in 1514. At Formigny, inland of Omaha Beach, that notorious battleground of nearly 500 years later, Kyriell's small English army, relentlessly bombarded by French artillery, were eventually forced to break ranks and counter-attack, with disastrous results. Three years later, in 1453, at Castillon-on-the-Gironde, the Paladin Talbot, aged seventy-one, lost his life and was hopelessly defeated when charging an entrenched French line plentifully supported by guns. Many years later, at Ravenna in 1512, when in a sound defensive position, the Spanish-Papal army suffered unendurable pounding by enemy artillery that forced them to come out and onto the offensive. At Bicocca in 1522, Swiss columns endeavoured to take a line of trenches in their usual irresistible fashion, but were thrown back in complete rout by weight of fire from artillery and hand weapons.

Gunpowder weapons had now come into tactical reckoning, but battles were still won in the same old ways, as at Fornovo in 1495 and Seminara in the same year, when the French beat the Spaniards (under Córdoba) by heavy cavalry charges; or at Novara in 1513 when fearsome columns of pikemen carried the day. Military thinkers of the day propounded the theory that a commander used to skilful manoeuvring and likely to indulge in frontal attacks against massed guns would win more battles than he would lose; they also maintained that against such a general enemy artillery would fire, reload and move far too slowly to be truly effective. In that context, Machiavelli, Italian military theorist and writer (1469–1527) believed that an enemy would not be able to get in more than two or three volleys at lightly moving and well-trained troops.

Early in the Pike-and-Shot period, massed phalanxes of pikemen, usually Swiss or German landsknechts, closely resembling the Macedonian phalanx or the Scottish schiltron, could sweep infantry and even heavily armoured cavalry from the battlefield. An overwhelming formation of pikes would make a steady but rapid advance that took the fight to the enemy, who never had the opportunity to attack them. Thus, they had the advantages of superior mobility and discipline, giving their attack increased shock by its momentum, and reducing the time they were exposed to the missile weapons of the enemy. Military historian Sir Charles Oman writes in his book *The Art of War*:

> The rapidity of the Swiss advance had in it something portentous; the great wood of pikes and halberds came rolling over the brow of some neighbouring hill; a moment later it was pursuing its even way toward the front, and then – almost before the opponent had time to realise his position – it was upon him, with its four rows of spear points projecting in front and the impetus of file upon file surging up from the rear.

The Swiss usually went into action in three bodies – van, battle and rear. The van, because of the desperate nature of its work, was called the *Verlorener Hauf*, from which is derived the old battle term

Forlorn Hope; the van and rear were each half the numerical strength of the battle, or main, body. Always of very deep formation and more-or-less oblong, the van marched straight for the selected point-of-attack in the enemy line; the following division moved parallel to the van, but a little to its rear, so that it could act as a reserve and throw its weight in where necessary. Impressively effective in their simplicity, these tactics of advance in echelon-of-divisions prevented the enemy wheeling inwardly to hit the attacking van in flank, because that would expose them, in turn, to a flank attack by the divisions advancing in the rear. Furthermore, such tactics left an open space in the rear of attacking columns to which they could withdraw if repulsed, without incurring that common eventuality in many mediaeval battles of throwing into confusion troops to their rear.

Moreover, the stands of pikes protected the vulnerable musketeers from cavalry attack in which was a throwback to the equally successful tactical formations of English bowmen and men-at-arms during the Hundred Years War.

The firmness of the Swiss infantry formations in the field was quickly proven on such occasions as the Battle of St Jakob-en-Birs in 1444 where a Swiss force of 1,500 pikemen attacked a French army 30/50,000 strong. Not surprisingly the Swiss were wiped out, but their determination and bravery in killing 3,000 Frenchmen discouraged them enough to make them withdraw. In the three battles of Granson (1476), Morat (1476) and Nancy (1477) in the war with Burgundy, the Swiss completely defeated Charles the Bold, who lost his life trying to cover the retreat at Nancy. These victories earned the Swiss the reputation of Europe's finest soldiers.

When pike phalanxes met there was a 'push-of-pike' and at the first impact most of the front ranks of both sides went down, so that masses of bodies checked all forward movement on both sides, forcing them to stand locked in a 'push-of-war'. Astute commanders placed one rank of arquebusiers or pistoleers between the first and second ranks of pike formation, to hold their fire until a moment before the clash, when they blazed away to bring down the front rank of the enemy – the officers and picked men. This had its snags because the fire-armed men had to reload, or else they would be completely helpless if the pike rank behind them continued to move forward; being jammed between two ranks of their own pikes they could not escape, and they must have greatly inconvenienced the pikemen, preventing them from fighting in their usual manner. It must have been interesting when both commanders used arquebusiers in this way!

In time, the vast formations of pikes were substituted by smaller corps with pikes and arquebus blended together, both acting on certain fixed principles.

At the Battle of Ceresole in 1544 between French forces of Prince of Enghien and Spanish troops of the Imperial force under Marquis del Vasto, events of the day confirmed that infantry – musketeers/arquebusiers protected by pikemen – could repulse cavalry attacks. The exception was when cavalry attacked in flank an infantry formation already engaged frontally by other infantry, shown by the destruction of 7,000 landsknechts fighting in Spanish pay. However, the unprotected arquebusier was no match for pike formations or cavalry, as shown by the rout of the Huguenot infantry at Jarnac in 1569 by Tavanne, for these infantry bearing hand-weapons were generally very effective but extremely vulnerable when reloading. Nor could rate of fire be raised sufficiently to protect them against 'push-of-pike', cavalry attack, or Spanish sword-and-buckler men, so the arquebusier had to be protected by pikemen at the same time as other arquebusiers (or crossbowmen in the French army) kept the enemy at a distance.

On the other hand, although he could cope with cavalry, the pikeman was very vulnerable to all types of fire-arms that could be turned upon him at a time when he was halted by physical obstacles such as trenches manned by arquebusiers – as at Bicocca in 1522, or when held up by cavalry attacks or threat of them, as at Moncontour in 1569, or earlier at Marignano in 1515. Notwithstanding these limitations of both arquebusier and pikeman, the combined effects of fire-power with offensive shock-action was of the greatest tactical importance during the sixteenth century. It was imperative at that time that there should be no forceful interruptions during the slow and painful process of forming-up a sixteenth-century army for battle. So arquebusiers were employed as skirmishers in front and on the flanks of pikes and halberdier columns; the French called them *enfants perdus*, which indicates the dangers involved in the tactical system.

As the sixteenth century pursued its course, the increased effectiveness of fire-arms allied to growing expertise in the use of fortifications forced commanders only to accept battle when they were certain of victory. This was not usually considered likely when facing Spanish armies, whose mutually supporting roles of their highly-disciplined arquebusiers and pikemen frustrated the majority of their enemies. This was achieved by a heavy type of formation, sometimes known as the 'Spanish Square', in which increased proportions of men bearing handguns were intermixed with units of pikemen in solid formations many ranks deep. By having front-rank men retire to reload while those to their rear moved up to the firing-line, a steady volume of fire could be maintained; the pikemen continued to bear the brunt of both offensive and defensive shock-action. Another tactic was devised by the French at the Battle of Coutras in 1587 during the Wars of Religion when Henry of Navarre, in anticipation of a Catholic cavalry charge, made his front-rank arquebusiers kneel in front of a standing second rank, so increasing the steadiness of the formation and doubling its fire-power. Towards the close of the sixteenth century, the lighter manoeuvrable arquebusiers became almost completely relegated to skirmishing roles, as the introduction of the musket increased the firepower of these heavy-infantry formations.

The new musket was longer-ranged but had a much slower rate of fire, and the fouling of musket-barrels sadly affected their performance. The methods of employment of musketeers enabled them to maintain a continuous fire by retiring to the rear of the six or ten-deep file when they had fired, or advancing to the front when they were ready to fire – in the one case the unit gradually retired and in the other it gradually advanced. Sometimes formations of musketeers were drawn up in small columns six or ten deep with an interval of at least one file between the columns; the front rank of each column filed off right or left of the interval, to the rear of the column, before starting to reload.

As the seventeenth century began, infantry tactics became elaborate, and because of the lack of distinctive uniforms, it became necessary to use badges, watchwords, or 'field-signs'. Actions usually commenced by the sending out of a 'forlorn hope' – a body of musketeers who fired and then fell back: On contact of the main bodies the musketeers would deliver two volleys, then the pikemen would charge. To prevent cavalry charges, infantry took shelter in ditches or behind hedges, not always possible in major engagements. In the English Civil War, Cromwell adopted the three-rank Swedish method of musketry for his New Model Army; Montrose also followed this practice. At that time, when each regiment dressed as its commander ordained, red was most commonly used in England and hodden-grey in Scotland.

At the beginning of the 'Pike-and-Shot' period, cavalry had not fully recovered from the harsh treatment they had received at the hands of English infantry formations in the first half of the fifteenth century and earlier, and did not regain much effectiveness until the sixteenth century was well under way. Although still forming a major element in all Western European armies, the dejected heavy cavalry-man struggled to find a solution to the Swiss tactical system, and even more to the advent of fire-arms. But he still existed as an essential part of armies because, often in conjunction with other arms, cavalry were still effective when charging or countercharging enemy thrown off-balance by artillery fire or by a prior infantry attack. The knight, man-at-arms, or heavy cavalryman was the last to wear personal armour. The increased weight of armour made them even more ponderous and although the height of development of armour had been reached, this coincided with numerous military innovations that assured its obsolescence. Even the finest armour was ineffective against the new and rapidly improving missile weapons that were employed by the gunner and the infantryman.

As the efficiency of fire-arms and artillery increased, and the combination of pike and arquebus supplemented the well-known resisting powers of the old Swiss phalanx, heavy cavalry made fewer desperate charges to break hostile lines and formations. Pikes could hold off cavalry, whose chances were greatly lessened if their ranks were being thinned by musketry whilst they were striving to break through the menacing out-thrust points of the pikes. Gradually, it became the practice only to loose heavy cavalry in attacks on infantry formations when that formation was under attack by other infantry, or to use the cavalry to thrust aside the enemy's equivalent force of horsemen who might be engaged with their own infantry. This situation prevailed at the Battle of Ceresole and in several combats during the French Wars of Religion.

Attempts were made to combat the redoubtable pike formations by arming heavy cavalry with a pistol, so that the fire-arm-equipped horsemen could force gaps in the serried ranks of the pikemen by 'caracoling' – riding up by successive ranks to fire, wheeling off to allow the following line of cavalry to discharge their pistols, each line swerving off to the rear and reloading as they formed up behind their preceding rank. But this caracoling had to be a very well disciplined and precise business, and only veteran troops could maintain their order after the first few firings, so that the ideal of firing a succession of pistol-bullets at close range into the packed pike-formation, so causing a gap into which following cavalry could penetrate, was not always successful. Defensive tactics against the caracole was either to use cavalry to charge the enemy pistoleers, or else have arquebusiers ranked in with the pikemen to shoot down the approaching pistoleers before they came close enough to do much damage, as the arquebus could out-range the pistol.

As noted in previous chapters, perhaps the most stimulating event of the latter part of the Pike-and-Shot period was the impetus given to the art of warfare by the rise of the new Swedish army, devised and inspired by their great warrior-King Gustavus Adolphus, the greatest captain of the seventeenth century. As demonstrated in the Battle of Breitenfeld in 1631, his organisation and tactics heralded a new era in warfare in which formations of cavalry, pikemen, musketeers and artillery, fighting in small, self-contained combat groups mutually supported each other in a tactical formation known as the Swedish Brigade System.

Conversely, the English Civil War (1642–51) which took place at roughly the same time as the concluding years of the Thirty Years War, was notable for lack of trained standing armies. Battles were decided more by luck than skill with a marked emphasis on amateurish lack of tactical direction. Most battles began through accidental contact, with 'forlorn hopes' blasting away at each other until their main bodies came on the scene. The resulting flurry of fire, both by artillery and muskets, would be followed by a wild charge.

Every age, every army, every battle displays tactics ranging from the most crude to the most skilful, because the art of disposing armed forces in contact with an enemy requires plans and means of carrying out a scheme or achieving an end. Those plans, allied to experience and foresight, reflect the innate ignorance or knowledge of the commanders, some whom History shows to have been fools while others are given the accolade of genius. The Pike-and-Shot period under review shows a bit of everything, with the advent of gun-powder and missile-weapons changing most aspects of warfare and tactics in a dramatic way only surpassed by the nuclear weapons of recent times.

8

The Weapons

BEFORE THE PIKE-AND-SHOT period began, in the early days of
the fifteenth century, hand-weapons developed more slowly than did
artillery. In the beginning handguns consisted simply of an iron tube
fixed to a long staff, sometimes a pike-handle. A slow-burning match
ignited priming powder sprinkled in a depression on top of the tube
(the pan), connected to powder inside the tube by a touch-hole also
filled with priming-powder. In the stress of battle, loading, aiming and
firing was difficult, and accuracy of direction or range was impossible.
Thus, these early handguns could not have had much direct effect
upon tactics or the conduct of a battle, and it was recognised at that
time that they could supplement but not replace the age-old familiar
longbow and crossbow. Around the middle of the fifteenth century
these crude weapons began to be superseded by the matchlock in the
form of the arquebus or hackbut, fire-arms which dominated military
tactics for more than a century. These early handguns were of
standard bore, weighed from nine to twelve pounds, and fired a ball
of about an ounce; they were called calivers or arquebuses-de-calibre.
As noted in the Introduction, they were fairly effective at ranges up to
100 yards, but difficult to aim accurately, they presented a tactical
problem in that the firer had no defence against attack while occupied
for several minutes when reloading with a wooden ramrod. In time,
this was solved by providing protection in the form of pikemen,
usually Swiss, or German landsknechts.

By the mid sixteenth century, the Spaniards had introduced the musket, a heavier handgun with a range of about 300 yards, which had to be fired from a fork-rest. Although it took longer than the arquebus to load and fire, this was accepted because of the weapon's greater range and striking-power. By the end of the century, the musket had largely taken over from the arquebus as the basic infantry arm. Fouling of the musket barrel frequently affected its performance, and a further complication was that the musket required a lot of match and, in the vicinity of the enemy, it was necessary to keep the match lighted, which was difficult in bad weather, which could literally disarm the musketeer.

Like primitive foot-soldiers through the ages, the Swiss began with the simple weapons of spear, axe, and shield and, because most of their foes were encroaching horsemen, they adapted these weapons accordingly. Thus they devised what was to become their national weapon, the halberd, an eight-foot long shaft, crowned with a heavy steel head featuring a broad, solid axe blade which, wielded by brawny Swiss arms, could shear through the best plate-armour and flesh-and-bone as though it were cheese, causing a contemporary chronicler to exclaim, 'this terrible weapon . . . cleaving men asunder like a wedge and cutting them into small pieces.' Incorporated in the head was a long spike with the point of a spear to thrust between armour-joints and, at the back, a curved blade or hook used to pull men out of the saddle. All Swiss armies contained halberdiers, some bearing other similar weapons – bills, guisarmes, and voulges – which had blades up to thirty inches long. As free men, armed with weapons of their own choice, some Swiss warriors preferred two-handed swords, or the 'morning star', a heavy cudgel plentifully studded with deadly long spikes. Men armed with halberds and these other tools of war were stationed initially at the rear of the pike formation and, if the onward surge of the phalanx was checked, they moved forward between the files to go into action in the front ranks.

To keep horses at a distance, the Swiss used a long spear or pike with a shaft eighteen to twenty-two feet in length, which they brought into prominence in a series of brilliant actions so noteworthy that the weapon ruled the battlefields of Europe for nearly two centuries.

As late as the mid sixteenth century, the famed English longbow was occasionally seen in Continental wars, although obviously outmoded by the increasingly common fire-arm. It was used to good effect by English archers at Bosworth Field in 1485 and Flodden Field in 1515, and more than 100 years later by Montrose's Highlanders in campaigns against the Covenanters in the 1650s. A Royal Ordinance of 1595 banned the longbow as the basic weapon of the militia train-bands, and each soldier had to provide his own arquebus, caliver or musket; however, repeatedly archers proved that they could shoot faster, farther, and more accurately than could most musketeers. In that context, it has been reliably claimed more than once that the English soldier was not provided with a hand-held weapon that surpassed the longbow in practised hands until the Enfield rifle issued to British regiments during the Crimean War of 1854–56.

True, the English were the last important European nation to officially adopt gunpowder small-arms, but as late as 1525 the French national infantryman was rarely equipped with an arquebus or caliver; those taking part in early years of the Italian Wars (1494–1515) were mainly crossbowmen from Gascony, a militant district of France. The arquebus superseded the crossbow in the later stages of this war, towards 1525, at that time being regarded with contempt as being a rather 'unsporting' weapon compared to the crossbow! Considering that it was the French who developed the finest artillery and artillerymen of the late fifteenth century in winning the Hundred Years War, it is surprising that it took to the middle of the next century to make them realise the dangers in relying exclusively on cannon.

In this part of the 'Pike-and-Shot' era, at the close of the fifteenth century, the Spaniards probably had the best-balanced military force in the world, seeming to have gone to much greater lengths than any other nation in exploiting cannon and small-arms, compensating for obvious limitations of these weapons by employing first-class sword and pike-armed infantry, and the competent use of field fortifications.

Cavalry bearing missile-firing weapons had been a feature of warfare for centuries – Saracen horsemen and their short bows were a scourge of the Crusaders – and when the Italian Wars began at the end of the fifteenth century the French light cavalry were using crossbows, an extremely awkward weapon to handle when mounted. They were replaced by arquebusiers-à-cheval, whose weapon must have been equally difficult to manage from a horse's back, as both crossbow and arquebus required the use of two hands. With only one shot to fire and the arquebus impossible to reload on the move, and necessarily fired at the halt – if the smouldering match was alight and manageable – the cavalryman had to make a choice between fire-power and horsemanship. Then, in 1544, it is recorded that, in a cavalry skirmish in Champagne, the French were surprised when German horsemen fired on them with 'pistols' – little arquebuses with twelve-inch barrels, and fired by a wheel-lock which did away with the tiresome match. Far better than the arquebus-and-match, pistols still presented the awkward problem of needing to be reloaded after firing, an operation requiring both hands, although, to achieve some semblance of sustained fire, the horse-pistoleer carried three weapons, two in holsters and one in the right boot.

Despite its drawbacks, such as the delicate wheel which was easily damaged plus the weakening of its spring if left wound-up too long, the pistol became very popular and was adopted by every army. The wheel-lock was also tried for infantry weapons, but it soon became obvious that it was too expensive and delicate to replace the tough and reliable matchlock on the prevailing infantry weapons. Able to use both hands for reloading, infantry continued to use the match until well into the seventeenth century, being superseded by the flint-lock not very long before the bayonet came into use, in the second half of the century.

Even more than tactics, formations and composition of armies, the most marked changes in the Pike-and-Shot period were probably those of weapons.

9

The Spaniards

THE MEDIAEVAL COMBAT formations of three massive 'battles' – dense blocks of mounted men and infantry – lingered on into the Pike-and-Shot Era, despite these unwieldy masses being outmoded and inadequate and besides being particularly vulnerable to fire-arms and artillery. Another throwback to tactics of earlier periods was de Córdoba's method of entrenching his Spanish armies, which, coupled with the Spaniards' early proficiency in the use of hand-fire-arms, was a 'gunpowder' replica of successful English longbow tactics.

It was the Spanish who took the first steps to modernise infantry tactics, using thorough methods of experimentation and improvisation, leading to de Córdoba's development of an entirely new formation.

In 1505 the Spanish created the *colunela*, a unit of mixed pikemen, halberdiers, arquebusiers and sword-and-buckler men. (The Spanish swordsmen could overcome the enemy pikemen but needed to be protected by arquebusiers in case the cavalry took a hand.) Organised in five companies totalling about 1,000–1,250 men, the *colunela* was the forerunner of the modern battalion and regiment, representing the first clear-cut tactical formation based upon the mutual employment of fire and shock weapons.

One of the more effective Spanish tactics was that employed by their sword-and-buckler men of running-in under pikes, particularly when locked in a frontal clash, their short stabbing sword being deadly in jammed formations. There are many recorded instances of combinations of sword-and-buckler men and arquebusiers slaughtering landsknechts, French infantry and even the renowned Swiss.

Over the next thirty years the Spanish gradually developed the *tercio*, a larger organisation consisting of three *colunelas* and totalling slightly more than 3,000 men. The title came from the triangular shape of the formation and because it was composed of about one-third of the infantry component of the average Spanish army. The *tercio* was the basic fighting unit of the army, consisting of pikemen and arquebusiers, while sword-and-buckler men and halberdiers were discarded, and it was a permanent formation large enough to fight independent actions, and with its own fixed chain of command. As the *tercio* became standardised, arquebusiers and pikemen formed the 'Spanish Square', with increased proportions of missile-men to pikemen formed up in several ranks and intermixed with pike formations. By having front-rank men retire to reload while those behind moved forward, a steady fire could be maintained while the pikes bore the brunt of both offensive and defensive shock action. Towards the end of the century, the introduction of the musket increased the firepower of these formations while the lighter, more mobile arquebusiers took on a skirmishing role. The reign of the Spanish *tercios* lasted for over 150 years, until the Thirty Years War, not being really discarded until Rocroi in 1643 ended the supremacy of the Spanish infantryman.

Emulating the Spaniards, in 1531 France formed regional legions, consisting of about 600 pikemen, 100 halberdiers and 300 arquebusiers. These legions were the forerunners of the famous French regional regiments of the seventeenth and eighteenth centuries.

THE BATTLE OF THE DUNES (DUNKIRK), 14 JUNE 1658

Early in 1657, in a Treaty of Peace and Friendship with France, Oliver Cromwell agreed to provide 6,000 men, to be known as the Lord Protector's Forces and to be commanded by their own officers, plus a fleet of naval vessels for a campaign against the Spanish in Flanders. The object of the Treaty was to reduce the three coastal towns of Mardyck, Dunkirk and Gravelines, and for England to take over the first two in pursuance of Cromwell's object of securing a

Continental naval station to check any attempted invasion from Spanish Flanders by Charles Stuart. Although the English contingent included numerous old soldiers, it was largely made up of drafts and new recruits, formed into six regiments under Sir John Reynolds (lost at sea before this battle and replaced by Sir William Lockhart), with John Morgan, Monk's right-hand man in the Highland War, as Major-General.

There was some campaigning in 1657, when Mardyck was taken, and in spring 1658 Marshal Turenne, with the combined Franco-British army, laid siege to Spanish-held Dunkirk. A Spanish relieving force, marching so rapidly along the sandhills that it left its artillery behind, arrived near Zudcote within three miles of Dunkirk on 14 June and took up a position with its right on the sea, intending to await the arrival of the guns.

This Spanish army was a motley host some 15,000 strong under the joint commands of Don John of Austria; Condé, the French Catholic leader; the Marquis Caracena; and James, Duke of York (later to be James II). Stretching across the dunes, the army's right wing consisted of 6,000 Spanish infantry, with four of their regiments, under Caracena and Don John, on a sandhill, considered the key to the position. On the left of the Spanish, the five British infantry regiments under the Duke of York were stationed: the King's Regiment of Foot Guards and Lord Muskerry's regiment (formed into one corps because of their small numbers) along with the Duke of Gloucester's regiment in the first line, and Willoughby's regiment and Ormond's regiment (under Colonel Grace) in the second line. The centre and left-centre of the line was held by Germans, Walloons, Scots and Irish, while on the left wing was Condé, with French and other infantry. The cavalry force was massed behind the foot in columns that stopped short of the beach, since they feared being fired on by the guns of the English fleet manoeuvring offshore.

The British regiments in the Spanish force consisted of some 2,000 men, three of them – James's own (Muskerry's), Ormond's and the Duke of Gloucester's – being Irish. Middleton's were Scots and the King's Regiment of Guards, made up mostly of refugees of 'gentle birth', were English.

Leaving 6,000 men guarding the siege-works, Turenne marched out at the head of 9,000 infantry, with forty pieces of artillery. The force included six of Cromwell's regiments, the Scottish bodyguard of the Kings of France, the Regiment Douglas (at one time the Scottish brigade of King Gustavus Adolphus) and Dillon's Irish Regiment, which was made up of men who in fact had fled from the wrath of Cromwell. The Cromwellian English were under the command of Sir William Lockhart and Morgan.

Turenne, one of the ablest generals of his time, formed up his army slowly and deliberately, coordinating his dispositions with the state of the tide, so that it was three hours before they were ready. The first line consisted of thirteen troops of cavalry on the right wing, a similar number on the left and eleven battalions of infantry in the centre; and the second line ten troops of cavalry on the right, nine on the left and seven battalions of infantry in the centre. Five troops of horse were posted midway between the two lines of infantry and four more were held in reserve.

The Cromwellian English outmarched the French and were first into action, supported by the guns of their fleet firing upon the Spanish right. Covered by a cloud of skirmishers, their pikes advanced steadily to the foot of the sandhill while the musketeers wheeled right and left to maintain a steady fire as the pikes halted to regain their breath. Then, shouting at the top of their voices, they surged so impetuously up the treacherous sand slopes into the Spaniards and their supports, the English Foot Guards, that, although fighting well and hard, both Spanish and English were fairly swept off the hill to retire in confusion, leaving seven out of eleven captains dead on the ground. James, Duke of York, tried to stop the rout by charging Lockhart's victorious regiment with his single troop of horse, but was beaten back; a second attempt broke into the infantry flank, but met such sturdy resistance that it too was pushed back. The remainder of the Cromwellian English regiments advanced quickly in support and, with the help of the French left-wing cavalry of the Marquis de Castelnau, completed the rout of the Spanish right wing.

Its seaward flank uncovered, the whole of Don John's line, now engaged by the French infantry, wavered and fell back, until the Walloon and German infantry were in full retreat, taking their 'rearward' cavalry with them. On the right of the Walloons, the regiments of the Dukes of York and Gloucester held on a little longer, but at last they broke and fled, together with all the English contingent but the Foot Guards. Standing firm as on their left they were passed by the first line of the French infantry and on their right

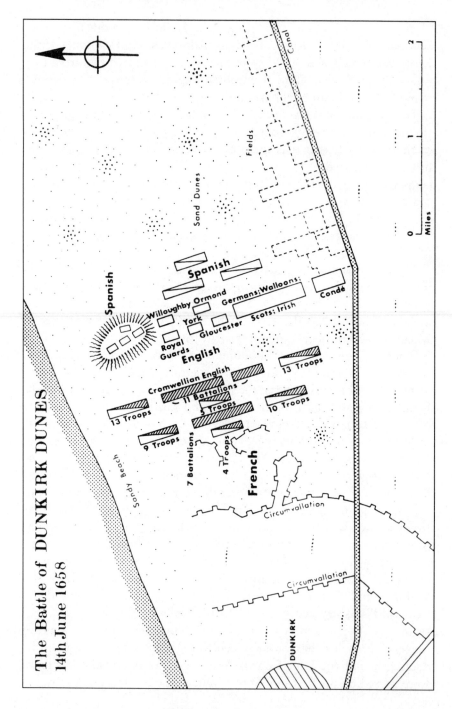

The Battle of DUNKIRK DUNES
14th June 1658

by some of Cromwell's regiments, they faced the second line of French, who called for their surrender. Then believing that they were the sole survivors of their army, they surrendered on advantageous terms.

On the extreme left of the Spanish line, Condé first successfully resisted the attacks of the French right wing, and his cavalry made a charge against the Marquis de Crequi that was only foiled by Turenne bringing cavalry from the French left wing, where they were unable to operate because of the incoming tide. Turenne's strategy of using the change of tide to enable him to carry out this cavalry envelopment of the Spanish left flank was a skilful use of local conditions. Ultimately Condé with all his troops was driven from the field, and the battle, which lasted from 8 a.m. to noon, ended in a complete victory for Turenne, with the loss of only about 400 men, mainly from the Cromwellian-English regiments. The Spanish lost 1,000 killed (their *tercios* were virtually annihilated) and 5,000 prisoners. Turenne pursued vigorously until nightfall, and the town of Dunkirk surrendered ten days later.

A notable omission in every report and on available maps of this battle is any trace of Turenne's forty pieces of artillery or indeed of their use. Perhaps the Spanish army's complete lack of guns caused the French Marshal to scorn employing his immense superiority in this field, or maybe the lengthy artillery deployment period made his troops so impatient that they stormed forward without waiting for artillery support, thereby masking their own guns.

10

The Swiss Armies

FOR THE FIRST TIME since the decline of the Roman legion, the Swiss – a poor mountain people, lightly armed and armoured and lacking horses – re-introduced infantry to offensive warfare through the experience gained in fighting the Hapsburgs for their independence, when they made the best possible use of local resources and difficult mountain terrain. In the process they became a mobile force capable of pushing all before their massed pike formations with a manoeuvrability, cohesion and shock-factor comparable to that displayed by the Macedonian phalanxes centuries earlier. At such battles as Laupen in 1339 they unseated the cavalryman, the symbol of chivalry and the feudal system, from his centuries-long dominance of Western European battlefields; at Mortgarten in 1315 and Sempach in 1386 they so profoundly influenced the tactics and strategy of their day as to change the whole accepted concept of mediaeval warfare, toppling an outworn social system into oblivion. The sturdy Swiss mountaineers carved a place for themselves in mediaeval Europe by exploiting skill and courage amid their mountainous valleys, successfully defying their feudal Hapsburg overlords after forming a league for self-defence against all oppressors in 1291. Swiss militia repeatedly repelled foreign attacks throughout the fourteenth century.

The Swiss infantry of this period displayed many unique features besides their inherent ability to make successful war; for example, they never worked under a commander-in-chief and there is no known instance of a Swiss officer rising to become a capable general. They were led by a committee of captains and their formations were controlled by 'old sergeant-majors', aged 'captains' who showed considerable skill in every sort of warfare including surprise, ambush, forced marches and other tactical manoeuvres. Pride in their formations and a strong *esprit de corps* were paramount, and any sign of cowardice saw the culprit handed over to the hangman. Stubbornly resisting to the last man even when defeat was inevitable, their vastly diminished numbers, in closed ranks, marched from the field, never dispersing or routing. The classic example of this was the battle of St Jakob in 1444 when a phalanx surrounded by French foes and outnumbered fifteen to one, fought on until reduced to a mound of corpses surrounded by twice as many dead enemy.

The first troops to do so since the Romans, the Swiss marched in cadence to the music of fife and drum, and carried a colour in each company, frequently that of their canton, plus local 'town' banners in their columns. Several of the cantons bore a huge horn which, when blown, was the signal for all to rally round it. Whenever possible, they marched rapidly and directly from march-column into battle, without deploying or going through the formality of forming a battle-line, although they were capable of forming formations such as line, wedges or square in a rapid and systematic manner. However, they preferred to fight in three heavy columns or phalanxes, echeloned to right or left rear, the frontage rarely exceeding thirty men, but from fifty to 100 men deep. Individual columns marched on parallel roads, or across country in combat positions; in other situations, the first column marched directly into the fight, the others peeling-off right or left, to come up on the first column's flank.

Charles the Bold, Duke of Burgundy lost his life at Nancy in 1477 at the third and last of three losing encounters with the Swiss within two years, first at Granson in 1476 which ended in an almost bloodless Burgundian rout; next at Morat in the same year, where even cannon did not halt the pike formation which completely routed Charles' force. At Nancy, the irresistible pike formations executed a turning movement covered by woods, to take the Burgundian army in front and flank, routing them and killing their commander. These impressive victories not only put into Swiss hands the complete Burgundian camp and baggage-train plus countless guns, but also

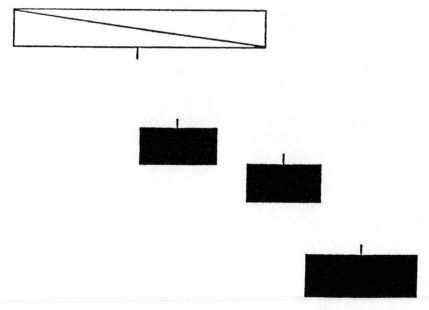

The attacking formation of the Swiss pikemen

killed numerous well-known soldiers along with their mercenary bands of English, Flemish, German and Italian troops. Moreover, the Swiss became the most sought after troops in Europe, and finding gain more profitable than patriotism, the Swiss became Europe's premier mercenary force. Their would-be hirers were more than convinced that the Swiss were as powerful in attack as tough in defence, that they were capable of resisting heavy cavalry in direct attacks, and that their fast-moving organised columns were far more than a match for Europe's ill-organised low-quality infantry.

Backed by their natural flair for warfare, Swiss tactics gave them superiority in Europe for more than fifty years and, in the open field, they were considered invincible against both infantry and cavalry. During much of this time, the Swiss battle-order consisted of three squares which could be between 1,000 and 10,000-strong, depending upon the size of their army on the day. Armoured pikemen covered the flanks with their eighteen-to-twenty-one-foot long pikes, and the main body was formed of halberdiers. When receiving a cavalry charge, a hedgehog was formed by upraised pikes so preventing the horsemen from penetrating the phalanx, then the halberdiers took advantage of the resulting confusion, cutting, slashing and pulling horsemen from the saddle.

However, the Swiss did not always have things all their own way and, as time passed, enemy commanders began to identify the conditions which led to either success or failure against the Swiss. Subsequently, instead of forming up their troops in flat, open fields, which was ideal ground for the Swiss phalanx, they selected terrain that was undulating, pocked by rocks and heavy undergrowth, or where natural ditches and dykes were likely to upset the cohesion of the phalanx. If the close formation became gapped then a lively enemy, such as Spanish sword-and-buckler men, could slip-in between the divided ranks and create havoc with their short swords, against which the long and awkward pikes were an encumbrance at close quarters. Perhaps those far-seeing commanders were classical scholars who had read of the occasion at Cynoscephalae in 197 BC when, for the first time, the flexible Roman legion and the Macedonian phalanx met on open terrain. Because of unsuitable broken ground, the phalanx – like their Swiss imitators and successors, always previously successful – had been divided and routed. The Greeks were no doubt just as incredulous as were the Swiss when it first happened to them!

Enemy commanders also learned from hard experience that when they had to meet a Swiss three-column force in echelon, with the right column leading, the simplest tactic was to lure it on to attack an entrenched position, strong with artillery and arquebusiers, backed by pikemen. Or, they could make a flank attack on the leading column, with cavalry or light troops, so forcing it to halt to beat-off the assault. This was because in the event of the pikes on the flanks having to come down to resist the charge, then the pikes in front had to halt to prevent the column breaking in two.

As it was with the earlier Macedonian phalanxes, the principal Swiss weapon was a twenty-one-foot pike, with an eighteen-foot shaft topped by a three-foot iron pointed shank capable of resisting the desperate slashes of attacking cavalry swords. Held at shoulder-height with arms apart and the hands grasping the weapon near the middle of the shaft, the Swiss kept the point directed downward, giving them an advantage when it came to push-of-pikes with an enemy formation. This was because when two pike columns clashed, points held high were likely to be pushed upwards by the enemy weapons, which then had a better chance of burying their points in opposing bodies because their points were downward. The Swiss formation meant that the heads of the pikes of second, third and fourth ranks projected in front of the first and foremost line; the rear rank held their pikes upright. The interior files of the column were occupied by halberdiers, whose role was to cut-down individual horsemen in a mêlée, when the pikemen had halted or repulsed a cavalry charge.

The soldiers of the cantons did not appreciate enforced changes in their proven national tactics, but grudgingly agreed in time that some concessions to gunpowder had to be made; a muster-roll dated 1444 reveals sixty-one handguns to be included with the crossbows of a 500-strong light infantry force. In earliest days, in addition to the basic pikemen, Swiss formations included a few crossbowmen – later handgunmen and arquebusiers – as skirmishers on the flanks of the columns. After the Battle of Bicocca in 1522 the three regulation Swiss phalanxes had flanking fire-arms-bearing men, sometimes as many as one in five or six, who were not part of the striking force but responsible for covering the column's flanks or going out to skirmish before the charge began.

The Swiss scorned gunpowder cannon and, during the fifteenth century, never really appreciated the vulnerability of their massed columns to effective artillery fire, possibly because of lack of field-artillery at that time. Their arch enemy Charles the Bold of Burgundy recognised this Swiss failure to understand the effects upon them of artillery and small-arms fire, but his relatively advanced tactical ideas in this field never bore fruit, due largely to his own rashness, as battle accounts indicate. Nevertheless, formidable soldiers as they were, the Swiss never recovered from their notable checks by artillery at Marignano in 1515 and Bicocca. In the first-named battle, which was a desperate two-day affair, the mutinous Swiss were given an unforgettable lesson by the French, their employers, whose guns extracted some 12,000 casualties; at Bicocca, their hasty assault on an artillery-protected position disordered their formations so much that they suffered a decisive defeat at the hands of German lands-knechts. In retrospect, things could have been different because, as early as 1444, it is known that a small number of culverins were brought into the field by the Swiss, although there is little record of their use.

These defeats, and that at Pavia in 1525, went a long way towards destroying prestige the Swiss had gained on so many fields, although these victories were surprisingly never followed up, and they showed a curious indifference to political or territorial gain. In fact, after their decisive victories over the Burgundians on the fields of Granson, Morat and Nancy, they could challenge any army in Europe. It was consistent with the Swiss national attitude towards resisting progress in their fighting methods that to them success failed to encourage change, except in the fact that the national trade of these mountain people became that of arms and fighting. Thus it was that their youth were trained from the cradle for the profession of bearing arms, encouraged to equate courage with national pride so that even children, bearing drums, flags and pikes, marched at the frequent feasts, fairs and similar semi-military occasions. Unfortunately, success brought arrogance, which manifested itself in a ruthless attitude towards prisoners, whom previously it had been the custom to spare for ransom. Their bloodthirstiness caused enemies to respond in kind. Moreover, they demanded such high fees as mercenaries that, in many cases, they priced themselves out of the market and were replaced by landsknechts. Insubordination, such as that which led to the Battle of Marignano, forced many would-be employers to lose confidence in them.

But none can take from them the accolade of being the Fathers of Modern Infantry.

11

The Landsknecht Armies

TOWARDS THE END of the fifteenth century the moral and tactical ascendancy of the Swiss infantry was such that no other European infantry could stand up against them, although other countries tried, with varying degrees of success, to put into the field a force that could provide reasonable opposition. So it came about that in the last quarter of the fifteenth century there arrived the landsknechts, very competent professional soldiers who were eventually to wrest a great deal of their supremacy from the Swiss, and who were the forerunners of the German infantry of the late nineteenth to mid twentieth century. They originated from Swabia which, being next to Switzerland, allowed them to learn the fighting methods of their neighbours and, because the Swiss were men of the mountains, the newcomers took the name of landsknechts, or men of the plains.

Maximilian of Hapsburg, plagued in his eternal and repetitive wars against the French House of Valois by the Swiss mercenaries, the infantry component of the French armies of the late fifteenth century, gave every encouragement to the creation of a German counterpart, the landsknechts. Organised, trained and equipped in the same manner as their Swiss rivals, soon the landsknechts became one of the toughest factors on the battlefields of Europe, and as mercenaries were almost as much sought after as the Swiss. Caring little on whose side they marched, landsknechts fought wherever there was fighting, prospects of loot, and good pay – bringing their weapons and gear with him, they were paid according to their quality. Whenever the landsknechts and Swiss came up against each other in battle – which was invariably fierce and bloody – the Swiss were invariably victorious, becoming even more bloodthirsty and ferocious than against other foes. But when landsknechts came up against landsknechts, they waged what they called 'good warfare' in which both sides spared the lives of prisoners.

Forming a separate caste, a sort of guild with its own laws and customs, in time the ranks of the landsknechts were composed of impoverished knights and lawless young men from the towns. They fought in most armies of the 'Pike-and-Shot' period, being no more reliable than were their eternal opponents, the Swiss, each possessing an overweening hatred for the other. Seemingly indifferent to national emotions, patriotism or loyalty (except to their own com-rades) they drifted everywhere in the sixteenth century, and could be found in French service, in Poland, Sweden and Denmark, a band of them even appearing in England, employed by Protector Somerset to put down Kett's Norfolk rebellion in 1549.

The strength of a regiment of landsknechts varied greatly, perhaps being made up of as many as thirty companies, sometimes only ten – the usual number assigned to a company was 400 – and their total force could reach as many as 10/12,000 men, when they would be strengthened by an artillery contingent. They were armed with the pike and the halberd and, over the years, with steadily increasing numbers of fire-armed men; they tended to hold pikes very low, always keeping the point slanting somewhat upwards, which put them at a disadvantage to their perennial Swiss opponents whose pikes were held shoulder-high with the point down, when in 'push of pike'. However, it seems unlikely that such a professional and experienced force as the landsknechts would have perpetuated this error, once its deficiencies had been revealed. There appears to be little record of specific drill or exercises for pike or halberd; their proficient employment would seem to arise from an innate national talent. As, like the Swiss, they fought in large columns, there was no need to acquire knowledge of the complicated manoeuvres so com-mon in the late sixteenth and early seventeenth centuries – their huge and tight formations were far too unwieldy for anything but the simplest evolutions. All that was required was for the men to fall-in by files, with sufficient distance and interval to allow each individual, on his own ground, to turn right or left and to competently wield pike or halberd.

In any event, few of their officers had any knowledge of drill procedures, being chosen instead for their bravery and experience, the colonel selecting his ensigns, delivering to each the colour of his company, and exhorting them to defend it to the death. These hardened, grizzled old warriors had the fife-and-drum of their company under their immediate command, enabling men to know the position of their company-colour by sound if not by sight. When the companies were formed into their squares, colour-bearers were positioned in the centre escorted by the colour-guards, who bore two-handed swords; then the colour-bearer (*Fähnrich*) would 'show the colours' by sweeping the staff about his head, using circular and figure-of-eight motions to fan out the cloth. To show them to friend or foe when the pikes were raised, he would hurl the colour high into the air, to fan out and hang briefly overhead like a kite, before coming down to be caught. Through a formalised system of movements, the colour-bearer could transmit basic military commands, such as 'March! Halt! Left/Right Turn!' and, on the march, he would signal the march-cadence of the fifes-and-drums without which the massive columns could not move in any order.

The colours of the landsknechts were very large and voluminous, probably to contrast with those carried by the Swiss, which were very small; the flag itself usually bore some heraldic colours or device relating to the colonel; territorial heraldic devices were only displayed if a regiment had been raised or paid by a specific town or district. It was the custom for the colour-bearer to display prominently in his personal costume the colour-scheme of the colour he bore. This was not difficult as the general costume of the landsknechts was strikingly bizarre, their dress being what it pleased each man to wear, and was invariably fantastically colourful and extravagant.

12

The Anglo-Scots Wars

DURING THE ELEVENTH century the four principal communities or kingdoms of Scotland – the Scots, the Picts, the Britons, and the Angles – united into a single kingdom of Scotland, under King Malcolm II (1005–34) and King Duncan (1034–40), but remained in a state of anarchy through almost constant internal wars and feuds. The kingdom was also subjected to many punitive English expeditions, arising from frequent Scots raids into the northern English provinces. During the reign of David I, much of Northumberland and Cumberland were conquered, despite a defeat in the Battle of the Standard at Northallerton in 1138; but both English provinces were regained by Henry II of England during the reign of Malcolm IV.

Supporting the feudal rebels and the sons of King Henry II of England in the Great Rebellion of 1173–74, Scots King William the Lion (1165–1214) was defeated and captured by Henry at the second Battle of Alnwick in 1174 and only gained freedom on payment of a ransom. His successor, King Alexander II, seeking to take advantage of the Baron's Revolt against King John of England, invaded in an attempt to seize Northumberland but was repulsed. From then on until the very end of the thirteenth century relations between England and Scotland were relatively peaceful. This suddenly changed in the 1290s following a dispute over succession in Scotland, leading to English intervention when Edward I of England, asked to mediate, gained acknowledgement of English overlordship and chose John Balliol as the new Scots king.

However, following Balliol's entering an alliance with France, Edward claimed the throne of Scotland and in 1296 invaded Scotland, defeated Balliol at Dunbar in 1296 and annexed the Scottish kingdom. In the following year, William Wallace, the Scottish leader, defeated the Earl of Warenne at Cambuskenneth Bridge, and raided into Northumberland and Durham. In 1298 Edward led an army of about 25,000 into Scotland, his aggressive advance forcing Wallace to fight at Falkirk on 22 July 1298, where was seen one of the first examples of the power of the English longbow. The Scottish schiltrons of pikemen were shattered by arrows before being destroyed by cavalry. Wallace was captured and executed, and Scotland annexed by England, but Robert Bruce continued to lead Scottish resistance.

In 1307, Edward II came to the throne of England. A weak ruler, during his reign Scotland virtually re-established her independence, provoking Edward to invade, but he was decisively beaten at Bannockburn on 23 June 1314, said by English historian Sir Charles Oman to be, 'The most lamentable defeat which an English army ever suffered.' For the next fifteen years or so, the Scots raided far and frequently into England, until 1328 when Scottish independence was recognised at the Peace of Northampton. It was a short-lived peace, because Edward III, now King of England, was a very different warrior to his predecessor and soon found an excuse to invade Scotland in 1333, when in the Battle of Halidon Hill he smashed the Scots, using infantry tactics which, within a few years, would make England masters of European warfare.

Warfare between English and Scots now became a desultory sideshow to the Hundred Years War (1337–1453) taking place in France, although in 1346 – the year of the victory at Crécy – King David of Scotland invaded England, only to be defeated and captured at Nevilles Cross. In 1388 there was a Franco-Scottish invasion of northern England by a force led by Earl James Douglas, who defeated Sir Henry Percy's English army at Otterburn, where Douglas was killed.

Throughout the fifteenth century, as in past years, there was almost continuous border warfare, perhaps less intense than in past centuries because of repeated internal struggles between Scots kings and their nobles. Taking advantage of the Wars of the Roses, during the reign of James III (1460–88) the Scots managed to recover those remaining areas of southern Scotland that remained in English hands.

The sixteenth century was that of the Tudors, dominated by larger-than-life Henry VIII and his colourful daughter Elizabeth I, who found time to carry on sporadic wars with Scotland whilst establishing the foundations of the great maritime empire of the future. In 1513, Henry VIII, warring with France, Scotland's traditional ally, caused sufficient provocation for James IV to invade England where, on 9 September 1513, he was soundly beaten by Thomas Howard, Earl of Surrey, at the Battle of Flodden. This great victory kept Scottish border ambitions on a low key, consisting only of endemic and indecisive warfare. In 1542 war was resumed as a result of religious differences between James and Henry VIII, who was renewing old claims of domination; a crushing Scottish defeat at Solway Moss on 25 November 1542, by an English invading army, began this period, which ended in 1547 when the Scots were defeated at Pinkie. This was the last formal battle fought between the national armies of the two countries, and resulted in the English occupying Edinburgh.

Following the execution of Charles I, his son Charles II was proclaimed King of Great Britain by the Scottish Presbyterians and, coming to an agreement to accept the Solemn League and Covenant, was crowned on 1 January 1651 in Scotland. Earlier, in July to September 1650, Oliver Cromwell led an invading army into Scotland, advancing on Edinburgh at the head of a force of 16,000 who encountered a larger Scottish force under David Leslie in a tight defensive attitude. They came to grips at Dunbar on 5 September 1650, when Cromwell's surprise dawn cavalry charge led to total victory. Leslie retreated to Stirling, leaving Cromwell in control of the route to Edinburgh and southern Scotland.

The last action of this concluding period of the English Civil War took place in June to September 1651, when Cromwell's ploy of threatening Stirling whilst leaving the road to London seemingly open, led to Charles II marching southwards with Leslie's army, followed by Cromwell's army marching at the rate of twenty miles a day down the east coast. At the subsequent Battle of Worcester, fought on 5 September 1651, a Scots army of 16,000 struggled hopelessly against twice their number; few survived to return to Scotland, and Charles was forced to flee to France.

THE BATTLE OF BANNOCKBURN 23–24 JUNE 1314

In June 1314 King Edward II, the unwarlike son of a warlike father, invaded Scotland with the objective of relieving Stirling Castle, whose English defenders had agreed to surrender to the Scots if aid had not reached them by Midsummer's Day. Robert Bruce, King of Scotland, attempting to intercept the English army, elected to hold a partly open plateau overlooking the marshy valley through which the Bannockburn meandered to join the Forth. His right flank was protected by the burn at the Newmiln bog and the left by a forest on Gillies Hill. The Scots right wing was further protected by three-foot-deep pits with a stake in each, lightly covered with sods and branches. Holes (or 'pottes') were dug in the road that ran behind them and iron calthrops with sharp points were strewn over areas where cavalry might be expected to charge.

Bruce divided his army of between 8,000 and 10,000 men into four 'battles' – the right commanded by his brother Edward, the left by Douglas and the young Stewart of Scotland, the centre by Thomas Randolph, the veteran Earl of Moray, and the reserve under his own command. With the exception of 500 cavalry under Sir Robert Keith, the Marshal, which were stationed about a quarter of a mile forward of the left wing, the knights were ordered to fight on foot like heavily armoured infantrymen. On the afternoon of 23 June Edward's army came into view. It consisted of at least 3,000 heavy horse, 5,000 archers and 15,000 infantry. The cavalry was divided into ten 'battles' in three lines of three battles each, with the tenth forming an advance guard. It was an impressive array, under gaily coloured pennons and banners, burnished arms and armour glittering in the sunshine.

Two companies of English cavalry came forward to reconnoitre the Scots position and, after Sir Henry Bohun had been killed charging at Bruce, one company was easily repelled by a force of 500 tightly packed Scottish pikemen.

There was no more fighting that day, and the discouraged Edward

[68]

ordered his men to build a wooden causeway over the marshland so that the packed infantry formations could reach the field of battle. Throughout a cold and uncomfortable night 20,000 men laboriously attempted to cross the stream and bog. Daybreak saw the English main body across the stream on the marshy flats milling about in disorder. Only Gloucester's cavalry vanguard was formed up for battle.

This situation so encouraged the Scots that they moved forward in echelon, causing Gloucester, without waiting for archers to support him, to lead his 'vaward' uphill in a charge at the Scottish right wing, which was slightly in advance of the other three 'battles'. The ponderous steeds of the knights lumbered into the forest of out-stretched Scottish pikes as the two formations clashed. For a few minutes they stood locked together, then Gloucester fell dead and his demoralised cavalry drew off. But their respite was short. The Scots charged in their turn, bearing down the floundering English soldiers with their pikes. Many of the cavalry were immediately unhorsed, to roll helplessly on the ground among their plunging horses.

Seeking a vantage point, a body of English archers ran forward to a position on the English right flank, whence they fired unchecked into the packed Scots ranks, bringing down man after man. Seeing this, Bruce ordered Sir Robert Keith and his cavalry to charge diagonally round the fringes of the morass into them. Caught by surprise in flank, without support and lacking spears, the archers were either cut down or dispersed in all directions, adding to the disorder in the English ranks. The Scottish cavalry so intimidated the English archers that they spent the rest of the battle firing flights of arrows from the rear over the heads of their own troops, doing little damage to their unseen targets.

The nine remaining English cavalry divisions now came lumbering up the slope towards the Scottish centre and, as the huge mass of horse and foot locked together, the battle developed into a confused mêlée between Scots pikemen and English men-at-arms. In such tight order and on such a narrow front only the foremost English ranks could strike the enemy, those in the rear being unable to move. Mounted knights and men-at-arms, in small bodies, made ineffective charges that all failed to break through the pike formations. So it came about that the English archers and spearmen waited in disarray behind their struggling cavalry until the piles of their own dead were so high that any forward movement was impossible. The English formations began to falter, and the tidal wave of defeat mounted when thousands of Scottish camp followers, who had been watching the fight from Gillies Hill, swarmed excitedly down the slopes waving banners and shouting 'Slay! Slay!' Imagining the rabble to be Scottish reinforcements, the English wavered and fled. Soldiers in the rear who had not even struck a blow stared incredulously at comrades fleeing past them, until panic took hold of them too and they ran for their lives, turning the defeat into a rout.

Down the hill came the Scots, driving the English into the bogs of the burn, where they were smothered or drowned, and soon the narrow ravine was choked and bridged over by the slain. Together with some of his knights, King Edward turned tail and galloped off to Stirling Castle, but was refused admittance and struggled on to the Castle of Dunbar. Behind him Stirling surrendered.

THE BATTLE OF FLODDEN FIELD 9 SEPTEMBER 1513

The longbow was to go out of military fashion in a blaze of glory, to achieve a victory in the old classical style that left a glow in the hearts of the yeomen of England, but no pangs of regret at its passing in the hearts of their enemies.

The events which led to the Scottish invasion of England in 1513 need not be recapitulated; suffice to say that King James IV of Scotland had crossed the border in mid-August of that year with, for that time, an enormous army of 40,000 men. They were well furnished with the latest artillery of the day. His leaders were all those of the highest rank in the Scottish kingdom; it may be fairly said that no grown-up member of any family of position was absent from the expedition. After some initial skirmishing, the Scots had Northumberland at their mercy; but after taking the castle of Ford, stronghold of the Heron family, James loitered in the neighbourhood whilst his army daily diminished. Said to have been infatuated by the captured Lady Heron, King James appeared to disregard the increasing desertions of those gorged with plunder in addition to those starved through the land being foraged-out. Finally, his army numbered less than 30,000, but those that were left represented the cream of the whole and were claimed to have been one of the noblest bodies of fighting men ever gathered together. To back them, James had a most efficient train of thirty pieces of artillery which had been cast for him at Edinburgh by the master gunner, Robert Borthwick.

Against the Scots was sent the veteran Earl of Surrey, over seventy years of age, and forced, on account of his rheumatism, to travel mostly by coach. Chiefly from the northern counties, he hastily gathered together an army of between 20,000 and 26,000 men. Whilst encamped at Alnwick, Surrey sent a formal challenge to King James, naming Friday, 9 September, as the day of battle; the challenge was duly accepted in the most formal manner. At the time of acceptance, James was encamped in the low ground and, according to the old rules of chivalry, his acceptance from this spot implied that he would give battle on that site. But before long James had moved his camp from there to Flodden Hill, an eminence lying due south of Ford Castle, running east and west in a low ridge. Here, on the steep brow of Flodden Edge, in the angle between the Till and its small tributary, the Glen, James's defensive position was so strong that no sane foe would dare to attack it.

Realising this, Surrey sent James a letter of reproach in which he pointed out that the arrangement had been made for a pitched battle, and instead James had installed himself in a fortified camp. He concluded by challenging him to come down on the appointed day and fight on Millfield Plain, a level tract south of Flodden Hill. King James refused even to see the herald who brought the message.

Surrey then marched his army up the River Till and put his vanguard with the artillery and heavy baggage across at the Twizel bridge, whilst the remainder of his force crossed at Sandyford, half a mile higher up. At this point James had an excellent opportunity of attacking the English whilst they were split into two parts. By failing to grasp it, James now found his foes placed between himself and Scotland; he was left with little alternative but to reverse his order of battle. Setting fire to the rude huts that his men had constructed on the summit of the hill, he moved his force on to Branxton Hill, immediately behind Flodden Edge; the movement was partially obscured from the English by the clouds of smoke that trailed over the brow of the hill. As they formed up on the ridge above Branxton, the Scottish army that had faced south were now drawn up facing north.

The two armies faced each other, both formed into four divisions and both with a reserve. Beginning on the English right, the first division was commanded by Sir Edmund Howard, the younger son of the Earl of Surrey; opposed to him were the Gordons under the Earl of Huntley and the men of the border under the Earl of Home. The second English division was led by Admiral Howard, who was faced by the Earls of Crawford and Montrose. The Earl of Surrey, with the third division, was opposed by King James himself; while Sir Edward Stanley, with the fourth division, had to try conclusions with the Earls of Lennox and Argyle, whose troops were mainly highlanders. The English reserve, mainly cavalry, was commanded by Lord Dacre; that of the Scottish under Bothwell.

It was not until four o'clock that the battle commenced. Then, as an old chronicler says: 'Out burst the ordnance with fire, flame and a hideous noise . . .' The Scottish artillery was far superior in construction to the English, which was constructed of hoops and bars; there were, however, more English guns. It seems as though the English gunners were superior to those serving the Scottish cannon, the latter committing the error of firing at too great an elevation so that their shots passed over the heads of the English and buried themselves in the marshy ground beyond. The old writer goes on to say, '. . . and the master gunner of the English slew the master gunner of the Scots, and beat all his men from their guns.' The early death of Borthwick, brought down by a ball, set up a panic in his men, who ran from their guns – but it was not by artillery fire that Flodden was to be won or lost. James realised this fact and ordered an attack; the border troops of the Lords Huntley and Home appear to have been the first to come to close quarters with the English.

In an unusual silence the Scots rushed forward, their twelve-foot-long pikes levelled in front of them; the initial impetus of their onslaught carried them far into the English lines, so that at first they achieved absolute success. The English right, under Sir Edmund Howard, was thrust back, their leader thrice beaten down and his banner overturned. The English fighting line was in disorder on this flank. Some Cheshire archers, who had been separated from their corps and sent out to strengthen the right wing, fled in all directions and chaos came to Howard's wing. John Heron, usually known as the Bastard Heron, at the head of a group of Northumbrians, checked the rout long enough for Dacre to charge down with his reserve. This committing of the reserve at such an early stage did not succeed in restoring the English line, but it did put Huntley to flight, whilst the undisciplined borderers of Home had no further idea of fighting. In a border foray, no more was expected after routing one's opponents; Home's men did not grasp that Flodden was no ordinary foray – 'We have fought and won, let the rest do their part as well as we!' was their answer to those trying to rally them.

Whilst this was going on, Crawford and Montrose were furiously attacking the division of Admiral Howard; so much so that the Admiral sent to his father, the Earl of Surrey, for assistance. But Surrey was fully occupied in holding his own against the division commanded by King James, strengthened by Bothwell, who had brought up the reserve and flung them into the struggle. The battle was now at its height and was being hardly contested all along the line; it seemed, here and there, as though the English halberds were proving more deadly weapons at close quarters than the long Scottish pikes.

On the English left, the archers of Cheshire and Lancashire, under Sir William Molyneaux and Sir Henry Kickley, were pouring volleys of arrows into the tightly packed ranks of the Scottish right, high-landers under the Earls of Lennox and Argyle. Galled by the hail of shafts which spitted their unarmoured bodies, the wild clansmen finally found it to be more than they could bear. Casting aside their targets and uttering wild, fierce yells, they flung themselves forward in a headlong rush, claymore and pole-axe waving furiously in a frenzy of anxiety to bury themselves into English flesh and bone. The bowmen and pikemen were shaken, so tremendous was the initial shock, their bills and swords, which had replaced the bows, reeling and wavering under the onslaught; but discipline prevailed and their formation remained unbroken. The archers on the flanks of the mêlée stood back and poured in volley after volley at close quarters, while the inner line of pikemen and men-at-arms held off the wild highland-ers. Their arrows gone, the archers threw down their bows and drew their swords and axes to fling themselves into the fray, both in front and on the flanks. It was a deadly struggle whilst it lasted, but gradually the clansmen gave way, fighting at first, but then, suddenly, in complete rout – both earls died trying to stem the tide.

Stanley pressed forward, won his way up and crowned the ridge. He did not make the error of pursuing from the field the thoroughly broken Scots whom his men had just beaten. Facing about, he charged obliquely downhill to take the Scots divisions of King James and Bothwell in flank. This struggle in the centre, between Surrey and King James, had been proceeding fiercely; the King was fighting on foot like the rest of his division, conspicuous by the richness of his arms and armour. Stanley's flank attack, coinciding with a similar attack on the other flank by Dacre and Edmund Howard, proved disastrous to the Scots. Hemmed in on all sides, they began to fall by hundreds in the close and deadly mêlée; no quarter was asked by either side and none was given. The blood flowing from the dreadful gashes inflicted by axes, bills and two-handed swords made the ground so slippery that many of the combatants were said to have taken off their boots to gain a surer footing.

As a battle, all was over by now and nothing remained but the slaughter. Surrounded by a solid ring of his knights, James refused to yield until he finally fell, dying with the knights who had formed a human shield around him. He was said to have been mortally wounded by a ball fired by an unknown hand; he had several arrows in his body, a gash in his neck and his left hand was almost severed from his arm. Ten thousand men fell on the Scottish side; to list the slain is almost to catalogue the ancient Scottish nobility. With the exception of the heads of families who were too old or too young to fight, there was hardly a family of top rank that did not grievously suffer. The English lost about 5,000 men.

On the Scots side, the archers of Ettrick, known in Scotland as the 'Flowers of the Forest', perished almost to a man. To this day the sweet, sad, wailing air known by that name is invariably the Dead March used by Scottish regiments.

THE BATTLE OF PINKIE 10 SEPTEMBER 1547

Like Marignano, Pinkie was a classic example of an old-fashioned infantry army being destroyed by a commander aware that cavalry and artillery were a deadly combination. The last tactical link in the long chain of battles where English combinations of weapons defeated the Scottish pike column, Pinkie was different in that it was won by horsemen and guns and not by a combination of bowmen and dismounted men-at-arms as at Dupplin, Halidon Hill, Neville's Cross, Homildon and Flodden. It highlighted the great lesson of warfare in this period – that cavalry could ride down musketeers who, in their turn, could mow down pikemen. To win battles a commander had to combine all his arms in the right proportion at the right place at the right time.

In September 1547 the Duke of Somerset, Lord Protector of England, marching parallel with Lord Clinton's fleet coasting along the shore, invaded Scotland with 16,000 men, about a quarter of them being cavalry, including foreign men-at-arms under Malatesta, 500 'Bulleners' (horsemen of the garrison of Boulogne), the Gentlemen Pensioners of the Royal Bodyguard, the Northern Horse (the 'Prickers' of the border marshes), and a troop of mounted arquebusiers under Pedro de Gamboa, a Spanish condottiere. Two of the foreign companies and 600 of the English infantry were armed with arquebuses, but the rest of the foot soldiers were the 'bows and bills' of the Flodden period.

Under the Regent Arran, the Scots army of 23,000 men had only 1,500 Border 'Moss Troopers' as their cavalry arm, and the bulk of the infantry were traditional Scottish pikemen. They took up a defensive position west of the River Esk where it ran into the Firth of Forth between Musselburgh and Inveresk, their long line running from the marsh on the river to the seashore, where guns were sited in an earthwork. It was a good unflankable position, protected by the sea on the north and on the south by the marsh, which could only be turned by a lengthy circular march over rough country. The River Esk was fordable in most places but, on the Scottish side, the steep and exposed slope of Edmonston Edge had to be climbed by attacking troops after fording the river. On the day before the battle English cavalry scouting inland fell in with the main body of Scottish horse, who were easily routed with heavy casualties by the stronger men-at-arms, and their morale greatly depressed.

Apparently inspired by the similarity of the Scots position to that of the Spaniards at Ravenna, Somerset determined to occupy the high knoll that projected almost into the Scottish lines, on which was built Inveresk church. He intended to plant all his heavy guns on it and sweep the Scottish line with flanking fire. So the English army began to march northward from its position on Fawside Brae, led by a body of light horse under Lord Ogle. The three infantry divisions – vaward, main-battle and rearward – followed, with the main body of cavalry and two heavy brigades making up the rear, and the guns spaced at intervals between the infantry divisions. Seeing the enemy moving towards the road that led to Dunbar and back to England, the Regent Arran incredibly surmised that they were about to retreat to Berwick, so he abandoned his intention of fighting the defensive battle for which his force was suited and ordered his men to leave their positions on Edmonston Edge, ford the River Esk and attack the English columns in flank as they moved across his front. In three columns of pikes the Scots came down the slope and across the river at the speed of horsemen rather than infantry. Their left wing under the Earl of Huntly was nearest the sea, flanked by a body of Highland bowmen; the centre, under Arran himself, included some artillery drawn by teams of men; and the vaward (right wing) under Angus had a few guns and the remains of the cavalry on its flank.

Greatly surprised by this unexpected Scottish move, Somerset hastily began to form 'front to flank' in a race against time; the arquebusiers and bowmen formed up on either flank of the billmen with some confusion and congestion in the centre as the guns were hastily pushed and pulled through the infantry, while the cavalry disposed themselves on the wings. Suddenly, as the tightly packed ranks of the Scottish left wing were crossing the river between the Inveresk knoll and the sea, they were hit by a broadside from the guns of the fleet lying offshore, completely dispersing the Highland archers on Huntly's flank, who fled in panic from the scene. The hissing roundshot from the ships' guns also ploughed into the mass of pikemen, causing heavy casualties, so that Huntly hastily shifted the disordered column inland out of range, where it coalesced with Arran's main battle into one great mass.

Unchecked by this reverse, although delayed by the difficulties of manhauling their guns across rough country, the Scottish columns splashed through the river and across the flat land beyond before ascending the slope to the crest where the English, now almost in battle order, awaited their onslaught. As Arran's four guns fell in on Huntly's left, the line re-formed, but the Scottish cavalry, still smarting from their rough handling of the previous day, hung back in echelon far to the right rear. This fact, with the disappearance of the light infantry archers, transformed the Scottish army into a great mass of pikes with totally unprotected flanks.

Somerset was a good enough commander to seize the opportunity of halting the infantry by successive cavalry charges, while his

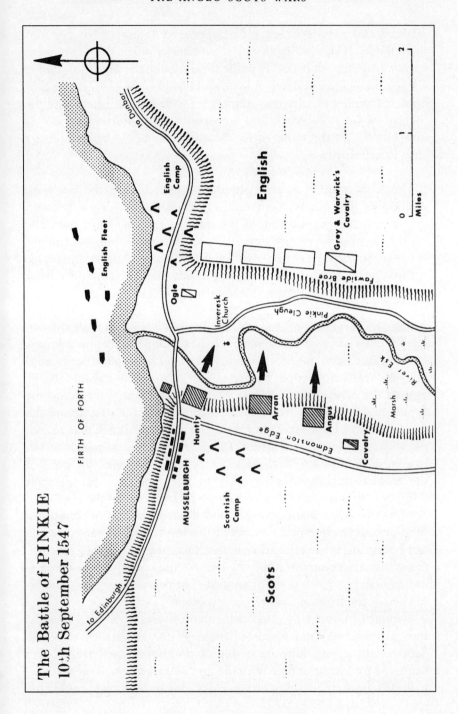

The Battle of PINKIE
10th September 1547

FIRTH OF FORTH

to Edinburgh

to Dunbar

English Camp

English Fleet

English

Grey & Warwick's
Cavalry

Fawside Brae

Ogle

Inveresk
Church

Pinkie Cleugh

MUSSELBURGH

Huntly

Scottish Camp

Scots

Arran

Angus

Edmonston Edge

Cavalry

Marsh

River Esk

Miles
0   1   2

artillery and missile-armed infantry poured a destructive fire into their flanks. The cavalry began their attacks when the Scots were halfway up the slope of Fawside Brae, amid the fields of Pinkie Cleugh, in an area of newly reaped stubble and low earth banks that hindered neither cavalry nor infantry. In went the 'Bulleners' and the 'Bands' of Grey, Norwich and Somerset – 1,800 horsemen striking into Huntly on the flank of the Scottish column. A contemporary chronicler records:

> The Scots stood at defence, shoulders nigh together, the fore rank stooping low before, their fellows behind holding their pikes in both hands, the one end of the pike against the right foot, the other against the enemy's breast, so nigh as place and space might suffer. So thick were they that a bare finger should as easily pierce through the bristles of a hedgehog as any man encounter the front of pikes.

Although charging courageously, the English horsemen were thrown back with relative ease, leaving great heaps of dead men and horses only six feet from the Scottish line. Intent on halting the Scots until his guns were in position, Somerset sent in a second cavalry charge against the Scottish main battle, the 1,600 horsemen including the Gentlemen Pensioners (the Royal Bodyguard), Vane's Band and the demi-lances of Lord Fitzwalter. Like the first, this attack was beaten off with great loss, some leaders falling and several standards put in jeopardy. By now the Earl of Warwick had positioned the guns of the English right wing and centre to bear upon the Scottish left (Huntly's division and parts of Angus's). Dramatically the elation of the hitherto triumphant pikemen was dashed by hails of roundshot fired into their close-packed ranks from less than 300 yards. At the same time arquebusiers and bowmen swarmed forward to fire into the stationary columns, while the horse-arquebusiers of the mercenary de Gamboa gave an exhibition of continental tactics by caracoling across the front of the helpless pikemen.

Hemmed in by heaps of dead men and horses, their ranks forced into a disordered and restricted mass by the cavalry charges, the Scots infantry was quite incapable of preventing itself from being shattered by weight of fire. With the cry 'Betrayed!' the Regent Arran galloped from the field. Left to carry on as best they could, his commanders took hasty, uncoordinated action. On the right Angus felt that it was essential to retire out of range of the guns. Trying to do this by falling back down the hillside, his retreat quickly turned into a rout as the disordered and now panicking pikemen cast down their pikes and fled instead of re-forming at the foot of the hill. Seeing this, the whole Scots line followed, and with Huntly's force, which had taken most punishment, all streamed off in a general stampede. The English cavalry charged again, to ride down and butcher the fleeing infantry as the Scots horsemen, who had never closed, rode away without loss. The Scots lost 10,000 to 14,000 men against English losses of about 250, mostly cavalry, for their infantry was hardly engaged.

13

The Turks and the Ottoman Empire

FOUNDED BY OTHMAN (Osman) in the early fourteenth century, the Ottoman Empire was the leading military power of South-East Asia throughout much of the Pike-and-Shot era, driving westwards against Europe on the two fronts of the Danube and the Mediterranean. Othman's son Orkhan organised the Ottoman Turkish State to create a military system superior to anything in Europe and, in 1356, the year of Poitiers in the Hundred Years War, the Turks crossed the Hellespont into Europe, taking Adrianople and flowing into the Balkans. Orkhan's successor, Suleiman I, was buried at Gallipoli, the first Ottoman ruler to be buried in European soil, and was succeeded by Murad I who continued to advance into Europe, until assassinated at Kosovo in 1389. His successor, Bajazet I, occupied Thessaly in 1391 and annihilated a Crusader army, mostly of Hungarians, at Nicopolis in 1396 but was defeated and taken prisoner at Angora in 1402 by Tamberlane's hordes, leaving his sons to fight between themselves for his empire.

Had Christendom been united, this was the moment when the Turks could have been driven out of Europe, but England and France were engaged in the Hundred Years War, and the opportunity was missed, allowing the Turks a long breathing space to re-form under such outstanding sultans as Mohammed I and Murad II. In 1444 the Turks were compelled to sue for peace after a series of defeats at the hands of a great alliance of Hungary, Poland, Serbia, Wallachia,

Burgundy, Genoa, Venice, the Greek Emperor and the Pope, their united armies being led by a Hungarian, John Hunyadi. Recovering from this, the Turks beat Hunyadi at Kosovo in 1448 and were now free to besiege the great city of Constantinople in 1453; Mohammed II, with an army of 100,000 men, battered down the fourteen miles of city walls and took the city. Then followed a series of resounding defeats of those European armies opposing the advancing Turks, and by the end of the fifteenth century steady Turkish expansion had conquered all the Balkans except Hungary.

The early years of the sixteenth century were the time of Turkey's supreme power and glory; their Sultan Selim I (1512–20) proved to be the greatest soldier of all the Ottoman rulers and he nearly doubled the size of their empire by decisive victories over the Persians and the Egyptian Mamelukes. However, his obsession with Asiatic campaigns deprived Turkey of the chance of capitalising on division in Europe. Selim was succeeded by his son Suleiman the Magnificent (1520–66) arguably one of the greatest rulers of the century. Again, a divided Europe was perhaps saved from Ottoman domination by Suleiman's repeated diversions of Turkish strength in wars against Persia. Although he conquered most of Hungary, he was thwarted in his attempts on Central Europe by the staunch defence of Vienna and other fortifications. Backed by an able admiral, Khair ed-Din Barbarossa, Suleiman built a strong Turkish navy and the Black Sea became a Turkish lake, but five years after his death, the long and slow decline of the Ottoman Empire was initiated by a decisive defeat at sea, at Lepanto in 1571, at the hands of Don Juan of Austria.

The decline slowly continued but not in a very apparent form as in the mid-seventeenth century the Turkish Empire stretched over three continents; the Red Sea and the Black Sea were both Turkish dominated, but there was a steady deterioration in the military strength upon which the Ottoman Empire depended. The janissaries, mainstay of the regular army, were becoming unruly, and the spahis and feudal cavalry were declining in numbers and quality, so that an increasing reliance had to be placed on Tartar horsemen from the Crimea, and on undisciplined and untrained militia and volunteers. Murad, last of the warrior-sultans, instituted military reforms in the janissary organisation, but these ended with his death in 1640. All these factors played a big part in the acceleration of decline in Turkish power by the end of the seventeenth century.

At the beginning of the fifteenth century only the English and the Ottoman Turks had regular standing armies, the latter giving allegiance to the Sultan as an individual in a manner comparable to the feudal system; both nations possessed a professional nucleus of infantry and cavalry. The Ottoman land forces were probably the most highly organised army in the world at that time, consisting of first-class soldiers who were well-trained and self-disciplined through religious zeal and strict sense of allegiance to the Sultan. However, it was an inflexible and over-centralised organisation, with the Sultan's absolute despotism cramping his generals' initiative; it was a mono-lithic structure with the marked defect of being particularly vulner-able to a war on two fronts, so that warlike threats from the West, allied to Persian threats, tended to disturb.

Turkish armies, save for the relatively small force of first-class janissaries, were composed almost entirely of cavalry, divided into light irregular skirmishers of the stradiot type, armed with bows; and heavier, lightly armoured and well-disciplined timariot (horsemen). Both were feudal levies formed into mounted units in which lancers and horse-archers were equally divided. Satisfied with the ability and effectiveness of their horse-archers, the Turks were slow to adopt cavalry fire-arms. They were capable of adequate shock-action against all but the heavily armoured Western men-at-arms of the fifteenth century, of the French-type gendarmeries; but even here their inferior shock-capability was somewhat counter-balanced by their greater manoeuvrability and general mobility. The role of these highly skilled horsemen was to form advance parties which pen-etrated deep into enemy territory, in the van of the army, pillaging, burning and rounding-up the terrified population as slaves. They were sometimes valuable for reconnaissance and for pursuit, but of little use in pitched battles, and were given captured territory in return for military service.

The elite cavalry of the Turkish army were the Sultan's Horse Guards, the spahis, which were permanent standing formations. More heavily armed and armoured than the timariots, they were capable of meeting the very best European cavalry and infantry on a level footing. They were highly paid and each one of them was responsible for recruiting and training from two to six additional horsemen, whom they brought into battle in the way a Western knight was accompanied by his 'lance'. In early times they wore little if any defensive armour, and were armed with bow, lance and short sword; in later times many of them were noblemen riding magnificent horses with accoutrements which were supreme examples of the art of the oriental armourer.

However, the cream of all Turkish armies were the highly trained and disciplined janissary infantry units. The most fearsome and dreaded of all Ottoman troops, they were first established by the Sultan Murad in 1360, when they were probably the world's first regular standing infantry. Taken when between ten and twelve as part of a recognised tribute due to the Sultan, the janissaries were trained in special communities and affiliated to a religious order of dervishes, receiving in their monastery-barracks a celibate education which made them fanatical Moslems. They received the best possible physical education, and were highly trained in the handling of their weapons. They were masters of attack as well as being experts in building fortifications, earthworks, ramparts and ditches and improvising defence. They were warriors who had neither family ties nor country and went into battle despising death and injury; they had a great deal in common with the Knights of the Hospital by whom they were regarded as worthy opponents. Belonging to a race whose only military tradition was that of cavalry, the janissaries were professional infantry at a time when infantry were out of fashion in the West. Perhaps the last-ditch stand of the Byzantine legions had taught the Ottoman Turks to appreciate the potential of a good infantry force. At the height of their greatness in the first half of the sixteenth century, the janissaries numbered between 12,000 and 15,000. Their basic tactical unit was the *orta*, which ranged in size at different periods from 100 to 3,000 men. The ranks of their many officers were taken from the titles of household departments – the Chief Soup Maker and the Chief of the Bloodhound Keepers. The commander of the janissaries was the Agha.

Never heavily laden with protective armour, in the fifteenth and sixteenth centuries the janissaries had a small round shield, a metal helmet shaped like a fez with a sharp point on top and possibly some light mail. Their original weapon was the short composite bow which they used with light arrows. Sabres and daggers were standard equipment and at various times they used slings, crossbows, javelins, lances, straight swords, pikes, axes, maces, scythes and whips.

In the seventeenth century, the janissaries were armed with a heavy

[83]

matchlock musket, a lance and the broad-bladed single-edged sword (known as the 'hand-jar'). At that time they wore blue caftans and high white caps, the uniform bearing the emblem of their corps – a wooden spoon. Their style of fighting was to sling the musket over the shoulder after firing and charge directly at the enemy; in the right hand was the sword, in the left a dagger – although sometimes this weapon was clamped between their teeth. If their first charge, invariably the bloodiest, was not entirely successful, further attacks were sometimes made with less enthusiasm. They played a major role in compensating for lack of steadiness when their highly mobile cavalry were engaged in a lasting and dour battle with a professionally balanced enemy by using field entrenchments that allowed the janissaries to provide a firm base of manoeuvre for their cavalry. Over the years, this tactic was frequently used by steadily augmented units of infantry janissaries.

The always-large Turkish armies who perpetually flooded west over the plains of Hungary could be said to have been a characteristic motley multitude of fighting-men gathered from every corner of their extensive country and acquired provinces. Perhaps on occasions they were more frightening in appearance than was justified, although they must have been impressive as they surged into action in a variety of national costumes, bearing traditional weapons and backed-up by hordes of servants, porters, drivers and the like. Every Turkish army carried innumerable such hangers-on, besides gunners, smiths, armourers and marines hired for single campaigns; there were also garrison troops known as the piyade; heavy guns and transport were drawn by bullocks and camels. Then there were the hordes of irregular troops formed by cavalry, known as akibi, and Bashi-Bazouks, who moved on foot – both types were unpaid and fought for loot and plunder.

The Bashi-Bazouks were a motley gang of rascals; many of them were Christians, such as Slavs, Hungarians and Germans fighting for plunder. The Ottoman method of fighting employed these irregulars as cannon-fodder by sending them in first with a line of 'military police' advancing behind them to encourage any waverers with whips and maces and behind the police came the janissaries, waiting to cut down any fugitive who got that far. Often the Bashi-Bazouks did very well in the first shock of an assault but they were easily discouraged if not immediately successful and the hopes of plunder receded. Against well-armed and disciplined defenders they were sometimes handicapped by their own numbers, getting in each other's way, and in scaling assaults most of the attackers could expect to be cut down before they reached the top of the ladder. But these irregulars worried the defenders and their corpses filled the ditches so that by the time the janissaries were thrown in the defence had weakened and success frequently followed.

Each unit of the Ottoman forces wore its own distinctive uniform bearing its emblem. Armour was of the mail type and was topped by a turban-shaped spiked helmet with a sliding nose piece. The Anatolian Turks wore both mail and breast-plates. The Ottoman equivalent of plate armour included fluted helmets, damascened in gold, brigandines (a kind of armour jacket, with exposed gold rivets) and heavy cloaks with luxuriant decorations. Since the scimitar was a weapon without defensive value, they also continued to use the small circular shield or target after it had gone out of fashion in Europe.

During much of their peak period, which lasted for more than 200 years, the Turkish armies revealed all the attributes of Asiatic cavalry armies in that they were extremely mobile and their fluid tactics – of the hit-and-run variety – were capable of demoralising all but the finest infantry and cavalry. In close hand-to-hand fighting, they were probably less efficient than their Christian opponents, who were able to risk their persons with greater boldness; but in their heyday the Turkish cavalry armies with their devastating combination of missile-power and shock-effect could handle most of the opponents that came against them. However, although their style of fighting was based on the solid foundation of well-disciplined and controlled janissaries, fighting from field entrenchments which provided a base of manoeuvre for their cavalry, they did have an obvious Achilles heel, peculiar to cavalry armies, in that they had to be constantly on the move to seek sufficient forage for their vast numbers of horses. This put them at a great disadvantage when attempting to carry on prolonged operations in a single region, particularly when they came up against European cavalry and infantry armies, based on strong, almost invulnerable fortifications, such as Vienna.

THE BATTLE OF MOHACS 29 AUGUST 1526

Although the opposing Turkish army, before whom the Hungarians had been slowly withdrawing, was numerically superior, the military pride of the Europeans caused them to stand and accept battle on the plain of Mohacs. Their army was made up of some 12,000 horse – 8,000 lightly equipped hussars and 4,000 fully armoured nobles and their retinues – and 13,000 foot, of whom 5,500 were veteran foreign mercenaries and the rest local levies experienced in border warfare in their mountain regions. The young King Louis of Hungary commanded the army, with Archbishop Tomori and George Zapolya as Generals-in-Chief, besides numerous soldier bishops and a veteran Polish condottiere, Leonard Gnomski.

The Turks had in the field an army of 60/70,000 men formed of 35,000 feudal horse (Roumeliot, Bosnian and Anatolian), 15,000 janissaries and regular horse, and a horde of ill-armed irregular horse and foot (adabs). Their very considerable artillery force was partly manned by Italian and German renegade gunners.

The Hungarians drew up for battle inland from the town of Mohacs, half a mile from the marshy bank of the Danube, overflowing through recent rains. The ground, flat and featureless and ideal for cavalry operations, sloped gently up towards the hills concealing the Turks. To avoid being outflanked, the Hungarians formed up in two long lines, the front line composed of 10,000 infantry in dense columns interspersed with 6,000 cavalry, including much of the feudal horse of the barons. Their twenty guns were placed in the centre. The right was held by the Croatian levies under Francis Bathiani, and the left was commanded by Peter Perenni, the Ban of Temesvar, who was greatly experienced in frontier fights against the Turks. The second line, in two ranks, was formed of 3,000 foot and 6,000 horse, with three squadrons of feudal horse in front of the King and his selected guard of 1,000 fully armoured knights, who were flanked by the Bishop's levies. Two small bodies of infantry were posted as flank guards, and there may have been a few light cavalry scouts beyond them.

The Turkish leader, the Sultan Suleiman 'the Magnificent', who had captured Rhodes in the previous year, formed his army in unusually deep order to counter the tempestuous fury of the charges of the heavy armoured knights, so that the Roumeliot horse occupied the first of three ranks, the Anatolian horse the second, and the janissaries, flanked by spahis and Silladar squadrons, the third. There were eighty guns, chained together in a huge battery between the second and third ranks. Parties of irregular cavalry called akindjis were scattered in front of the army, and about a mile forward, out on the left front, more of them, plus 4,000 Bosnian horse, were placed behind hills to form an outflanking force when battle was joined.

Concealed behind the hills, the main Turkish army was slow getting into battle order, and it was not until three hours after noon that the lance-heads and pennons of the Turkish horse appeared on the hill-tops. The Hungarians, who had been drawn up since early morning, opened fire as soon as the Roumeliot horsemen came within range, but with little effect, and then, as the Turkish horse seemed about to charge, the whole Hungarian front line surged forward to push everything before it, thrusting the Roumeliot horse back on the Anatolian cavalry of the second line in a mêlée in which the lighter Turkish cavalry suffered heavy casualties. It is likely that this relatively light resistance by the Turkish horse was a tactical move to disorder the Hungarians, whose infantry could not keep up with their charging horsemen, and draw them on to the massed Turkish guns.

Messengers from the fighting came back to the King with news that the whole Turkish army was giving way and now was the time for the Hungarian 'Main-Battle' to advance and clinch the victory. So, passing through their own guns, the second Hungarian line rolled forward up the slope to reinforce the tumultuous mêlée. Fighting fiercely, the Hungarians forced their way through the wilting ranks of both Anatolian and Roumeliot horse until they reached the janissaries of the third line and the chained guns. Here they were brought to a halt, milling about on open ground, charging and countercharging as salvoes of roundshot at ranges of less than 100 yards caused them heavy casualties.

As the Croatian infantry on the Hungarian right had struggled forward, trying to maintain contact with their cavalry, the Turkish outflanking cavalry force had come thundering into them, to send them reeling back and forcing the cavalry of the second Hungarian line to throw back their right squadrons to form a new front. Then, in

[87]

the 'killing ground' before the Turkish guns, the sadly stricken Hungarians began to wilt and the disordered cavalry and infantry of their left wing gave way, to retire to marshy ground near the Danube, where they tried to rally. But then the centre, unable to endure the point-blank discharges any longer and much affected by the suffocating smoke, gave way in great disorder. They passed through their own guns and skirted the camp on the outskirts of Mohacs, which was already being attacked by Turkish light horsemen. Completely beaten, the Hungarians made no attempt to rally. The Turks were prevented from carrying out a general pursuit by trumpets ordering every man to muster by a standard and remain in his original position.

About half the Hungarian army perished – only 3,000 out of the 13,000 foot got away, with 7,000 or 8,000 cavalry. The heavily armoured knights, having charged so fiercely that their armoured horses were too exhausted to carry them out of the battle when the rout began, fared far worse than the light hussars. Every Hungarian leader was left on the field, and all the noble houses of Hungary suffered loss; only five of the numerous prisoners were spared, the remainder being decapitated on the spot. The body of King Louis was found two months later, the subsiding Danube floods revealing the heavily armoured rider and horse at the bottom of a gully a mile from the battlefield. Turkish losses, although heavy, were much less than those of the defeated Hungarians.

THE SIEGES OF VIENNA BY THE TURKS, 1529 AND 1683

Vienna, through its geographical position and political importance, has been subjected to several sieges over the ages, and those in 1529 and 1683 must rank high in the annals of siege warfare.

In May 1529 Suleiman II led a large army into Hungary and in five days in September besieged and captured Buda, massacring most of the garrison, before marching onwards, pillaging, ravaging and destroying everything that lay before him. He reached Vienna on 23 September and lay siege to this capital of Austria and of the whole Western Empire, since the house of Austria was said to occupy the throne of Charlemagne. Accompanying the Turkish army was a flotilla of boats on the Danube which, within a few days, had sailed past the city to cut the line of communications to Bohemia. The

Ottoman army was said to exceed 80,000 men and included the janissary force which had just subdued Persia; its numerous light cavalry ravaged all of Lower Austria.

The garrison of Vienna, numbering about 17,000 men, was commanded by Philip, Count Palatine of Austria, but de facto leadership lay in the hands of Count Nicholas of Salm and Marshal William von Roggendorf, who inspired their men to labour night and day to prepare the city's defences. It was obvious that the ancient mediaeval walls, with their few artillery bastions, were insufficient to halt the Turkish onrush, so a field of fire was provided by levelling the land around the walls; lines of entrenchments and crude fortifications were dug within the walls; and all wooden and thatched roofs likely to burn were torn down.

The siege began on 27 September and from then on there were incessant Turkish bombardments and mining attempts, punctuated by fierce assaults. The defenders withstood it well, and their counter-mining, allied to frequent sorties, did great damage to Turkish positions and mineheads. The defenders detected underground enemy activity by observing agitation of water in bowls positioned on walls and outworks, and then furiously countermining. Truly, the citizens of the besieged town were intrepid and, when a mine threw down a section of wall, men, women and children laboured to construct new barriers. At one point, in early October, heavy Turkish assaults were twice beaten back; twice they were rallied by the Sultan and returned and for four hours the fighting flowed back and forth, until the attackers were repulsed.

The major assault began on the night of 13 October, and continued at daybreak, when a massive Turkish attack took place which lasted for twelve hours, before the attackers were thrown back. It was enough for Suleiman. Winter was now approaching, and after forty fruitless days before the city, with very heavy losses to his army, he murdered all the male prisoners and withdrew. Throughout October and November the Austrians vigorously pursued and harassed the Turkish enemy, who were handicapped by early snow, frosts and tempests, so that transport had to be abandoned. The Turkish river flotilla, carrying the siege artillery, took heavy losses when pushing past the batteries at Pressburg (Bratislava).

*

More than 150 years later, the Turks were still pursuing their ambitions in Europe, and in March 1683 the Sultan Mohammed IV personally led a Turkish army of nearly 200,000 men from Adrianople towards Belgrade, from where they continued north, under the actual leadership of Kara Mustafa. In June they invaded Austria via the Danube, marching through a countryside filled with refugees and fugitives while ravaging, burning, slaughtering and pillaging, to reach Vienna on 14 July 1683, which was immediately invested. Leopold and his court fled to Passau and Duke Charles of Lorraine, with his Austrian army of about 30,000, retreated to Linz, leaving Count Rudiger von Starhemberg, Governor of Vienna, to defend the city with a garrison of about 15,000 men.

The stirring events that followed are colourfully described in true Victorian style by an unnamed author in *The Great Sieges of History*, published by George Routledge & Sons of London in the mid 1870s:

The approaches to Vienna were easy. The trenches were opened on the 14th of July, in the faubourg of St. Ulric, at fifty paces from the counterscarp; the attack was directed against the bastion of the court, and that of Lebb. Two days only advanced the works as far as the counterscarp where the ditch was dry. With the Turks, there were daily mounds raised, works advanced, new batteries, and a fire which augmented every instant; with the Austrians, it was, in an equal degree, a display of the most intrepid valour and firm resistance. Starhemberg, who at the first approaches had been wounded by a fragment of stone struck off from the curtain by a ball, though only half-cured, animated the whole defence by his looks, his actions, and his humanity. He treated all his soldiers like brothers; he praised and recompensed all distinguished actions; and, not content with being with them during the day, he passed the night upon a mattress in the *corps de garde* of the emperor's palace, which adjoined a bastion of the court comprised in the attack. By the 22nd of July, the besiegers were at the palisade, which was only defended by the sword. They were so near, that they grappled each other across the pikes in death struggles. The count de Daun, a general officer of distinguished merit, had scythes fastened to long poles, which destroyed a vast number of the infidels, but which could not diminish the presumptuous confidence which animated them. The enemy did not obtain possession

A contemporary print showing early cannon at a Middle Ages siege.
(From a fifteenth-century manuscript.)

A fourteenth-century archer, wearing light armour consisting of a small iron cap, a mail hood, a mail hauberk and a small breastplate. He is armed with a sword and dagger as well as his longbow, and he carries a small, round buckler.

A musketeer, from an early seventeenth-century tract.

A pikeman, from an early seventeenth-century tract.

Sixteenth-century cavalry, armed with handguns.

A mercenary.

The Marquis of Montrose.

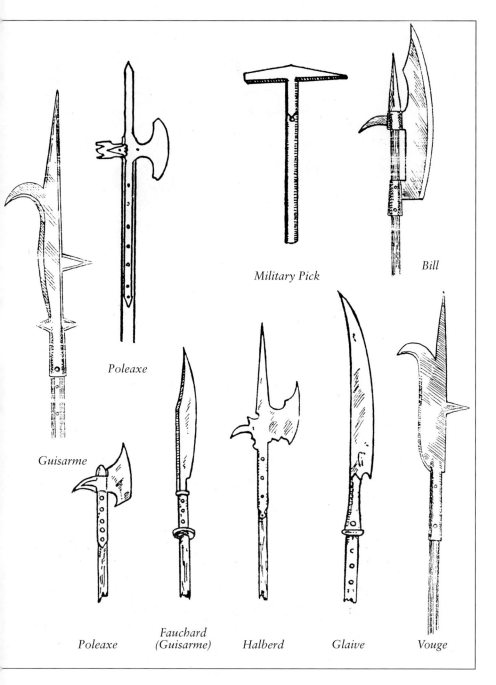

Military Pick

Bill

Poleaxe

Guisarme

Poleaxe

Fauchard
(Guisarme)

Halberd

Glaive

Vouge

A variety of weapons.

Incendiary missiles fired from longbows and muskets (mid-seventeenth-century).

Chainshot and 'Firework Weapons' (end of sixteenth-century).

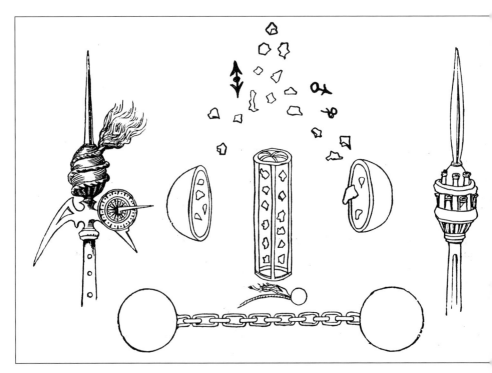

Spanish pikeman.

Swiss halberdier.

Swiss (Bernese) pikemen, at the Battle of Morat 1476.
(A contemporary print.)

German professional foot soldier, wearing 'mail Bishop's mantle,'
carrying a two-handed sword and one with S-shaped quillons.

An Ottoman Turk.

A Turkish janissary.

An archer; a crossbowman; a crossbowman firing from behind a pavis (
pavisier); and the standard of Richard
Earl of Warwick. (Wars of the Roses
period – fifteenth-century manuscript.

Foot soldier of the Wars of the Roses,
armed with a handgun.

(Left) A cavalryman of the French Religious Wars period, armed with lance, sword and pistol. (Right) A Dutch pikeman of the mid-sixteenth-century. (Below left) Soldiers of the Thirty Years War 1618–48. (Below right) Pikeman of the Cromwellian period.

A Cromwellian Ironclad.

A musketeer at the time of the War of the Grand Alliance 1689–97.

of the counterscarp before the 7th of August, after twenty-three days' fighting with a great effusion of blood on both sides. The count de Serini, nephew of the famous Serini whom Leopold had brought to the scaffold, had retarded the taking of this work by a thousand actions of bravery. There was no sortie in which he was not conspicuous. His ardour on one occasion prevented his feeling that he had received an arrow in his shoulder. The Turks had come to the descent of the ditch; no people equal them in turning up the ground. The depth of their work was astonishing: the earth they threw out was carried to the height of nine feet, surmounted by planks and posts in the form of floors, beneath which they worked in safety. Their trenches differ from those of Europeans in shape: they are cuttings in the form of a crescent, which cover one another, preserving a communication like the scales of fish, which conceal a labyrinth from whence they fire without inconveniencing those who are in front, and whence it is almost impossible to dislodge them. When the janissaries had once entered them, they scarcely ever left them. Their fire became progressively more active, whilst that of the besieged relaxed: the latter began to husband their powder, and grenades were short. The baron de Kielmansegge invented a powder-mill and clay grenades, which proved of great service. Industry employed all its resources but the hope of holding out much longer began to diminish. The enemy's mines, the continual attacks, the diminishing garrison, the nearly exhausted munitions and provisions, everything conspired to create the greatest anxiety; and not content with so many real evils, they invented imaginary ones. A report was spread that traitors were working subterranean passages by which to introduce the infidels. Every one was commanded to keep watch in his cellar; and this increase of fatigue completed the weakness of the defenders of Vienna, by robbing them of their necessary rest. Others spoke confidently of incendiaries hired to second the Turks. A young man found in a church which had just been set fire to, although most likely innocent, was torn to pieces by the people. But the Turkish artillery was more to be dreaded than all these phantoms. The inhabitants were incessantly employed in extinguishing the fires which the bombs and red-hot balls kindled in the city, whilst the outworks were falling in one continued crash. The half-moon had already suffered greatly; the ramparts presented in all parts vast breaches;

and, but for the invincible courage of the inhabitants and the soldiers, Vienna must have been taken.

On the 22nd of August it appeared certain that they could not hold out more than three days, if the Turks gave a general assault. From that melancholy period, one mine seemed to precipitate itself upon another. The half-moon was taken; breaches of from eighteen to twenty toises laid open the two bastions and the curtain; soldiers served instead of walls. A mine was advancing under the emperor's palace, already beaten to pieces with bombs, and close to the bastion of the court. Other mines, like snakes, were winding about in all directions; several were discovered; but the Austrian miners were timid, and could not be persuaded to go under ground when once they had heard the enemy at work there. The artillery was no longer able to respond, most of the cannons being either broken or dismounted.

By this time the defenders were reduced to about half-strength, and were running short of ammunition and other vital supplies. In this extremity, Leopold turned his eyes towards Poland and Jan Sobieski, held in considerable respect by the Turks, and perhaps the only sovereign of that Age to be a Great Captain simultaneously. The Pope appealed to the Polish leader to come to the assistance not only of the Austrian Empire, but the whole Christian world. Instantly responding to the summons, Jan Sobieski marched to the relief of Vienna with about 30,000 men, covering the 220 miles from Warsaw in the then exceptional time of fifteen days. He crossed the bridge of Tulin, five leagues above Vienna on 5 September 1683, united with the Austrians and Germans west of the city, and advanced on the Turkish camp on 11 September. This completely surprised the Otto-man leader, Kara Mustafa, as is described in *The Great Sieges of History*:

The Poles, after crossing the bridge, extended themselves to the right, exposed during twenty-four hours to being cut to pieces, if Kara Mustapha had taken due advantage of their position. On the 7th, all the German troops joined their allies, and the army was then found to amount to about seventy-four thousand men. There were four sovereign princes among them, – John Sobieski of Poland, Maximilian Emanuel, elector of Bavaria, John George III, elector of Saxony, and Charles V, duke of Lorraine; and twenty-six princes of sovereign houses.

When about to march, Sobieski gave out the following order of battle, written with his own hand: 'The corps de *bataille* shall be composed of the imperial troops, to whom we will join the regiment of cavalry of the Marshal De la Cour, the Chevalier Lubomirski, and four or five squadrons of our gendarmes, in the place of whom some dragoons or other German troops shall be given. This corps shall be commanded by M. the duke of Lorraine.

'The Polish army will occupy the right wing, which will be commanded by the grand-general Jublonoswski, and the other generals of that nation.

'The troops of MM. the electors of Bavaria and Saxony shall form the left wing, to whom we will give also some squadrons of our gendarmes and of our other Polish cavalry in the place of whom they will give us some dragoons or some infantry.

'The cannons shall be divided; and in case MM. the electors have not enough, M. the duke of Lorraine will furnish them with some.

'The troops of the circles of the empire will extend along the Danube, with the left wing falling back a little on their right; and that for two reasons: the first, to alarm the enemy with the fear of being charged in flank; and the second, to be within reach of throwing succours into the city, in case we should not be able to drive the enemy as soon as we could wish. M. the prince of Waldeck will command this corps.

'The first line will consist entirely of infantry, with cannons, followed closely by a line of cavalry. If these two lines were mixed, they would doubtless embarrass each other in the passages of the defiles, woods, and mountains. But as soon as they shall be on the plain, the cavalry will take its posts in the intervals of the battalions, which will be arranged with this view, particularly our gendarmes, who will charge first.

'If we were to put all our armies in three lines only, it would require more than a German league and a half, which would not be to our advantage; and we should be obliged to cross the little river Vien, which must be our right wing: it is for this reason we must make four lines; and this fourth shall serve as a body of reserve. For the greater security of the infantry against the first charge of the Turkish cavalry, which is always impetuous, it will be desirable to employ *spanchéraistres*, or *chevaux de frise*, but very light, for convenience of carriage, and at every halt place them in front of the battalions.

'I beg all the messieurs the generals, that as fast as the armies shall descend from the last mountain, as they shall enter the plain, every one will take its post as it is set down in this present order.'

There were but five leagues between them and the Turks, from whom they were separated by that chain of mountains which surrounded the vast plain on which they were encamped. Two routes presented themselves: one by the more elevated part; the other, by the side where the summit, sinking, became more practicable. The first was fixed upon: it was true it was the more difficult, but it was the shorter. On the 9th of September all the troops moved forward. The Germans, after many attempts to bring up their cannon, gave the matter up in despair, and left them in the plain. The Poles had more spirit and perseverance.

By manual strength and address they contrived to get over twenty-eight pieces, and these alone were used on the day of battle. This march, bristling with difficulties, lasted three days. At length they approached the last mountain, called Calemberg. There was yet plenty of time for the vizier to repair his faults: he had only to take possession of this height, and mark the defiles, and he would have stopped the Christian arms. But he did not do so; and it was at this moment that the janissaries, indignant at so many blunders, exclaimed: 'Come on, come on, ye infidels! The sight of your hats alone will put us to flight.'

This summit of Calemberg, still left free, discovered to the Christians, an hour before nightfall, both the innumerable hosts of the Turks and Tartars, and the smoking ruins of Vienna. Signals incontinently informed the besieged of the succour at hand. Sobieski, after having examined all the positions of the vizier, said to the German generals, 'That man is very badly encamped; he is an ignorant fellow: we shall beat him.' The cannon, on both sides, played the prelude to the grand scene of the morrow. It was the 12th of September.

Jan Sobieski assumed command of the allied arms, with the Poles on the right wing, the Austrians, under Charles of Lorraine, on the left, and the German Corps in the centre, advancing slowly because of difficult terrain. It is recorded that the intention was to attack at daybreak on 13 September, but noticing that Turkish resistance seemed half-hearted, Sobieski ordered a general attack at 5 p.m. on the 12th; simultaneously, the Vienna garrison attacked the Turkish siege-lines. An inconclusive struggle between opposing infantry surged between the river and the Ottoman camp; then Sobieski's Polish cavalry charged irresistibly on Kara Mustafa's headquarters-camp, creating a general panic and causing the Turkish leader and his army to flee, having suffered heavy losses. Darkness now enveloped the field and Sobieski halted pursuit for fear of ambush; thus the Turkish army escaped destruction.

The Great Sieges of History paints a colourful picture:

The Christian army descended with slow and measured steps, closing their ranks, rolling their cannon before them, and halting at every thirty or forty paces to fire and reload. This front widened, and took more depth as the space became greater.

The Khan of the Tartars drew the vizier's attention to the lances ornamented with banderoles of the Polish gendarmerie, and said, 'The king is at their head!' – and terror seized upon the heart of Kara Mustapha. Immediately, after having commanded the Tartars to put all their captives to death, to the amount of thirty thousand, he ordered half of his army to march towards the mountain, whilst the other half approached the walls of the city, to give a general assault. But the besieged had resumed their courage. The hope, and even the certainty of victory, had rendered them invincible.

The Christians continued to descend, and the Turks moved upwards. The action commenced. The first line of the Imperialists, all infantry, charged with so much impetuosity, that it gave place for a line of cavalry, which took part in the intervals of the battalions. The king, the princes, and the generals gained the head, and fought, sometimes with the cavalry and sometimes with the infantry. The two other lines urged the first on warmly, protected by the fire of the artillery, which was incessant and very near. The field of the first shock, between the plain and the mountain, was intersected with vineyards, heights and small valleys. The enemy having left their cannon at the beginning of the vineyards, suffered greatly from those of the Christians. The combatants, spread over this unequal ground, fought with inveteracy up to mid-day. At length the infidels, taken in flank, and driven from hill to hill, retired into the plain, lining their camp. During the heat of the *mêlée*, all the bodies of the Christian army having fought sometimes on the heights, and sometimes in the valleys, they had necessarily doubled over each other, and deranged the order of battle. A short time was given to re-establish it; and the plain became the theatre of a triumph which posterity will always feel difficulty in believing. Seventy-thousand men boldly attacked more than two hundred thousand! In the Turkish army, the pacha of Diarbeker commanded the right wing, the pacha of Buda the left. The vizier was in the centre, having by his side the aga of the janissaries and the general of the Spahis. The two armies remained motionless for some time, the Christians in silence, whilst the Turks and Tartars emulated the clarions with their cries. At length Sobieski gave the signal, and, sabre in hand, the Polish cavalry charged straight upon the vizier in the centre. They broke through the front ranks, they even pierced through the numerous squadrons which surrounded Mustapha. The Spahis disputed the victory; but all the others, the Wallachians, the Moldavians, the Transylvanians, the Tartars, and even the janissaries, fought without spirit. In vain the Ottoman general endeavoured to revive confidence: they despised him and disregarded his words. He addressed himself to the pacha of Buda, and to other chiefs, but their only reply was desponding silence. 'And thou!' cried he then to the Tartar prince, 'wilt not thou assist me?' The khan saw no safety but in flight. The Spahis were making their last efforts: the Polish cavalry opened and dispersed them. The vizier then turned his back, and spread consternation by his flight. The discouragement extended to the wings, which all the bodies of the Christian army pressed at once.

But all dispersed, and all disappeared, as if by magic; that vast camp, which the eye could not measure, resembled a frightful desert. Night stopped the victorious progress of the Christians, who remained upon the field of battle till daybreak.

Thus, without much bloodshed, the valour and skill of John Sobieski saved Vienna, the empire and religion. In fact, if Vienna and been taken, as at Constantinople, churches would have been changed into mosques, and nobody can say where Mahometanism, which already was spread over so much of the globe, might have ended. Starhemberg came, immediately after the victory, to salute the preserver and liberator of Vienna, into which city the hero entered over ruins, but amidst the acclamations of the people. His horse could scarcely pierce through the crowd who prostrated themselves before him, who would kiss his feet, calling him their father, their avenger, the greatest of monarchs. Leopold seems to be forgotten – they only saw Sobieski.

THE SIEGE OF CONSTANTINOPLE FEBRUARY–MAY 1453

Throughout the fourteenth century, Muslim invaders poured westwards in a steady stream out of Turkestan; the flood was briefly stayed as at Kosovo in 1389, but resumed at the second battle of Kosovo in October 1448, leaving the Turks firmly established at Adrianople. This left the Bulgarians and the Hungarians uneasily balanced on their borders, and the ancient city of Constantinople thrust temptingly forwards at the mercy of any Turkish force determined to take it by siege. This was encouraged by the knowledge that Constantinople was but a shadow of its former power and glory, saddled with a large population unlikely and unwilling to bestir itself against the threatening hand poised to take over. When the blow eventually fell upon this city which had, in past centuries, been known as 'the impregnable city', it was marked by the first classic bombardment to bring about the fall of an empire and a civilisation.

The warlike Turkish ruler Mohammed II, who had succeeded his warrior-father Murad II in 1451, began his campaign against Constantinople by constructing, in the face of accusations and protests, the fort of Roumelia-Hissar on Greek territory opposite that built by Bajazet I on the Asiatic shore. Within five miles of Constantinople, the two forts commanded the narrowest part of the Bosphorus. Halfheartedly, the inhabitants of the city set about strengthening their defences as Constantine XI began to muster his forces, numbering less than 10,000, including auxiliary contingents of mercenaries from Venice, Genoa and Crete. Subordinate commands were entrusted to the leading soldiers of fortune at his disposal; the veteran condottiere John Justiniani of Genoa, as the most doughty and experienced commander of them all, was given responsibilities that virtually made him commander-in-chief.

In his definitive work *The art of War in the Middle Ages* Sir Charles Oman describes Constantinople as it was at that period:

> Constantinople was the most perfect of all Eastern fortresses: on its landward side it had a triple enceinte and a deep ditch in front of the outermost face. The first wall was commanded by the second, and the second by the third, each overtopping the line below it, and all three furnished with military machines capable of playing upon the siege works of the beleaguering army. Moreover, the two first walls were loopholed at a stage below the battlements, so that the garrison could fire not merely from the parapets, but from a well-protected second line of openings. Piercing this landward wall were, from north to south, nine gates, of which the most important were the Xylo Porta, the Adrianople Gate, the central Gate of St. Romanus (Top Capou-Cannon Gate), and the Golden Gate.

With a circumference of about sixteen miles, the city was roughly triangular in shape, its longest side fronting the Sea of Marmora, where the fortifications were virtually inaccessible and therefore unassailable; its base traversed the southern shore of the Golden Horn, across the mouth of which was a huge cable denying access to the long and narrow inlet beyond; the third side, facing the land approaches from Adrianople, was about five miles in length and vulnerable to assault. It constituted an extensive area to be defended and so few were the available defenders that some of the seaward-facing towers were garrisoned by squads of as few as half-a-dozen men.

The Turkish leader Mohammed was fully alive to the fortification-destroying capabilities of artillery, a relatively new weapon that truly appealed to his Eastern imagination. A skilful Wallachian cannon-founder named Urbin furnished him with a battering-train far superior to any previously fielded and within three months Urbin had produced an enormous piece of ordnance, with a bore two feet

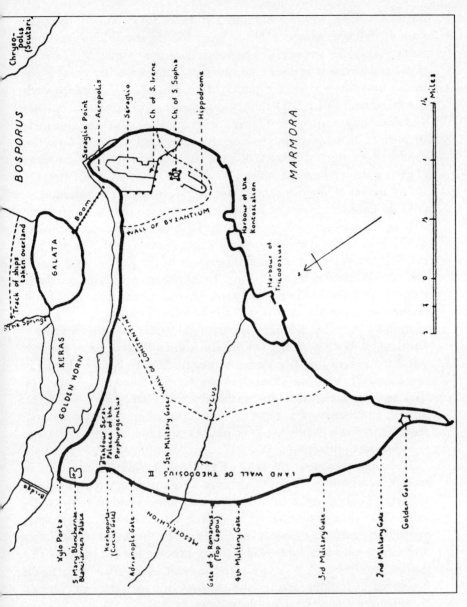

The Siege of Constantinople 1453

six inches wide, which could hurl a stone-ball weighing up to 1,500 pounds, but was only capable of being loaded and fired seven times a day. When he was ready to march to Constantinople, Mohammed possessed fourteen batteries, consisting of thirteen of the great bombards, and fifty-six smaller pieces of varying sizes. To convey each bombard from Adrianople, thirty waggons had to be linked together and drawn by sixty oxen or horses, with 200 men marching alongside to prevent slewing while another 200 men went ahead to level the road and strengthen bridges: It took two months to draw the huge convoy a distance of 150 miles.

On arrival at their destined positions in front of the beleaguered city, the monster pieces of heavy ordnance were dragged into place to a background cacophony that must have brought fear to the hearts of the bewildered garrison – the staccato beating of drums and the clashing of cymbals, the shrieking prayers of the priests, wild shouts and caterwauling that split the air. Triumphantly surveying the scene from his gorgeous red-and-gold tent, pitched on the slope of the hill facing the Blachernae quarter, a little beyond the site occupied by the Crusaders in 1203, Mohammed gave the order to open fire on 5 April 1453. With a mighty bellow and a great flash of flame the first bombard roared out its message of destruction, to begin a day-and-night assault that was to last for six weeks. During the hours of darkness the scene was illuminated by flares stuck on the end of lances. Simultaneously, battering rams, tunnelling-and-mining, and mobile siege-towers played their part as sideshows to the first great bombardment of history.

Mohammed came at the head of an army of about 80,000 regular troops, of whom the famed janissaries were the most terror-inspiring element, backed by Bashi-Bazouks and other undoubtedly well-armed but quite undisciplined irregulars. This concourse of recognised fighting-men were greatly outnumbered by the multitude of slaves and camp-followers who traditionally accompanied armies of the period, forced by whip or sword to the front of the army in battle or employed as human fascines at sieges, serving as fodder to exhaust the enemy who had to strike them down.

While Mohammed was investing Constantinople by land, his fleet, of about 250 sail, advanced to the Dardanelles; this allowed the Turks, as masters of the port, to establish batteries on the side nearest the sea while the army pressed the city on the land side. Then, he had constructed across the top of the Horn, a 2,000-feet long barrel-bridge, with an eight-feet wide central roadway, thus uniting the two wings of his army and establishing a new artillery position from which the bombardment could be intensified.

Mohammed put into effect his plan for a great assault that was to bring crashing down the city walls. Trusted subordinates pinned down defenders of the ramparts – Zagan Pasha at Galata and the Golden Horn; Caraje Pasha the ramparts between the Xylo Porta and the Adrianople Gate to the north; Isaac Pasha the area to the south between the St Romanus Gate and the Golden Gate. Synchronised with the sustained and increasingly accurate bombardment of the walls, the Turkish leader had planned an attack on the boom and chain defending the entrance to the Golden Horn, an obvious means of further dispersing the city's already inadequate garrison. He had at his disposal some of the most skilful engineers of Asia and Europe, secured by fair means and foul, and they secretly assembled timber for the construction of ships' cradles, plus a corduroy track and slipway sufficient to stretch from eight to ten miles. Simultaneously, covering parties, plus mobile artillery, were sent out to the Pera area to draw the attention of the garrison, while warning-off the neutral Genoese in Galata.

As night fell on 18 April, Mohammed launched his onslaught with a wild rush of howling Bashi-Bazouks and undisciplined irregulars, scrambling into the ditch which quickly became filled with their bodies, serving as a bridge for the crossing of the regulars who carried the main burden of the attack. From the walls came a devastating fire of missiles from the defenders' arquebuses, bows and crossbows, catapults and wall-guns, breaking the attackers' momentum and then halting them until eventually, slowly, sullenly but still defiant, they withdrew from the assault. Infuriated by the failure of both land and sea assaults – the marine attack on the boom had also been unsuccessful – Mohammed redoubled the bombardment of the battered walls, with the fleet joining in, hoping to pin the maximum numbers of defenders to walls fronting the sea and the Golden Horn.

During the hours of darkness on 21/22 April, seventy or eighty ships were hauled from the water, one after the other, and man-handled by labouring slaves and patient bullocks, with the aid of cables, cradles and rowers, over more than two leagues of wooden track, made slippery with the grease of slaughtered sheep and oxen.

There was no attempt at secrecy, drums and fifes vied with shouting and cheering, as the ships, lit by torches and flambeaux, with sails unfurled and pennants fluttering, pilots at the peak and steersmen at the helm, moved inexorably as though at sea. In turn, each vessel was relaunched in the placid upper waters of the inlet, and at dawn the Greeks, bewildered by the nocturnal tumult, saw at dawn Moslem standards flying from a host of vessels in their port.

On land, every form of military engineering was tried: mines, counter-mines and trenches were dug, though most were detected and blocked before reaching the walls; several breaches were made, on which a number of unsuccessful attacks were attempted and repulsed by defenders who not only repaired the breaches but made some lively counterattacks. It is recorded that Mohammed considered raising the siege; he had believed that the city might well be reduced to submission through starvation, but a similar feat was beginning to haunt the Ottoman camp, as supplies for the vast horde of besiegers had denuded the surrounding countryside. Advised that unless the city walls were stormed within a month, the siege would have to be raised, Mohammed resolved to make one last all-out attempt.

Meanwhile, sporadic attacks were being made, with relatively major massed assaults being made on the sector around St Romanus Gate, on the 7th and 12th of May; both were beaten back by defenders, inspired by their leader Justiniani, exacting heavy losses; nor did sapping and mining attempts fare any better. Then the Turks employed a 'Helepolis', a wheeled wooden tower, with platforms, scaling-ladders and built-in artillery, moving it up until it overhung a breach in the walls. From it the Turks hurled down rubble, earth, stones and fascines to make a causeway for their assault parties to seize the breach. Justiniani led his desperate defenders throughout the day as they threw back wave after wave of attackers; when the assaults ceased, the defending mercenaries blew up the abandoned Helepolis by casting barrels of gunpowder into the ditch.

Notwithstanding the sterling example set by the condottiere, the citizens of Constantinople refused not only to be drawn from their secure places to man the walls, but also could not be persuaded to part with their money and riches to pay the mercenaries, who steadfastly refused to return to their posts without their promised pay. Thus, the garrison was reduced to a mere 4,000 effectives, a fact relayed to Mohammed by spies within the city, prompting him to make his final attack on 29 May, issuing a proclamation to his soldiers that the plunder of the city would be abandoned to them.

Three principal points of attack were chosen, with the centre of assault in the St Romanus Gate sector, which was considered to be the point of decision; the wall between Tekfour Serai, just south of Xylo Porta, and the Adrianople Gate; and a supporting attack on the Third Military Gate. At three o'clock in the morning, Mohammed sent in about 30,000 of his lesser irregular troops – Bashi-Bazouks, Kurds, and Dervishes – whose heaped bodies would fill the ditch and facilitate the progress of his 10,000 janissaries and other regulars. All were encouraged to the point of desperation by the promise of three days' uninterrupted freedom to loot the city once it fell into their hands.

Justiniani and his small band were soon engaged in hand-to-hand fighting with pikes, swords, lances and axes and, for a while, held the enemy at bay, then were forced back behind stockades built to strengthen the battered walls. By now it was sunrise, and Mohammed ordered trumpeters to sound a fresh signal, at which the artillery opened fire from all quarters, quickly driving away from the wall those defenders who had taken up positions thereon.

The inevitable began when the Turks discovered that Justiniani had left unguarded the Kerkoporta or Circus Gate – only half-a-mile from where he and his men had fought so valiantly to throw back the first tide of the assault. This fault allowed a party of janissaries to make their way unhindered down the inner enclosures, to take the defenders by surprise and in the flank. In the confusion that ensued the Turkish attackers at St Romanus forced their way into the city in considerable strength.

The position was truly desperate for the defence, although it was not beyond the Justiniani's powers of leadership to rally the sorely pressed defenders and give some time for a reorganisation; but Justiniani was struck down at that crucial moment and carried mortally wounded from the field. In a last desperate attempt to turn back the Ottoman horde, the Emperor Constantine led a few of his guards and some faithful servants into the thick of the battle, sword in hand to fight bravely until a Turkish scimitar sliced off half his face. With his death all attempts at organised resistance dissolved in panic; thousands of citizens were ruthlessly cut down, and a savage pillaging began that was to last three days.

Thus fell the Roman Eastern Empire which had existed for 1,143 years, and the blood-red Turkish standard replaced the flag of St Mark. The Turks did not let their European foray finish there, and were not stopped until the King of Hungary faced them at Belgrade in 1456.

14

The Hussite Wars 1419–34

DURING THE FOURTEENTH and early fifteenth centuries three widely separated developments – the Swiss pikemen, the English archers, and the wagon-fortress tactics of Jan Ziska and the Hussites of Bohemia – led to the decline of armoured cavalry as a dominating force on the battlefield. Their long supremacy was broken by steady, disciplined infantry armed with a combination of missile and shock weapons such as longbows, handguns and pikes. In fierce warfare, Sigismund's vastly superior forces of German Knights of the Holy Roman Empire were repeatedly defeated by tactics two centuries ahead of their time. The Bohemian victories owed much to the genius of one-eyed Jan Ziska. He towers above the military thought of the age as the first commander to use armour-protective fire-power as a manoeuvrable arm in a technical combination of cavalry and infantry as a mobile defensive/offensive system, prefiguring the modern concept of movement in armoured personnel carriers. His daring and ingenuity, coupled with swiftness of movement, particularly when following up victory, was compared by Sir John Fortescue with that of Napoleon.

At his fortress base of Tabor, Ziska drilled his followers, transforming them from poorly equipped, untrained peasants, who knew nothing of crossbows or handguns and had never been in battle, into a well-trained and balanced fighting force that, while never exceeding 25,000 men, defeated armies up to seven or eight times their own numerical strength. The knights and infantry of these vast armies wore armour that resisted both arrows and crossbow bolts at normal battlefield ranges, so Ziska armed one-third of his infantry with the handgun. The Hussite Wars were religious struggles and the strong beliefs that they valued more than their lives together with a high degree of nationalistic fervour gave the hymn-singing Bohemian peasants an almost fanatical enthusiasm. Demanding from both officers and men the utmost discipline and devotion, Ziska trained his force into a unique combination, enforcing harsh laws and introducing vigorous but controlled conscription to provide man-power for his army.

Over and above all these qualities, the Hussites evolved a new weapon system by adapting the wagon-fort as a tactical unit and revolutionised warfare by new concepts of fire-power and manoeuvre. A factor in the Roman defeat by the Goths at Adrianople in AD 378, the wagonlaager had been used as a manoeuvrable fortress for centuries by migrant tribesmen. It was employed as a defensive barrier to protect its occupants from attack, much in the manner of the Western settlers against Red Indians. After early victories, Ziska discarded his improvised wagons and constructed wheeled forts designed specifically for fighting. These mediaeval predecessors of the tank were built of solid heavy slabs of wood reinforced with iron and leather, their chest-high sides pierced with slots for firing bows and handguns and fitted with chains to link them together when under attack. Each wagon was a unit, crewed by twenty men – ten musketeers who fired from inside the wagon and ten pikemen who defended the space between the wagons. There were wagons and carts mounting medium and heavy artillery such as rock-throwing catapults and iron cannons firing stone balls.

At first the wagons did not actually attack but moved into position and then were chained together to form forts, still sufficiently mobile to be quickly hitched up. Ziska believed that they could also be effectively used in offensive operations, and soon his wagoners were so highly trained that the heavy draught-horse drawn wagons could advance to the attack in a series of parallel columns; they could form squares or rectangles, circles or triangles at a given signal, and under virtually all conditions. At their peak, the Hussites were so adept at mobile warfare that they could take their wagons into the midst of an attacking army before forming their battle line.

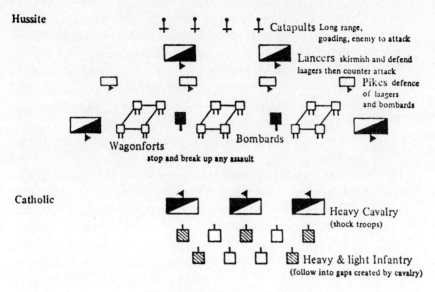

The Hussite Wars 1419–34

At that time, the Hussite army was formed of two-thirds wagon-fort troops armed with handguns and pikes, and one-third light cavalry armed with lances and crossbows. If Hussite tactics had a major defect it was that they lacked cavalry to exploit a victory, although Ziska did have a body of highly trained horsemen who rode with his combat wagon trains. Most of them were mounted crossbowmen capable of reloading their weapons and remaining mounted. These Hussite mounted archers acted as light cavalry, scouting and skirmishing and pursuing when necessary. In a pitched battle they took refuge in the wagon-forts and added their fire to that of the crews.

Well in advance of their time and anticipating a new age of tactics, the Hussites' style of warfare was never really comprehended by their foes who saw them in an aura of invincibility which often saved the Hussites the trouble of fighting a battle. Lacking the ability to enforce discipline, opposing commanders could not keep a fighting force in the line to stand up against the Hussites, but in time their adversaries took advantage of the Hussites' well known zeal in counter-attacking and used it to their advantage by feigning retreat so that the Hussites abandoned their battle formations and pursued. Then, shorn of their armoured protection, they were cut off from their primary weapon system and defeated, for without their wagons the Hussites were no match for the overwhelming numbers of their enemies. The armies of the Catholic Knights were often over 100,000-strong, formed of one-third heavy cavalry consisting of mounted knights armed with lance and sword, one-third heavy infantry formed of nobles and men-at-arms armed with the pike and sword, and one-third peasants who were mostly poorly armed light infantry and included a few archers.

The victorious ability of the Hussites lay in disorganising the enemy by the inherent armour-protected fire-power of their vehicles, and then following up with a powerful counter attack. The usual Hussite battle formation consisted either of one of the well rehearsed geometric configurations or a battle line of wagon-forts across the front, with pikemen or artillery in the gaps and cavalry on the wings. The battle began with the Catholic heavy cavalry, goaded by missiles from catapults and by the skirmishers, surging forward to the attack, assailed with missiles from the bombards and by the handguns at close range. This high rate of fire-power usually halted the attack, but on the rare occasion when the remnants of the cavalry actually came up to the wagons, they were unable to penetrate further because of the armoured walls and the stands of pikes in the intervening spaces. When the frustrated and sorely stricken enemy began to withdraw, the Hussites launched the counter-attack, chasing the retreating cavalry back into their own advancing infantry, causing confusion and dismay. Then the wagons were unchained to take up an offensive formation which thundered across the battlefield, their crews firing throughout, while the Hussite cavalry harassed the enemy flanks. No quarter was given.

Such tactics required well disciplined and confident troops, even though the Catholic Knights fought to rigid feudal ideas and lacked co-ordinated strategy. Typical Hussite victories included Prague in 1419, when they repelled a frontal attack from an entrenched position on a hill beneath the city walls with their guns sited so as to give a destructive cross-fire; at Kuttenberg in 1422, the wagon-laagers stopped the German frontal attack and then Ziska put in a furious counter-charge with mobile artillery support to destroy the enemy; in 1426, after Ziska's death, the Hussites under Prokop defeated the Germans at the Battle of Aussig, breaking up their formations by a strategic wagon attack and then a cavalry charge into the disordered ranks. In their time the Hussites fought in Hungary, Austria, Silesia, Saxony, Bavaria, Thuringia and Franconia. After Ziska's death, Bohemia split into two opposing groups and Ziska's commanders divided amongst themselves, forgetting the true strength of their tactical concept.

Ziska's use of field fortifications was an imaginative offensive-minded system, causing his battles to be models of offensive/defensive tactics, but he did not introduce field-artillery in its truest sense, nor did he use gunpowder weapons in a tactically offensive manner. After Ziska's death, his successors failed to maintain his strategic initiative, and the increasing efficiency of field artillery and small-arms exposed the extreme vulnerability of the wagon-fort, leading to its disappearance from the field of war.

15

The Wars of the Roses 1455–85

THE POWER STRUGGLE between the House of Lancaster (the Red Rose) and the rival House of York (the White Rose) ebbed and flowed for nearly thirty years, eventually shattering the feudal system in England. The general policy of 'slaying the nobles and sparing the commons' resulted in a great loss of leaders while demonstrating the rancorous spirit of the time. During this lengthy struggle, there were eighteen relatively major pitched battles and innumerable skirmishes and sieges. The Hundred Years War had just finished and England was full of unemployed soldiers cast adrift after the loss of France. They had been trained in an undisciplined school so that treachery, plundering, brutality and barbarity were the habitual background to the war.

At St Albans in 1455, Richard of York used his cannon and bowmen to engage the Lancastrians defending the town while Warwick took a force of cavalry to attack the Lancastrians' rear and scatter them. Here Warwick's company of Burgundian musketeers were the first soldiers to use hand fire-arms in England. Towton in 1461 was probably the bloodiest battle ever fought on English soil when Edward, with about 15,000 men against 20,000 Lancastrians, sent out archers in a blinding blizzard, who fired a few volleys and then fell back. Replying blindly, the Lancastrian archers used up their arrows ineffectually before Edward successfully attacked and gained the victory. Archers played a big part in the Wars of the

Roses; those of York wreaked great slaughter in the close confines of the streets of St Albans during its second battle in 1461, when Queen Margaret's army contained large numbers of Scots and Welsh bor-derers-mercenaries who followed any leader for loot. Foreign soldiers of fortune were freely employed and on the field of Stoke, 2,000 Germans armed with halberd and pike fought on the losing side, standing fast until they were cut down to the last man. At Barnet in 1471, Edward brought from the Continent 300 Flemings armed with handguns. In this battle both armies blindly advanced in a fog; the Yorkist left wing was routed by a Lancastrian force who, on return-ing to the battle, blundered into the rear of their own centre who had changed their position during the fighting. Shaken by this apparent treachery, the Lancastrians were routed, with Warwick their leader (who had changed sides) being killed.

In 1471 at Tewkesbury the Lancastrians were defending a slope behind a brook under fire from Yorkist bombards, while Somerset led the Lancastrian right wing in an outflanking movement only to fall into an ambush prepared by Edward. On returning to the main battle line, Somerset personally killed Lord Wenlock, commander of the Lancastrian centre, who had failed to support his charge! The Yorkists advanced, pushed back the enemy centre and rolled up their right wing to rout the Lancastrians. At Tewkesbury the Lancastrians were well aware of the inferiority of their troops compared to the well armed soldiers of Edward (who had command of the arsenals and the wealth of London). Edward IV and his brother Richard were the best generals of the war. In fact Sir John Fortescue claims that the rapidity of Edward's decisions and his marches stamp him as a soldier of no ordinary talent and in many respects far ahead of his time. The final battle of the war took place at Bosworth in 1485 where the armies of Richard III and Henry Tudor (whose force included some 200 French auxiliaries under Bernard, a Scottish captain of Free Lances) disposed themselves in a similar order of battle with the archers in front, the billmen behind them and the horses upon the wings. The armies deployed on open ground, with Sir William Stanley holding back on high ground to the north-west while the force of his brother, Lord Stanley, did the same to the south-east. When Richard ordered his left wing to advance the Earl of Northumberland refused to move, and at the same time Stanley's force defected to the Lancastrians. Richard led his loyal remnants in a fierce charge at the Lancastrian centre, hoping to defeat Henry in single combat but was overwhelmed and killed. But the Battle of Bosworth Field did not truly end the Wars of the Roses.

The Wars of the Roses showed unmistakeable signs of the changes that were coming over the art of war, and a slow tactical revolution occurred as improved gunpowder weapons were introduced. Although mainly fought by knights, men-at-arms and archers, new weapons made their appearance in the hands of foot-soldiers – principally hired bands of Burgundian or other foreign handgunmen. A duel of artillery became the regular preliminary to general action as more artillerymen were trained; wheeled and manoeuvrable cannon were used and large bombards or cannons, mounted on carts protected by baskets of earth, were laboriously pushed into position by soldiers. Aiming devices were almost unknown and the recoil of the guns presented a disturbing problem.

At one stage the Lancastrian party regarded it as an atrocity that the Yorkists were 'traitorously ranged in Bataille . . . their Cartes, with Gonnes, set before their Batailles.' The common soldier, known from his peculiar weapon as a billman, began to supplant the dismounted man-at-arms, restoring him to his proper station as a cavalryman.

The tactics of the Wars of the Roses usually consisted of straight-forward frontal assaults. There were few instances of tactical refinements in this war where headlong courage and brute strength prevailed rather than military tactics or skill. The only degree of surprise rested in the dispositions of the various types of troops and the use to which they were put. The most notable exceptions were Salisbury's feigned retreat at Blore Heath in 1459, Falconbridge's ruse in the blizzard at Towton, and Edward's tactics at Tewkesbury when he ordered Gloucester's division to simulate a withdrawal. Otherwise it was the normal practice for both armies to line up about 450 yards apart, facing each other, often conforming to their opponent's frontage. As the war dragged on, the old order of battle in three lines became obsolete and at Bosworth both armies were drawn up in a single line with the cavalry on the wings; the cavalry itself was beginning to forsake the column formation for that of line.

Clad and armed alike, both sides only knew each other by their different coats of arms and badges, and it was not infrequent for soldiers to mistake badges and unwittingly fall upon men of their own side. This occurred at Barnet, causing cries of 'treachery', which was always readily suspected. Leaders frequently changed side as did the Stanleys at Bosworth Field. Civil Wars are always fiercely fought and those leaders who had defaulted from one side to the other fought with obstinacy and bravery, aware that defeated traitors had no prospect before them but exile or death.

THE BATTLE OF BARNET 14 APRIL 1471

This battle was fought during the Wars of the Roses between the Yorkists under Edward IV and the Lancastrians under the Earl of Warwick.

Returning from exile in March 1471, Edward IV landed in York-shire and marched south. Warwick's opposing forces manoeuvred until the night of Saturday 13 April, when they positioned themselves near Barnet, the men lying down in their ranks behind a long line of hedges. During the night the Yorkist army reached Barnet, Edward marching them up to Warwick's position in the dark (a rare accomplishment in those days) and drawing them up as best he could. Edward was a good soldier, and realised the necessity of forcing his enemies to fight before they could gather their full strength against him.

Edward drew his troops up in battle order facing Warwick's army on the lower ground beneath the road. In the darkness, Edward's right wing extended beyond Warwick's left, and the latter's right outflanked Edward's left. Realising the enemy were at hand, Warwick opened a fruitless cannonade from his guns posted on his right.

Edward formed his army up in three bodies, commanding the centre himself, and giving his younger brother, Richard, Duke of Gloucester, command of the right wing and Lord Hastings command of the left. The Lancastrians were formed up in four groups, with Warwick himself leading the left wing, Exeter on his right, then Montagu, and finally Oxford commanding the right wing. The Lancastrians had 15,000 men and the Yorkists 10,000.

Both armies are known to have had artillery, but Warwick's was the better served. The foot soldiers were equipped with new weapons, for both Edward and Warwick had hired bands of Burgundian handgun men. Apart from these professionals, the armies were formed of nobles and their retainers; during the Wars of the Roses the nobles frequently changed their allegiance, so that men were now fighting alongside each other who, in past days, had been bitterly opposed; there were doubt and suspicion of treachery in the air.

The battle began on Easter Sunday, 14 April, in thick fog between 4 and 5 a.m., with both sides advancing slowly and cautiously, Edward's army having to ascend rising ground. At no time during the day was visibility more than about twenty yards, and as men loomed out of the mist, archers and cannon opened fire. Edward and Montagu were the first to find each other, and rushed in to engage at close quarters. On the Yorkist right Gloucester suddenly came upon Exeter's left flank, which turned and faced him, besides bringing Warwick in on its left, so that Gloucester was engaging both groups. On the Lancastrian right, Oxford, an efficient soldier, hit Hastings' left flank, causing his force to break in sudden rout; the broken remnants were chased by cavalry down the road as far as Barnet itself.

Unaware of these events, Warwick could not take advantage of the success of his right wing, so Oxford's pursuit had no effect upon the rest of the battle. Unaware that his left was in the air, Edward continued pressing Montagu hard and getting the better of his West Country bowmen and billmen. Exeter, with his men well in hand, appears to have given some assistance to Montagu's hard-pressed force. Montagu had told his men to keep in line with Exeter's, who, to meet Gloucester's attack had turned to face eastwards; both armies had gradually turned anti-clockwise until they were at ninety degrees to their starting positions.

Oxford halted and reformed his men, to return to where the Yorkists should have been, and came upon the exposed flank of a large body of men looming out of the mist. This force, which was actually Montagu's Lancastrians, mistook Oxford's de Vere badge of a star for Edward's sun device, and fired a volley of arrows as Oxford's men charged into them. Suddenly recognising each other, both sides raised the cry of treason, always common in the Wars of the Roses, and many fled towards the Yorkists, who simply cut them down. There was general confusion.

Oxford, convinced that he had been betrayed, left the field. The cry of treason passed from man to man down the already hard-pressed centre of the Lancastrian army; Montagu and his men found

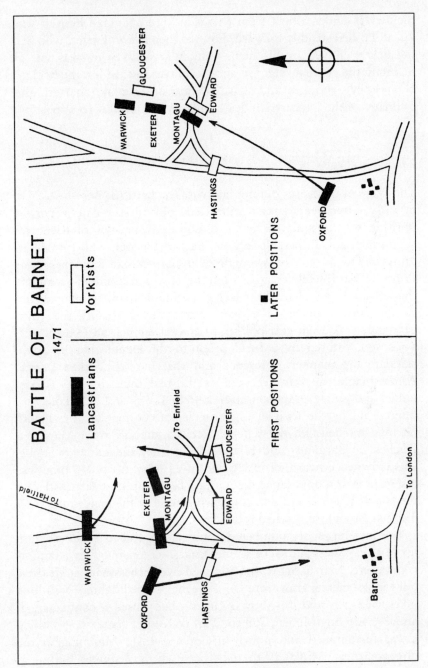

The Battle of Barnet 14 April 1471

themselves under attack from two sides and Montagu himself was killed. Pushed steadily forward, Edward then fell on Exeter, who fled the field followed by his men. Only Warwick's wing was left to maintain the combat, but, seeing that all was lost, he left the field, to be speedily overtaken and slain. Edward ordered 'no quarter', and estimates of the Lancastrian dead range from 4,000 to 10,000.

THE BATTLE OF STOKE FIELD 16 JUNE 1487

The Wars of the Roses did not end with the Battle of Bosworth Field in 1485 – two years later a short-lived plot to stimulate a Yorkist uprising was formulated by Lord Lovell, a survivor of Richard's supporters, and Robert de la Pole, Earl of Lincoln, who formed an army in Dublin on the strength of declaring that with them was Prince Edward, lately escaped from the Tower of London. Seemingly this solved the problem of the lack of a suitable royal figurehead who would draw support to a rebel army, but in reality the royal candidate was a ten-year-old boy, Lambert Simnel, an Oxford artisan's son, tutored by a local priest to the extent that he could simulate the manners, presence and speech of a Yorkist prince. Astonishingly, he was accepted as the real thing by pro-Yorkist nobles and gentry and, taken to Ireland by Lovell and de la Pole, was offered aid by the Irish in his struggle for the throne of England. Gaining momentum, the scheme received support from Margaret, Duchess of Burgundy and Edward IV's sister, and Lambert Simnel was crowned Edward VI in Dublin on 24 May 1487. No time was lost, and eleven days later, the Yorkist fleet landed at Piel castle, on the Isle of Foudray in Lancashire, where one of the conspirators, Sir Thomas Broughton, owned much land.

The invading force numbered about 9,000 and its main strength lay in 2,000 Swiss and German mercenaries commanded by a famous condottiere, Martin Schwartz, supplied by Duchess Margaret; these tall foreign mercenaries were landsknechts, skilled fighters with long pikes, halberds and crossbows. Lincoln had raised a contingent of about 3,000 Englishmen, and the Earl or Kildare had brought along 4,000 ill-equipped and poorly disciplined Irish. Marching in the direction of the Midlands, the rebels crossed the Pennines, halting at Masham from where the Earl of Lincoln sent a messenger requesting permission to enter York; this was refused, so the army continued on to Southwell, reaching it on 14 June, and then proceeded to cross the River Trent at Fiskerton Ford. Support was gathered as they marched, most notably that of John, Lord Scrope of Bolton and Thomas, Lord Scrope of Masham.

King Henry was at Kenilworth when he heard of the rebels' landing on 4 June and, setting out by way of Coventry and Leicester, he gathered troops to his banner *en route*. Reaching Nottingham on 14 June, he was met by Lord Stanley (the Earl of Derby) and his son Lord Strange (the Earl of Oxford) and Lord Pembroke, whose men brought the army up to a strength of 12,000. Carrying the Royal shield was Thomas Brandon, whose brother Sir William was killed at Bosworth when performing the same duty. The vanguard was commanded by the veteran Earl of Oxford, of whom it was said that 'no finer soldier fought for King Henry VII'. It is said that morale in the King's army was on the low side, and his march towards Newark was marked by desertions. On 16 June, the army was early on the move and they encountered the Yorkist rebel army drawn up astride a ridge in the Trent Hills above the small village of East Stoke, with the River Trent covering their right flank and part of their rear.

The battle that ensued was fought in two stages. Lincoln put his own 'battle' on the right wing, the Irish, 'beggarly, naked and almost unarmed', on the left. Commanding the vanguard, the Earl of Oxford out-marched the rest of the royal army and initially confronted the rebels alone; Lincoln's army descended the slope to meet them, before the odds became overwhelming, and held them up for three hours. Trying to deploy to counter the rebel formation, Oxford's men became disorganised and suffered heavy casualties while many of them fled from the field in panic. The crossbow-armed landsknechts did great damage and it was not until Henry's archers – longbowmen all – arrived that the tide of battle began to turn, when standard-bearer Robert Brandon led on the Royal second line and Martin Schwartz, Lincoln and Broughton were killed. The Irish contingent were no match for the fresh and well-armed Royal troops now surging into action, and were cut down in large numbers, with many killed trying to cross the River Trent at Fiskerton Ford. The route to the ford, a narrow defile, became known as the 'Red Gutter' where, in the congestion, 4,000 rebel soldiers were slain. The key moment in the battle was the death of the mercenary leader, Martin Schwartz, for it was his landsknechts who held the rebel line together for three hours, while the cloth-yard shafts of the English longbowmen cut them down remorselessly. But the Swiss and Germans stood their ground and, in the classic novel *Kenilworth* a ballad is quoted by Giles Gosling:

> *He was the flower of Stoke's red field*
> *Where Martin Swart on ground lay slain.*

The King planted his royal Standard in a 'burrand' bush, and knighted Robert Brandon on the field. Only one rebel leader escaped, Lord Lovell forcing his horse through the river at the ford. He disappeared and was never seen again. The impostor Lambert Simnel was captured and, in an extraordinarily merciful manner for the day and age, was spared, but made to work as a menial in the Royal kitchens.

And so ended the Wars of the Roses, in a relatively small battle which, along with Bosworth, has been claimed as the really decisive conflict of the wars.

16

The Italian Wars 1494–1544

WHEN IN 1494 CHARLES VIII of France led an expedition of 30,000 men to Naples, he came up against the City States together with Spain and the Papacy. The French force was most impressive in this era, with a large artillery train, while French cavalry with mercenary Scottish archers and Swiss pikemen made up the bulk of the infantry. This lengthy war caused a great upsurge in the development of warfare. From then onwards, every battle out-dated its predecessor as Europe advanced from the sprawling mediaeval brawl via the tactics of Greece (exemplified by the Swiss pike phalanx) and Rome (the sword-and-buckler fighting of the Spanish infantry) to the effective fire-power in the science of war. There now dawned a new, Spanish-founded tactical age of pike and arquebus, with both sides using static and mobile artillery. The invention of the wheel lock and snaphaunce gave a foretaste of the new power of the infantryman.

It was in keeping with the age of the Renaissance that these wars were fought between curiously constituted armies in which lances came up against cannon, crossbows vied with arquebuses, mercenaries fought side-by-side with patriots while military scientists buried the few remaining exponents of chivalry. In an age of great names, Gonzalo de Córdoba, the 'Great Captain', devised a system of combining sword-and-buckler tactics with weapons of gunpowder. Pedro Navarro, the foremost engineer of the day, tried new techniques of siegecraft and fortification for the Spanish invaders of Italy;

Fernando Devalos, Marquis of Pescara, was responsible for new styles of infantry training, formations and tactics which possibly moulded the warfare for the entire century, while the Duke of Ferrara brought success to the French through his improvements on the mobility of artillery.

In 1495 at Fornovo, a French army of about 8,000–10,000 men took ten minutes to completely crush the stilted and contrived tactics of 30,000 Italian *condottieri* who, expecting to engage in the traditional cautious *condottieri* style of warfare, received a most unpleasant surprise when the French heavy cavalry smashed straight into their centre. They broke and fled, leaving 3,500 casualties on the field against French losses of 100, without either commander realising that a new age of deadly warfare had permanently banished the polite scufflings of chivalry.

At Barletta in 1502 Gonzalo de Córdoba, with 500 cavalry and 1,500 infantry trained in a tactical combination of the Roman legion's short sword-and-buckler, plus arquebus and field fortifications, came to close quarters with the hitherto invincible Swiss and rendered their pikes useless as they got under them and thrust upwards with their short, stabbing swords. It was an historical echo of the clash between the Roman sword and the Macedonian sarissa at Pydna in 168 BC, and again sword defeated pike. In the following year, the Battle of Cerignola was probably the first in history to be settled by gunpowder small-arms – Córdoba entrenched his new arquebusiers and, by sheer fire power, brought to a standstill the advancing Swiss pikemen and French infantry. Then the French, counter-attacked by Spanish infantry and cavalry, broke and fled. In this battle, where their own artillery became useless because its powder supply blew up, the Spanish captured the magnificent French artillery train which had never been in action.

During the next decade the French devised new tactics for their mobile artillery and at Ravenna in 1512 they won a pyrrhic victory over the Spaniards. Pedro Navarro and the Marquis of Pescara relied on entrenched arquebusiers; the French infantry and German landsknecht mercenaries stood firm under the deadliest fire so far experienced on any battlefield for three hours while Ferrara moved twenty-four French cannon onto the enemy's extreme right and blasted their infantry out of the trenches with enfilade fire. Then the landsknechts rushed in to crush the shaken Spanish sword-and-buckler men as French cavalry struck them in the rear.

Marignano in 1515 was the last battle of the Middle Ages and the first great battle of modern times – its cruel fighting and heavy losses setting the pattern for future battles, with armies building trenches and earthworks to protect themselves from artillery fire. The Swiss, employed by the Spaniards, were about to accept a French bribe and return home when reinforcements arrived from Switzerland to bring their numbers to 25,000. Deciding to fight, they advanced in their customary manner with three columns of pikemen in echelon, ignoring the massed French cannon tearing bloody lanes through their ranks, until they were halted by a furious cavalry charge personally led by Francis I of France. Repeatedly the Swiss renewed their attacks, which were repulsed by artillery followed by cavalry charges. The battle halted at midnight and resumed again at dawn until, with only 3,000 men left after receiving more than thirty cavalry charges in twenty-eight hours of fighting, the Swiss withdrew from the field. Marignano ended the Swiss reputation of invincibility, and this battle was followed by a steady diminishing of their prestige after similar disasters when they frontally attacked cannon and entrenched arquebusiers.

The decisive battle of the Italian Wars occurred at Pavia in 1525 when, besides devising tactics to counter the mobility of the French artillery, the Marquis of Pescara established infantry tactics which were to be used for the next century. The guns kept up a sustained fire as the musketeers took up their positions; the pikemen protected the musketeers who, in turn, cleared the way for the pikes and the cavalry – this was how it was to be until the invention of the bayonet. King Francis had his army of 20,000 men entrenched before the city. They were attacked at dawn by the same number of Spaniards in columns. The Spaniards were soon disordered by the French concentration of artillery but managed to hold their ground against a French cavalry counter-attack, which masked their own artillery. Pescara deployed 1,500 specially trained arquebusiers. In the words of the chronicler Brantôme 'these picked troops had been trained . . . without word of command . . . to wheel round, to face about, from this side to that, now here, now there, with the utmost rapidity.'

Attacked by landsknecht pikemen, the arquebusiers flayed their ranks from the cover of walls and hedges. Then the Spanish attacked again and the battle turned into a vast mêlée, dominated by Spanish fire-power, until the French were overwhelmingly defeated and King Francis himself was taken prisoner.

Using a mixture of Roman-style infantry tactics allied to the power of the handgun, the Spaniards showed at Pavia that they had achieved the most effective infantry fire-power tactics yet known in the age of gunpowder, and for many years the Spanish military system was considered to be so superior that no other army felt capable of offering battle on equal terms.

THE BATTLE OF RAVENNA II APRIL 1512

This battle was the first example of an action won by complete dominance in artillery – in this case under the control of an intelligent commander, and of Ferrara, one of the foremost artillerymen of his time. To relieve Ravenna, besieged by a French army commanded by Gaston de Foix, Duke of Nemours, the Spanish-Papal force, led by Ramón de Cardona, had taken up a position some two miles from the city in a flat waterlogged area backed by the River Ronco and flanked by marshy ground. Except for a twenty-yard gap left between its northern end and the high bank of the Ronco, and a similar gap left at the southern end to allow cavalry to charge out in close column, the Spanish line was solid. They planted their thirty guns along the centre of the entrenchment. It is recorded that they also had some two-wheeled 'carts', each with a long frontally projecting spear and flanking scythe-blades, mounted with a bunch of arque-buses which, by mechanical means, could be fired as one. It seems that the carts were to be pushed forward by a long pole so as to break up the formation of an attacking column or to blunt a cavalry attack. There is no record, however, of their use at Ravenna.

Gaston de Foix marched out at the head of 23,000 men, leaving 2,000 Italian foot to guard his camp and trenches and hold off sorties from the beleaguered city. He formed up his army facing and conforming to the Spanish position, largely with the infantry drawn back in the centre and the cavalry thrown forward on the wings. La Palice, with 900 lances, was placed on the river flank with thirty guns and 3,500 Gascon foot, mostly crossbowmen. On their left were 500 German landsknechts under Jacob Empser, next to 3,000 Picard and Gascon infantry under the Seneschal of Normandy. To the left again were 780 French lances, flanked by 2,000 Italian infantry. The right wing was completed by twenty-four guns under the Duke of Ferrara, a famed artillery expert of the day, flanked by 2,000 French light horse composed of mounted arquebusiers, cross-bowmen and stradiots (light cavalrymen).

The Spaniards allowed the French army to advance within cannon-shot of their entrenchments, although Colonna, the Spanish cavalry leader, was refused permission by Cardona to charge out and attack the vulnerable heads of the columns as they were crossing the river by the French bridge. The advancing French halted and gazed at the Spanish position, but could see only masses of cavalry on the right and left and some ominously sited guns. The cavalry were Colonna's 670 Italian lances next to the river and Pescara's 1,700 light horse (Spanish ginetes and Italian mounted arquebusiers) on the Spanish right; there was a reserve of 565 lances on the river bank in the rear of the position. Four bodies of Spanish infantry, each 1,000 strong, were lying down behind the trench in the flattest part of the position, and three Spanish foot regiments and 2,000 Italian foot of the Papal levy remained in reserve, making a total infantry strength of about 11,000.

This was a period when armies attacked once they were in position, but at Ravenna Gaston adopted different tactics, holding his troops in check for two hours whilst his artillery pounded the Spanish lines. The guns in front of his right wing and near the river played upon the only target they could see – Colonna's cavalry – while Ferrara's guns enfiladed Carvajal's and Pescara's light horse. The Spanish guns in their turn so effectively hit the Gascons that they fell back against the flanks of the landsknechts. With neither army showing any inclination to come to grips, Gaston de Foix sent d'Alégre with two guns to a position on the far side of the river whence they could fire into the rear of Colonna's cavalry.

Realising that there was little point in allowing his cavalry to be decimated without striking a blow, the Spanish commander sent Carvajal's corps and Pescara's ginetes from his right wing out over the marshy ground in a series of charges on the French light horse and the Ferrarese guns they were guarding. After a surging cavalry mêlée into which Cardona fed his cavalry reserve, the French reinforced their horsemen and eventually drove the Spanish cavalry back. Simultaneously, on the other flank, Colonna's cavalry had charged La Palice's cavalry, but they were driven off in confusion, the survivors fleeing south-westwards down the road to the protection of the entrenched Spanish infantry. The victorious French cavalry pursued on both flanks.

While the cavalry battles raged on the wings, Gaston de Foix ordered his infantry, which had been taking heavy punishment from the Spanish artillery, to advance, and 2,000 Gascon crossbowmen supported by 1,000 Picardy pikemen went forward. As they neared the enemy position, the Spanish infantry rose and at close range poured such a blast of fire into them that the French foot soldiers melted away, their survivors fleeing back to safety.

In spite of the serious impediment of a drainage ditch across their line of advance, Empser's landsknechts, in a great column of pikemen, now assaulted the Spanish position. When they closed in combat, Spanish sword-and-buckler men from the rear ranks slipped in among them and extracted heavy casualties. After a short, sharp struggle the landsknechts were thrown back, leaving many dead before the entrenchment. The Spaniards, sensing victory, raised a loud shout, but that was quite misplaced because the dispersal of their flanking cavalry had already lost them the battle.

In a second charge Gascon and other French infantry and the German landsknechts traversed the ditch before being repelled with heavy losses, the Gascons being charged in flank by the remnants of Colonna's cavalry. At the same moment two companies of Spanish infantry charged forward from their position and broke into the shattered Gascon ranks, fighting their way through until they found themselves isolated in the rear of the French line.

The infantry battle seemed to have reached deadlock, but the position was dramatically changed as masses of French cavalry, mainly from La Palice's division, began to penetrate the gap at the river end of the Spanish position. Charged by cavalry in flank and rear and attacked again in front by rallied French foot, the Spanish infantry battalions broke. All were ridden down except a solid body of about 2,000 who escaped in close formation south-eastwards down the Cesena road. Attempting to escape also, along a narrow raised path by the river, the broken column of the two isolated Spanish companies previously mentioned was pointed out to Gaston de Foix, the French commander. At once, with his personal staff of some fifteen to twenty gentlemen, he charged up on to the raised path to intercept them, only to be met by a volley of arquebus fire, followed by a charge with levelled pikes that brought down and captured every French horseman, including the army commander!

So ended one of the bloodiest battles of the age, with both armies suffering huge losses. The vanquished Spaniards were almost exterminated, only some 300 cavalry and about 3,000 infantry remaining out of the 16,000 who had stood seemingly secure behind entrenchments at dawn.

Gaston de Foix, the French commander, used his superior artillery strength skilfully against entrenched infantry and artillery. Had he halted his infantry outside the range of the Spanish artillery, his losses would have been far less. The Spanish defensive tactics required a superiority of artillery fire they did not possess, for to win this battle the Spanish had to silence the French artillery with fewer guns – an impossible task. With every part of the position within reach of cannon shot, the Spanish cavalry were sitting ducks, and the rest of the army, in a murderous cul-de-sac with a river at their backs, had as their only line of retreat one extreme end of their position that was under artillery fire.

THE BATTLE OF PAVIA 24 FEBRUARY 1525

This decisive battle of the Italian Wars of the first half of the sixteenth century was a 'victory by surprise', when an incautious enemy was caught before he could get into battle array. From 28 October 1524 throughout the worst months of winter, Pavia and its garrison of Spanish troops and landsknecht mercenaries were besieged by a French army led by King Francis I.

After three months of gross discomfort, made worse by lack of pay, the troops of both armies had become discontented to the point of mutiny. Then, in late January, came a relieving Imperialist army under the joint command of Lannoy (the Spanish Viceroy of Naples) and the Marquis of Pescara, but, with only 1,000 cavalry and some 17,000 infantry, they were much inferior to the French in numbers. So, rather than engage against the odds in a pitched battle, they endeavoured to force Francis to abandon the siege by threatening his communications with Milan and France by throwing up defences on the eastern back of the Vernacula brook, a deep-sunk and very muddy tributary of the River Ticino that in winter formed an almost impregnable barrier. To counter this, the French dug two miles of earthworks from the Ticino in the south, with their northern end resting on the wall of the Park of Mirabello, a hunting palace three miles north of Pavia; the south park wall was demolished to facilitate troop movements.

Then, as Italian and Swiss mercenaries blockaded the western aspect of Pavia, the two armies exchanged intermittent fire across the brook, in some places separated by only forty yards of mud and water, both praying that the hard weather, general discomfort and lack of pay would cause the enemy's unreliable mercenaries to desert and go home. In mid-February that was what happened, for both of Francis's mercenary Italian companies disbanded when their leader died through wounds, and only two days later 6,000 Grison Swiss mercenaries marched off to clear their borders from an invading Milanese army. Thus, in a three-day period, the French lost 8,000 men.

Francis was now in the unenviable position of attempting to besiege Pavia while holding off the relieving force with an army reduced to 1,300 mounted men-at-arms, 12,500 landsknechts, 5,000 Swiss of various cantons and about 9,000 French and Italian infantry. Even so, his force possessed numerical parity with Lannoy's and was stronger in cavalry.

The Imperialists were also having trouble with their own Swiss mercenaries, who were demanding overdue pay or immediate battle, which fact, coupled with the encouraging news from the enemy camp, decided them to take the offensive. On the night of 23–24 February, with their artillery vigorously bombarding the entrenchments on the far side of the Vernacula, the Imperialist army marched two miles upstream in what the terminology of the time called a 'camisade' – because they wore shorts over their armour for recognition on the dark, wet and windy night. There were five divisions of infantry in this attempt to turn the French flank: the first division comprised Italian and Spanish arquebusiers with 200 light horse, preceded by 2,000 pioneers carrying battering rams and tools; the second consisted of Spanish infantry under Pescara, followed by half the cavalry; the third Lannoy and the German landsknechts, followed by the other half of the cavalry; the fourth a corps of German mercenaries under the renegade Constable Bourbon; and the last a rear column of Spanish and Italian foot.

Reaching the north-east corner of the park walls without interruption, they breached them and passed through into the park to form up in an area of partly opened rides and lawns, suitable for limited manoeuvres. With considerable difficulty the foremost units were restrained from dispersing to plunder the French base camp, where the light cavalry were left. Francis, finding his flank turned and the enemy forming up steadily behind his headquarters, left the greater part of the French infantry holding the southern section of the Vernacula and, in the early light of dawn, formed up the main body of his gendarmerie, with the landsknechts on their right and the Swiss on the left. He could not use the Italian infantry watching the west walls of Pavia because they were occupied by the distraction of a pre-arranged sally from the city. The Duc d'Alençon, with 300 lances and some companies of Italian and French foot, remained in camp to the north-east of Pavia and never came into action at all. Advancing with his cavalry and a few guns, Francis opened fire upon the last enemy column (the Spanish-Italian division) as it was passing through the broken walls, then charged with two squadrons of gendarmerie, to send them fleeing back as far as the Vernacula and abandoning several pieces of artillery on the way. The rest of the French cavalry coming up, Francis placed himself at their head and charged across the front of his own guns (so masking their fire) into the hindmost of the two Imperialist cavalry brigades in the centre of the enemy line. Their leader killed, the Burgundian and Austrian horsemen of this brigade scattered, leaving a gap in the left centre of the Imperialist army into which Francis led his horsemen in repeated charges on the neighbouring infantry columns, putting them into disorder but failing to break them. The French numbers rapidly diminished, however, as man after man was brought down by the fire of arquebusiers sheltering in hedges and copses out of reach of their lances, and they were falling into disarray.

At that point the Swiss and landsknecht mercenaries approached, but the former, moving slowly while being harassed by volleys from del Vasto's arquebusiers on the Imperial right wing, only succeeded in putting in a desultory 'push of pike' before retreating *en masse* along the Milan road. Knowing their impetuous ferocity in the past,

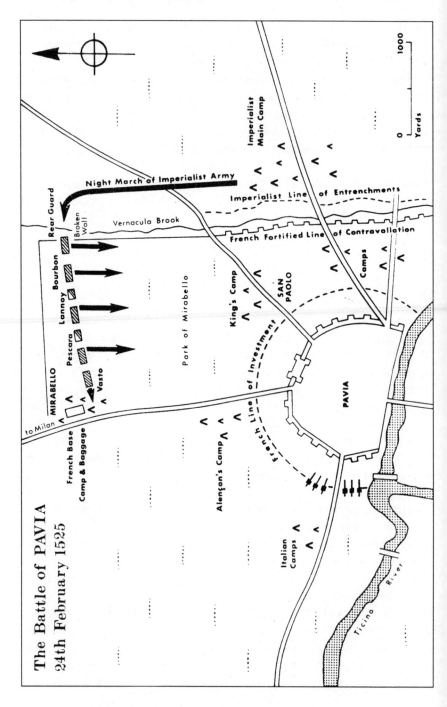

The Battle of PAVIA
24th February 1525

Night March of Imperialist Army

Imperialist Main Camp

Imperialist Line of Entrenchments

French Fortified Line of Contravallation

Rear Guard

Broken Wall

Vernacula Brook

Bourbon

Lannoy

Pescara

Vasto

MIRABELLO

French Base Camp & Baggage

to Milan

Park of Mirabello

King's Camp

SAN PAOLO

Camps

French Line of Investment

Alençon's Camp

PAVIA

Italian Camps

Ticino River

1000

0

Yards

both friends and foes were astonished by their lack of dash. The fact was that the outmoded tactics of the Swiss three years earlier in 1522 at Bicocca had cost them so dearly that they had lost their aggressiveness.

On the French right the landsknecht Black Bands launched themselves headlong into a column of their countrymen commanded by Lannoy. The fighting was desperate until they were taken in flank by the other body of Imperialist landsknechts and wiped out almost to the last man. Finally the French infantry came up from the lines of contravallation to be immediately attacked and routed by the same columns of landsknechts who had exterminated the Black Bands. The King and the remnants of his cavalry fought on until Francis was brought to the ground and captured.

Seeing that the day was lost, d'Alençon, who had remained passively out on the left throughout, taking no part except for a little feeble skirmishing with the Imperialist light horse, now marched from the field, taking with him the Italian troops who had been holding the western front of the lines of investment. The French lost 8,000 men at Pavia, the slaughter among their nobility resembling that at Agincourt 110 years earlier. The Imperialists had 700 casualties, mostly from the cavalry corps ridden down by Francis early in the action.

Tactically, Pavia was an interesting battle, as both armies were on the move and came together in an irregular manner, with each division as it reached the front finding itself engaged by hostile troops. The battle emphasised the growing importance of small-arms, as the arquebus fire was decisive in delaying the advance of the Swiss infantry, caused heavy casualties on the flanks of the French landsknecht column and, perhaps most important of all, disorganised the French gendarmerie. Possessing few arquebusiers, their infantry being mainly armed with ineffective crossbows, the French were unable to send a force of light infantry against the Imperialist arquebusiers. Pavia encouraged the captains of the period to mass their arquebusiers, and led to a mistaken neglect of the pike, an essential weapon to repel cavalry.

THE BATTLE OF CERESOLE 14 APRIL 1544

The Battle of Ceresole was unique in that both sides drew up their forces in careful array with the fixed intention of fighting, although each commander was aware that hazarding all on a general action was a dangerous business. It was an engagement that emphasised that the infantry of the day – arquebusiers, Swiss and landsknecht pikemen – when fighting with other infantry, were helpless if attacked by cavalry, and that the latter, by repeated charges, could pin steady infantry without necessarily breaking them.

During the winter of 1543–44 the young Enghien was besieging Carignano, a strongly held Spanish fortress sited in the middle of an area of French positions, in an attempt to force the Spanish Marquis del Vasto to try and relieve it. His action stimulated 100 gallant young noblemen of the French Court to post full speed to the area in the hope of winning glory and fame. Closely watched by French light cavalry, del Vasto came into the area with a force of 7,000 lands-knechts, 6,000 Italian foot, some 5,000 Spanish and German infantry who were veterans of African campaigns, 300 Florentine and 300 Neapolitan light horse and 200 Spanish and Italian heavy armed gendarmerie, and twenty guns. Del Vasto believed the steadiness of his German infantry, plus large numbers of arquebusiers, would balance his shortage of cavalry.

Determined to fight on his own chosen ground, Enghien selected a position on a long, low hillside, facing a similar ridge. The flanks could only be seen from the centre sections of the ridges as both centres stood higher than their wings. A farm and outbuilding lay before the centre of the Spanish line and another in front of their right wing, and there was a small wood on the French right. The French army was divided in the old style into three corps – 'Battle' (centre) under Enghien, 'Vaward' (right) under de Boutières and 'Rearward' (left) under Dampierre. There was no second line or reserve. The line running from right to left comprised three companies of light cavalry (450/500 men); 400 French infantry; de Boutières with eighty men-at-arms of the gendarmerie; a pike column of thirteen veteran Swiss companies; Enghien himself at the head of three companies (250) of gendarmerie, 150 light horse and the 100 gentlemen volunteers from Paris; 3,000 so-called Swiss pikemen provided by the Count of Gruyères; six companies of Italian infantry; and, on the extreme left, 400 mounted archers acting as light cavalry.

Both armies were endeavouring to keep under cover – the French/ Swiss mercenaries were lying down behind the crest of the hill – and neither side was fully visible as the Imperialists began to deploy on the forward slope. In an effort to discover the French dispositions, and perhaps turn their flanks, del Vasto sent out a screen of 800 arquebusiers to skirmish with their counterparts from the French and Italian companies in a scattering of fire-fights that flickered up and down the slopes between the lines for nearly four hours. It is said to have been 'a pretty sight . . . for they played off on each other all the ruses and stratagems of petty war.' Meanwhile both sides brought up their artillery, the Spanish placing their twenty guns beside the two farms, and Enghien deploying two batteries each of ten guns, one in front of the Gruyères contingent on his left and the other in front of the Swiss in the centre. While the skirmishers bickered, the guns fired incessantly in a largely ineffective manner, as both sides were still under cover. Del Vasto sent the Florentine horse to take the arquebusiers in flank, but Enghien replied by pushing des Thermes' light horse forward on his right wing and easily scattered them.

Now del Vasto took the general offensive by advancing across the dip between the two armies, revealing on his left wing the Italian foot under the Prince of Salerno flanked by the 300 Florentine horse; 7,000 landsknechts in the centre; 200 lance-armed gendarmerie on their right under his own command; and Cardona with 5,000 Spanish and German veterans, flanked by Lannoy with 300 Neapolitan horse, on the right wing. The shaken Florentine horse were pushed back on to the pikes of Salerno's infantry, who were simultaneously assailed by des Thermes' horsemen following up. Although disordered, the Italians held their ground, but in the time required by Salerno to get them under control, the Spanish centre had run into real trouble.

Here the 7,000 landsknechts had advanced well up the slope while the Gascon infantry of the French right centre had moved downhill to attack Salerno's Italians. Seeing their exposed flanks, the Gascons swerved diagonally left towards the German column. Excellently controlled, the great mass of landsknechts split, one group swerving to face the French foot as the other marched onwards towards the Swiss. The Gascons and the landsknechts came together with a great crash that brought down the entire front rank on each side – both had placed a rank of arquebusiers or pistoleers immediately behind the front rank of pikemen, and, at the moment of impact, each rank poured in a deadly volley. The second and third ranks, propelled forward by the men in their rear, met in a fierce 'push of pike', trampling on the corpses of their comrades. At this point the concealed Swiss in the French centre rose to their feet and rolled down the hillside in solid formation to crash into the column of landsknechts approaching them, so establishing a vast 'push of pike' along the entire centre of both armies. The final blow was supplied by de Boutières' small force of gendarmerie charging into the flank of the landsknechts to send them reeling back down the hill. Supporting Spanish cavalry on the right of the landsknechts made a perfunctory move forward towards the Swiss flank, but recoiled from their pikes and rode to the rear, carrying the wounded del Vasto with them. The landsknechts, jammed together so that only their rear ranks were able to throw down their pikes and flee, were hacked down by the ruthless Swiss and the Gascons, losing 5,000 out of their original 7,000 men. Following this disaster in the centre, the Prince of Salerno marched his force off the field, accompanied by the survivors of the Florentine light horse.

The Imperialists' fortunes had prospered better at the other end of the battlefield, where Cardona's pike column of Spanish/German veterans, flanked by swarms of arquebusiers, had surged irresistibly forward against the infantry of Gruyères and the Italians, who broke and fled without offering any serious resistance. Laying about them on all sides, the Imperialists pursued, oblivious of Lannoy's Neapolitan light horse on their right, driven from the field by Dampierre's cavalry.

Enghien, the French commander, seeing his left wing swept away while the Imperialist landsknecht column was still battling and was yet to be defeated in the centre, led his gendarmerie and the gentlemen volunteers against them, now well behind the French position. Halting, the Imperialists turned to receive the cavalry, whose first charge broke in a corner of their column, pushing right through to the rear, but at the cost of many casualties. The infantry closed ranks and their flanking arquebusiers poured in a heavy fire as Enghien's cavalry re-formed and made two more indecisive charges, the last being joined by Dampierre and the remnants of his light horse, who had returned from pursuing Lannoy's Neapolitans. The undulating ground separated this mêlée from the rest of the battle, and Enghien, who could not see what was happening elsewhere and now had less than 100 horsemen remaining, was full of despair when a courier galloped up with the news that the battle was won.

Cardona's infantry column, sensing defeat, began to retreat towards a wood in its rear, followed by Enghien and the survivors of his cavalry. They were reinforced by a newly arrived company of Italian horse – arquebusiers who, dismounting, firing and remounting, harassed the retreating column, slowing them up. The victorious Swiss and Gascons from the French centre re-formed as they ran side by side across the battlefield to join in the attack on the enemy columns, which were moving off under cover of salvoes of arquebus fire. It was the final blow to the outnumbered Imperialist infantry and, seeing the French cavalry preparing to charge, they threw down their pikes and surrendered.

Del Vasto lost this battle because both his wings were paralysed by cavalry charges, while the landsknechts in the centre, who might have held the Swiss, were outweighed by the Gascon foot, who themselves should have been contained by Salerno's Italians on the left wing. But they, in their turn, were affected by the inability of the Imperialist left-wing light horse to hold the cavalry of des Thermes. The Imperialist leader was wrong in his assumption that his considerable cavalry inferiority would be balanced by his superiority in arquebusiers, because the combination of enemy infantry and cavalry was too much for his unsupported infantry when deserted by their own cavalry.

Little quarter was given at Ceresole, the Imperialists losing 6,000 to 10,000 men against French losses of 1,500 to 2,000.

17

The French Religious Wars 1562–98

WHEN THESE WARS began, the French infantry unit was the regiment of about 1,000 pikes and 'shot' in fairly equal numbers, forming into squares after the Spanish system with the arquebusiers retiring to the rear to reload after firing. These standardised tactics favoured the Catholics who had the majority of the regular troops and mercenaries. The Protestants' main strength lay in a cavalry force composed of noblemen and their retinues. With horsemen armed with the newly invented pistol, these wars became a testing ground for new cavalry tactics. The Protestants employed German reiters (heavy cavalry, wearing helmet, cuirass and high leather boots) who introduced the caracole style of cavalry attack, riding up in successive lines, firing their pistols at close range before wheeling back to reload and re-form their ranks. Although it exposed them to cavalry counter-attack and required exact timing, the caracole frequently achieved its objective of shattering squares of pikemen. The Protestants' own horsemen fought in columns, hurling themselves impetuously on the enemy, discharging their pistols and then laying-to with their swords; they had a force of mounted infantrymen much in the style of the Dragoons of 100 years later. The Catholics still clung to the old concept of lancers charging in lines.

At Dreux in 1562, the Catholics narrowly won a hard-fought battle in which both Swiss mercenaries and landsknechts fought each other, and the two opposing commanders, Condé and Montmorency, were both captured. At St Denis in 1567, Montmorency was killed when his 16,000 men were held off for several hours by Condé's 3,500. In 1569 at Janac, the Huguenot army were surprised and badly defeated; Condé was captured and killed. In the same year at Montcontour, the Catholic commander, Tavanne, with 7,000 cavalry, 18,000 infantry and fifteen guns, defeated Admiral Coligny's force of 6,000 cavalry, 14,000 infantry and eleven guns when Catholic cavalry and Swiss infantry routed the Huguenot cavalry and then the Swiss ruthlessly slaughtered their infantry.

From repeated defeats over a ten-year period, the Protestants evolved a new and successful system of warfare based on the rapidly improving gunpowder weapons. Lacking protective pikemen, they posted their arquebusiers between cavalry squadrons and on both wings, breaking up enemy cavalry attacks by fire power or being cut down. Later the Protestants were superior in siege-craft and fortification, reinforcing unreliable mediaeval stone walls with outlying palisades, entrenchments and gun emplacements; they adopted the musket which was a devastating weapon of great stopping power and a range of 300 yards, although slow to load. Their three principal victories were gained by the good positioning of their few guns.

When Henry of Navarre took command, the Protestants began to win battles. At Coutras in 1587 this talented leader skilfully deployed his 6,300 men on a narrow front amid wooded heights, whilst between his cavalry squadrons he placed arquebusiers, with the front rank kneeling and the second rank firing over their heads, thus doubling his fire power. The Catholic cavalry attacked in two thin lines followed by infantry squares, only to be shattered by the fire of the arquebusiers and artillery at twenty yards' range. Then the six-deep columns of Protestant horses plunged into the enemy formations and broke them. Ensuing strikes from flanks and rear destroyed Joyeuse's army as a fighting force in less than fifteen minutes.

At Arques in 1589, the Catholic League's new commander, Mayenne, threatened Henry (who had less than 9,000 troops) with a force of 20,000 footmen and 4,000 horses. Henry lured Mayenne into the defile of Arques where the Catholics, unable to take advantage of their superior numbers, attacked on a 400-yard front defended by trenches and gun emplacements. When Mayenne drew his battered troops off, they were struck by a succession of cavalry attacks supported by the fire of a small Huguenot battery concealed in a castle overlooking the defile. Eventually the much larger Catholic army streamed away in defeat.

The Battle of Ivry, fought in the same year, was the most decisive of the war and, from a tactical standpoint, the most instructive of the century. The Protestant army of 11,000 had three times as many musketeers as pikemen; the Catholics had 15,000 men. Each army was drawn up in a single line of cavalry squadrons alternating with infantry units; the longer Catholic line enveloped the Huguenot flanks. Mayenne's reiters were immediately thrown into confusion by the flanking fire of arquebusiers so that their caracole tactics failed; withdrawing they blundered into the Catholic lancers and Mayenne's cavalry lost its momentum all along the line. At once Henry sent his squadrons into the unloaded reiters and the crowded lancers, to cut their way through, turn and charge back again, putting the Catholic squadrons to flight. At this, the majority of the Catholic soldiers threw down their arms and surrendered. It was an action where both the caracole and the lancers failed against cavalry using the pistol as a prelude to shock attack, while the volleys of the relatively small number of arquebusiers were far more effective than the pikes of both sides.

Horrified at the thought of a Protestant monarch on the French throne, Philip II of Spain sent 15,000 men from the Netherlands under the veteran Parma, the best soldier of the day. He frequently outwitted Henry by skilful strategic and tactical manoeuvring. On his death, Henry formally returned to the Catholic faith, preventing a large-scale Spanish invasion.

THE BATTLE OF DREUX 19 DECEMBER 1562

Condé and Coligny, marching their Huguenot army towards Dreux on the morning of 19 December, reached an area between the villages of Epinay and Blainville to find the Catholic army positioned across their route. Having neglected to put out scouts, they were completely surprised. They had forewarned the enemy of their approach by the sound of their drums, and the Catholics, commanded by the shrewd seventy-year-old Constable Montmorency, were formed in a single line some 2,500 yards long across the road to Dreux, with their right wing resting on Epinay and their left on Blainville, two villages protected by thick woods and rivers, so that they could not be turned. Personally leading the 'main-battle', Montmorency had divided his army into two instead of the usual three divisions, with the Marshal St André commanding the right. The Duke of Guise, although probably the greater captain, was serving in St André's division at the head of his own double-strength *compagnie d'ordonnance*.

With four guns in front of Epinay and another four across the road just west of Blainville, the Constable's troops occupied the space between the two villages. Sansac, commanding eight companies of light horse (400 men), was on the extreme left, and the Constable himself, with eighteen *compagnies d'ordonnance* (2,500 cavalry and retainers), lay next to the barricaded village of Blainville and the guns. To the right of the Constable's men stood twenty companies of French infantry (4,000 men) from Picardy and Brittany, and in the centre the solid phalanx of twenty-eight companies of Swiss pikemen (5,600 men). St André's division continued the line to the right with three companies (each fifty lances) of gendarmerie under Damville, the Constable's son; then came ten *enseignes* (companies) of German landsknechts (2,000 men), and twenty *enseignes* (each 200 men) of French infantry, mainly from the 'Old Bands' of Piedmonte. St André lay slightly ahead of the latter with twelve companies (each fifty lances) of gendarmerie, and on the extreme right were fourteen companies of Spanish infantry (4,800 men). The greater part of St André's 'vaward' was screened by the houses of Epinay and by the wood; the cavalry were dismounted and the infantry had their pikes lowered so that they were hardly visible. St André's fourteen guns were placed east of Epinay, bearing on the road. The Duke of Guise held 200 horse (including some noblemen volunteers) in reserve behind the village. The total Catholic army comprised 3,000 cavalry and 16,000 infantry.

The light horse that headed the Huguenot column of route came under fire from the Constable's artillery as soon as they appeared, and the leading squadrons were forced to seek the shelter of a dip in the ground. Condé and the Admiral Coligny rode out in front of their halted army to view the partly screened Catholic position. Sure that the Catholics would not leave their defended location, Coligny advised that the Huguenots should turn westward and march up the Treon road to avoid a general action, so the baggage and all the guns save five light field pieces set off in this direction. At the same time the Huguenots deployed from column of march to a fighting front in case the Catholics made a sudden attack on the exposed flank of their army moving across its front. They deployed in two divisions but with a second line and reserves; facing Montmorency was Coligny with the 'vaward' consisting of 400 French heavy cavalry, four companies of German reiters (about 1,000 pistoleers), then eleven *enseignes* of French and six of German landsknechts (some 3,500 foot). On his left, facing the eastern third of St André's division, was Condé with the 'main-battle', comprising 500 gendarmes, six companies of reiters (1,300 men), 400 argoulets (light cavalry) and horse arquebusiers, and twelve *enseignes* of French and six of German landsknechts (some 4,000 foot soldiers). The total strength of the force was about 4,000 horse and 8/9,000 foot.

The two armies in battle order faced each other a mile apart for about two hours, until at noon Condé, believing that the Constable would not leave his defensive position, decided to follow the artillery and baggage moving westward to the Treon road. The Huguenots had barely begun to move when the Constable's line started to come downhill to fall upon their flank, so Condé faced his army to the front again and began the general advance that had been his original intention. The Huguenots attacked in two lines, an unusual formation for the day, with French cavalry in front and reiters in support, followed by infantry, with a small cavalry reserve of 100 lances. Condé did not move against the fortified village of Epinay or the artillery alongside it, but masked the area with the infantry of his column and two squadrons of reiters.

In the eastern half of the field towards Blainville, the Huguenot attack was completely successful as Coligny's French horse, supported by his reiters, rode down the lesser numbers of the Constable's cavalry. In spite of his seventy years, the old man fought in the front line and was captured. In the fashion of the time, the Admiral's cavalry got out of hand and pursued the flying Catholics, so it was some time before Coligny could rally sufficient men to move across to the other wing of the field, but his 3,000 infantry played a small part in defeating the Constable's company of French foot, and apparently remained in much the same place throughout the battle. The gendarmerie, under the Prince of Porcine, completely routed the French infantry and Sansac's light horse in and around Blainville, to capture the village and the guns in front of it.

Things had gone very differently on the western side of the battlefield, where Condé attacked the Swiss, the best soldiers in the Catholic army, with all his troops, but a small infantry group and two reiter squadrons remained opposite the Catholic left wing. At first Condé's attack went well as the gendarme companies of de Muy and Araret carved their way right through the Swiss formation to come out on the other side – but without causing it to break up. Then the main body of Huguenot horse, French and reiters, charged the Swiss in flank and pushed them back, so that they left the guns they were guarding. But still they refused to break, although falling back towards St André's line. He sent three companies of his gendarmerie to their aid, but they were routed by two squadrons of reiters, their survivors falling back and rallying on Guise's small cavalry reserve. Determined to smash the stubborn Swiss, Condé withdrew the six landsknecht foot companies facing St André's front and threw them in, but the Swiss, seeing their old enemy in front of them, advanced and easily drove them from the field. In desperation Condé then sent forward the last of his cavalry, the 100 lances held in reserve, but they too were repulsed, and the frustrated Huguenot units fell back from the battered but triumphant Swiss pike phalanx.

Knowing that the last of the Huguenot cavalry had been used up, Guise at the head of 200 gendarmes led by 500 arquebusiers, and with the Spanish infantry and the French 'Old Bands' infantry, came out of the woods in front of Epinay to attack the Huguenot line at a point where the only opposition was a reiter squadron and two squares of raw French infantry who, attacked by both foot and horse, broke at once. Simultaneously St André charged out with what he had left of his cavalry and ten companies of Catholic landsknechts and, with Guise's force, fell upon the German infantry who had just been beaten off by the Swiss. Said to have been the most cowardly lot of landsknechts who had come into France during the forty years of war, the Germans threw up their pikes and surrendered. The disordered exhausted squadrons of Condé's gendarmes and reiters, dispirited at the collapse of their infantry, began to leave the field, and Condé, after vainly trying to rally them, charged into the Catholic mass at the head of a handful of horsemen and was captured.

The battle died down, and St André and Guise believed it to be over until, through the December dusk, they saw coming upon them from the south a large body whose white scarves revealed that they were Coligny's cavalry from the other wing. The Admiral had rallied about 1,000 reiters and 300 gendarmes and formed them in three troops. Guise and St André, taken somewhat by surprise, formed a new front in and about Epinay, where confused but fierce fighting was still going on when darkness fell. The Huguenots rode down the Catholic horse and captured St André, who was almost immediately killed by a man who bore him a grudge. Hard as they fought, however, the newly arrived Huguenot cavalry were unable to defeat the Catholic infantry, who resisted stoutly from houses and trees; and after many attempts to dislodge them, Coligny withdrew in good order, with two of the five Huguenot guns, to a camp three miles from the battlefield, where he was joined by the remnants of his infantry.

An indecisive battle where each side lost between 3,000 and 4,000 men, including prisoners, Dreux was notable in that day and age for (a) the incredible failure of an army with superior cavalry not knowing that the enemy were within a day's march of them, (b) a lack of preliminary skirmishing, (c) the remarkable generalship displayed by Guise in holding back until Condé's horse were exhausted, (d) the battle's duration of five hours instead of the usual short, sharp clash, (e) the capture of both commanders-in-chief, (f) the fact that steady infantry can win a battle without being able to exploit their victory if the enemy still has in the field a superior cavalry force that can block pursuit, (g) the fact that the defeated army retreated without pursuit and in good order, and (h) showing that simple linear tactics are always dangerous and that reserves of both arms should always be kept.

THE BATTLE OF COUTRAS 20 OCTOBER 1587

The Huguenot leader, Henry of Navarre, and his cousin Condé, had gathered together a small army of formidable veterans, their arquebusiers mounted on a motley assortment of horses to keep up with the cavalry, and were marching south towards a much larger Royalist army under the King of France's favourite, Joyeuse. When the strong Huguenot cavalry vanguard led by La Tremouille vanquished a similar scouting force of Mercurio's stradiots in a dusk skirmish through the long main street of Coutras, Joyeuse halted his army ten miles from the town. Henry took up a position in ideal defensive ground, 700 yards wide, with woods backed by rivers on each flank. If he was defeated, however, the lack of exits would make the position a death-trap.

Joyeuse marched at midnight but did not achieve surprise, as the 200 light horse and eighty men-at-arms sent out by Henry to patrol the road engaged in a running fight with the same stradiots who had been bested on the previous night and with 400 gendarmes. They were slowly driven back towards Coutras, the heavy arquebus fire warning Henry of the approach of the Royalists. Joyeuse's long column came on the scene in early daylight and wheeled from line of march into line of battle. The weary army took until 9 a.m. to position itself, with infantry on the wings and cavalry in the centre on open ground to the left of the high road. On the left were two very strong infantry regiments – one of them, the 'old Picardie', the senior infantry corps of the French Army, and the other Tiercellin – totalling 1,000 pikes and 1,800 arquebuses, so that each was twice as big as the small Huguenot regiments. In the centre were Mercurio's stradiots, several bands of light horse and 500 lances under Montigny. The ground to their right was occupied by the rest of the gendarmerie companies, some 1,200 lances in a long line; the front rank consisted entirely of 'great lords', with Joyeuse's personal company and his banner in the centre. On the extreme right of the cavalry stood the infantry regiments of Cluseau and Verduisant – some 2,500 men – with a scattering of mounted arquebusiers between them and the Pallard Marsh.

Henry's men had all slept comfortably in Coutras and were fresh. The right of the line was held by three foot regiments (2,000 men) in the Warren, a ditch-bordered enclosure of low shrubs from which they would only be dislodged by first class infantry, as it was unsuitable ground for cavalry. On their left, stretching as far as the high road, stood five bodies of cavalry. Those who had been skirmishing before dawn, supported by Gascon and Poitevin horse under La Tremouille and Turenne (about 400 in all), were placed nearest the infantry, and then came 600 cuirassiers in two columns, fifty men wide by six deep, under Condé and Henry. The former commanded the right of the battle and the latter the left. Soissons, with a column of 200 Northern horse, was to their left. The interval between each cavalry block was occupied by *enfants perdus* – detachments of arquebusiers five deep, the front rank kneeling. They had been strictly enjoined not to fire until the enemy came within twenty yards of them, so that they would not be ridden down. Henry intended to receive the charge and only to strike himself when the enemy, shaken by musketry, would be close and in a state of confusion.

Just before the battle began, Henry received the reinforcement of three guns brought by his gunnery specialist, Clermont d'Amboise, escorted by three foot regiments, sent to reinforce the Warren. The guns were positioned on a mound to the right of Soissons' cavalry. The left flank was held by *enfant perdus* and 300 arquebusiers detached from the regiments in the Warren.

The Huguenot force totalled 5,000 infantry, 1,300 cavalry and three guns against the Catholics' 2,000 horse, 8,000 infantry and two guns.

Not allowing the latter to settle down, Henry ordered Clermont d'Amboise to take some long shots at them. The first ball knocked over Joyeuse's personal banner and others carved bloody lanes in the flank of an infantry regiment. The return fire from the enemy guns, placed ineffectively in low-lying ground, did little damage, and, smarting under the galling fire, the Catholic line moved forward. At the eastern end of the battlefield their infantry engaged the Huguenots in the Warren but made little impression, while on the extreme left of the Huguenot line the detached arquebusiers, far from just containing the enemy, as they had been ordered, charged into the wood and pushed back the Catholic pikemen; the fierce struggle that developed here was still going on when the battle had been won and lost elsewhere. But the first clash of horse in the centre saw Montigny's gendarmes, the light horse and Mercurio's stradiots attack the

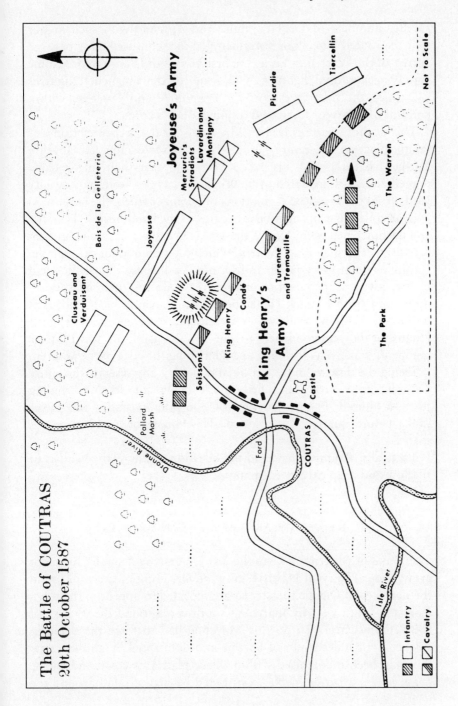

The Battle of COUTRAS
20th October 1587

Joyeuse's Army

Tiercellin

Picardie

Not to Scale

The Warren

Mercurio's Stradiots

Lavardin and Montigny

Joyeuse

Bois de la Gelleterie

Cluseau and Verduisant

The Park

King Henry's Army

Condé

King Henry

Turenne and Tremouille

Soissons

Pollard Marsh

Dronne River

Castle

Ford

COUTRAS

Isle River

Infantry

Cavalry

smaller numbers of La Tremouille and Turenne with such vigour that the routed Huguenot horsemen fled in a confused mass past the corner of the Warren as far as the first houses of Coutras. After some sprawling confused fighting, with some of the Huguenot fugitives swimming the river to escape, La Tremouille and Turenne, with a handful of survivors, managed to join Condé's corps.

This Catholic success was of little avail, for the decisive action was taking place in the centre, as Henry of Navarre intended. Joyeuse charged so early with his 1,200 horsemen that their line became ragged and gaps appeared in it. When the cavalry were only twenty yards from the five-deep formations of *enfants perdus*, the latter fired a great volley that brought down scores of men and horses. Then the reeling horsemen were hit by the six-deep blocks of the Huguenot squadrons charging in at the trot, which took them right through the Catholic line at every point. In five minutes Joyeuse's battle line had melted away as panic-stricken fugitives rode for their lives in all directions. In this attack Henry performed valiantly but Condé was unhorsed. With no enemy left to attack, some of the victorious Huguenot horsemen turned to cut up the flank of the Picardie regiment, which was frontally engaged along the edge of the Warren.

Seeing the disaster in the centre and lacking any reserve, the entire Catholic army broke and fled, many being cut down, including Joyeuse himself, in the slaughter of 400 nobility and 3,000 lower ranks before quarter was granted. The Huguenot losses were less than 200.

Tactically, Coutras answered the question of the relative values of shallow and deep cavalry formations.

THE BATTLE OF ARQUES 21 SEPTEMBER 1589

The Duke of Mayenne's Catholic army, pursuing a small Huguenot army under Henry of Navarre (now *de jure* King of France), found the defences of Dieppe too strong and decided to approach the town from the south-west by marching southwards round the estuary of the Béthune River. To do this Mayenne had to force the defile of Arques, four miles south of Dieppe and dominated by an old castle that had been modernised with artillery platforms commanding the road. It was a perfect defile, constricted by high ground around the village of Martin Eglise on one side and by the Fôret d'Arques, a steep and thickly wooded hill, on the other. The road, traversing an area not more than 400 yards wide, was bordered on one side by river marshes at its lowest point; where it was narrowest, there was a chapel, La Maladerie.

Across the defile at a point by the chapel where it was sunken and narrow, the Huguenots dug a trench and threw up an earthwork, with gaps at either end for the cavalry to sally out. The chapel, in the centre of the line, was barricaded and its parapet covered by a battery of four guns sited on a mound of earth. Five hundred yards back, where the road was sunk and bordered by a high hedge that provided cover for the arquebusiers, a second trench was dug from the edge of the marsh to the foot of the wooded hill. This trench and the area around it was commanded by the guns in the castle, but the first trench and the chapel were out of their range.

Henry had his army of about 8,000 men positioned before dawn, with the first line held by 1,200 pikes of the Royal Swiss, 600 landsknechts and about 1,200 men of five depleted regiments of French arquebusiers. The second trench was held by Galatti's Swiss Guard and the rest of the French infantry. His 1,000 cuirassed pistoleers were placed behind the first trench on each side of the high road, and there was a small cavalry reserve by the second trench.

At the head of 4,000 horse and more than 20,000 infantry, half of them Catholic-Swiss and landsknechts, Mayenne came up to the position in a long column headed by masses of horse. He sent forward Collato's landsknechts to push through the closely grown timber on the steep hillside to the right of the first trench. Two French foot regiments were to follow. The landsknechts arrived disordered and scattered at the edge of the wood, where they put their caps on their pikes, crying that they were good Protestants and would not fight their friends. Completely deceived, the occupants of the trench cheered and welcomed them, allowing the Germans to collect round that end of the defences. When a large group had assembled, the supposed deserters suddenly formed their ranks and flung themselves on the surprised and unprepared Swiss, pushing them back in disorder, so that they abandoned their position and allowed the landsknechts to push along the line, taking it and the chapel from the rear.

In the front line at the time, Henry of Navarre was carried back by the fleeing Swiss infantry, crying out: 'Are there not fifty gentle-men of France who will come and die with their king?' This urgent appeal was answered by his horsemen charging forward at May-enne's three squadrons of Royal Horse (800–900 men), who were pouring through the gaps at the ends of the line. Although there were only about 150 of them, the Huguenot cavalry charged and counter-charged to drive the Catholic horse back beyond the chapel in a sprawling mêlée that lasted for an hour. Then the arrival of four more of Mayenne's squadrons pushed the Huguenots slowly back until they were able to rally on some 150 of their own cavalry under the Count Auvergne. Together they went forward again, driving the enemy before them to the turn of the road, when they could see a huge mass of some 3,000 Catholic horse, who pushed them back past the abandoned first trench and the chapel until halted by flanking fire from Huguenot arquebusiers lining the hedgerows of the sunken road.

While all this was going on, attempts by Huguenot infantry to storm the first trench had been beaten off by the landsknechts, and now both Huguenot cavalry and infantry had to retire to the second trench. Here the Swiss guard had remained firm and their pikes, backed by the fire of flanking arquebusiers lining the hedgerows, brought the Catholics to a complete standstill. Mayenne's men were so tightly packed as to make manoeuvre impossible, and he tried to break the deadlock by turning Henry's left with 500 horsemen sent through the marsh; but their chargers sank to their bellies in the mud, causing their riders to abandon them and struggle out on foot. Pistols empty and swords blunted, Henry's cavalry managed to rally and again went forward, only to see Mayenne's entire force stretch-ing back along the road, rolling towards them.

The end of the unequal struggle seemed to be nigh when the fog that had been lying low over the battlefield throughout the morning suddenly lifted to reveal a perfect massed target to the impatient gunners standing on the parapet of the castle of Arques. At once they opened fire on the tightly packed ranks of the approaching Catholics, their shot causing lanes and gaps to appear in their column, so that they were forced back out of artillery range round the bend in the road. Seeing themselves left behind by their cavalry, the landsknechts occupying the first trench put up a poor resistance as Henry advanced with his Swiss, both the rallied and the reserve, in a column flanked with arquebusiers, to storm the chapel and earthworks and send the German mercenaries fleeing back up the road.

Henry's Huguenots halted and occupied their original position as the enemy withdrew. The Catholics had employed only a third of their infantry and half of their cavalry, whereas Henry had used every man in his army. The casualties were not very heavy, Mayenne losing 600 men against the 200 of the Huguenots. So ended the extraordinary Battle of Arques, certainly one of the most notable recorded cases of the defence of a defile, where superior numbers were useless if they could not be deployed.

18

The Dutch Revolt in the Netherlands
1566–1609

WAR IN THE LOW COUNTRIES followed a pattern of its own; battles were few and indecisive with the open country in the south easily dominated by regular troops, while the canals, dykes, marshy estuaries and broad tidal waters prevented normal troop movements and encouraged coastal sea power, fortification and siege-craft. An early Dutch effort to raise a mercenary army of German landsknechts and reiters under Louis of Nassau met disaster at Jemmingen in 1568 when the Duke of Alva, with a smaller Spanish force, overwhelmed the mercenaries with superior fire power, then dislodged them from a strong defensive position by skilful frontal and flank attacks, causing 7,000 losses against 100 Spanish dead.

In the long drawn-out struggle, the dogged courage of the rebels was matched by the discipline, confidence and audacity of the Spaniards, as when 3,000 Spanish troops took the Island of Zierikzee in 1576, making a night-crossing by wading through water four feet deep on the top of a submerged dyke, holding their powder and muskets over their heads. Although harassed throughout by Dutch boatmen armed with harpoons and arquebuses, the Spanish veterans captured the island.

Many towns were besieged – at Haarlem, Dutch arquebusiers on skates made frequent and effective sallies; Antwerp held out for fourteen months and Ostend, resisting its besiegers from 1601 to 1604, so drained Dutch military strength that in the desultory warfare that followed they were only able to hold their own because of control of the sea. Leyden held out for eleven months before cutting the dykes and flooding the Spaniards out of their positions. The Dutch became the fortification experts of Europe, strengthening their fortresses by wet ditches that were drained before they froze, while mines and counter-mines were sunk in the frozen soil, with subterranean fighting taking place in galleries far below ground.

Water being a great ally of the Dutch, there was a rise of Dutch sea power, and their sailors (the Sea Beggars) won many victories over Spanish coastal shipping. During the relief of Leyden, flat-bottomed boats fought a naval battle, manoeuvring among half-submerged trees and farmhouses in flooded countryside, with the Sea Beggars, using harpoons as weapons, destroying the Spanish vessels and their crews.

In 1584 William was succeeded by his seventeen-year-old son Maurice of Nassau, who proved to be not only the greatest general of the war but also the creator of a new school of tactics. Believing that manoeuvring and siege-craft were more likely to gain independence than costly pitched battles, Maurice used inland waterways to move the entire Dutch army and artillery on barges from one end of the country to the other, audaciously raiding and striking throughout the Netherlands with a compact force that seldom exceeded 10,000 men. He organised the first dependable Dutch standing army, formed of German mercenaries plus English, Scottish and Huguenot volunteers, in a practical combination of Roman tactics and gunpowder weapons. Comparable in size to a cohort, Maurice's regiments consisted of 250 pikemen, 200 arquebusiers and 100 musketeers, formed in companies each of a single arm. They were positioned in three lines in a chequerboard array while still maintaining Vanguard-Main Battle-Rearguard; Maurice disapproved of the current practice of throwing a whole army into battle at once. His formations had their width of front increased by reducing the depth of the musketeers to ten ranks and drilling the pikemen to take three-foot intervals instead of standing shoulder-to-shoulder.

Other aspects of the Dutch army improved by Maurice included the cavalry and the artillery. Reiters and cuirassiers were armed as, and fought in the style of, the German reiters, organised in troops of 120 men and subdivided into three groups. Posted on the flanks, they worked in separate bodies, independent of their infantry. The Dutch artillery consisted of 48, 25, 12 and 6-pounder guns, all mounted on horse-drawn, wheeled carriages. Spanish artillery at this time consisted of cannon (huge), demi-cannon (heavy siege guns), quarter-cannon (normal field piece) and Falcon (light field piece). The last two had wheeled carriages.

Spanish generals relied on infantry squares, with the musketeers retiring for protection *inside* the formation; Maurice reversed this by training his musketeers to take refuge *outside* the pikemen on both flanks, stationing themselves parallel with the fourth or fifth rank, able to continue firing even during close combat. If push-of-pike failed to gain a decision, then the flanking musketeers charged home. Most of the footmen were armed with muskets, although the skirmishers favoured the arquebus; constant drilling developed speed and precision in reloading and in preserving perfect order while filing back to the rear. The densely packed *tercios* presented an inviting target to the steady volleys of the highly trained Dutch musketeers.

Maurice struck with 7,000 troops at Tournhout in 1597. Taking advantage of bad weather to march rapidly to attack an isolated Spanish force of 6,000, he killed 2,000, including their commander, for 100 Dutch dead. The Dutch leader's only major battle was at Nieuport in 1600 where each army was composed of about 10,000 foot-soldiers and 1,500 cavalry. With Dutch warships firing ineffectually from the sea, the two armies met on the exposed beach at the turn of the tide. Driven inland to the sand dunes, the four great blocks of Spanish infantry were greatly handicapped by the broken ground. Both sides attacked and counter-attacked before the Spaniards, exhausted by several days of hard marching, were defeated by Maurice's mobility and reserve strength.

Maurice conducted numerous successful sieges, working at astonishing speed and aided by heavy artillery concentrations. He took every advantage of Parma's absence in France until Philip of Spain realised that he could not reconquer the lost provinces any more than the Dutch could hope to gain ground in the southern Netherlands. The deadlock was broken when the Spanish monarch virtually conceded the independence of the new republic.

THE BATTLE OF NIEUPORT 2 JULY 1600

This, the most brilliant victory achieved by Prince Maurice of Orange during his long military career, was a most interesting fight from a tactical point of view. Maurice intended to besiege Nieuport, and numerous Dutch ships bearing provisions and munitions from Ostend, having sailed in conjunction with his army, were moored in the tidal estuary of the River Yser. A recent mutiny in the Spanish Low Country forces had led the Dutch to believe that they would be uninterrupted, so that Maurice was surprised when he received the news that the Austrian Archduke Albert, ruler of the Spanish Netherlands (Belgium today), was close at hand with a field army of unknown strength, having recaptured numerous recently taken small fortresses and positions. By thrusting himself between Maurice and his base at Ostend, and with a fortified town behind him, the Archduke had forced the Dutch leader either to accept battle or embark his army, probably losing at least his rearguard in the process.

The Archduke had been able to raise an army because the Spanish soldiers, although in a state of mutiny, were proud of their military reputation and hated the thought of the Spanish Netherlands falling into Dutch hands. They responded, therefore, to the Archduke's desperate appeal to their religious fanaticism and *esprit de corps*, and agreed to join him, provided they served under their own standards and chosen officers, with an honourable place in the vanguard during the battle.

On hearing of the Spaniards' approach, Maurice sent Ernest of Nassau with Edmond's Scottish Regiment of Foot, Van de Noot's Zealand Foot Regiment, 400 horse and two field pieces, to delay the Spaniards by seizing the important bridge at Leffinghem, unaware that the Archduke had already captured it. Coming upon the enemy in force, Ernest was almost cut to pieces, only two fugitives arriving back at Nieuport to reveal the disaster.

At 8 a.m. on 2 July, when the water was low enough to uncover the fords, Maurice pushed his 'vaward', under Francis Vere, across the river, to deploy on the broad dry beach and cover the passage of the rest of the army, as the incoming tide made it essential for them to have plenty of time to cross and form battle order. The 'vaward', far stronger than the 'main battle' or the 'rearward', consisted of forty-one companies of foot – 4,000 of the best infantry in the army, made up of the Veres' two foot regiments (Francis with thirteen companies and Horace with eleven), a strong Frisian regiment of seventeen companies under Colonel Hertinga, and two companies of Maurice's own Foot Guards, and more than half the Dutch cavalry force (nine units out of the seventeen), mostly picked troops under Count Louis of Nassau, Lieutenant-General of the Horse, and including cuirassiers and three cornets (or troops) of light horse. The cavalry led the advance, with the light horse well forward in a scouting role. The 'vaward's' six field guns, served by sailors, were planted on the dry sand at the foot of the Dunes, with six companies of Frisians in support.

The 'main-battle' followed, and much later the 'rearward', which had remained before Nieuport in case the garrison was tempted to sally out and destroy the ships stranded on the mudflats. This force was still crossing the estuary when cavalry skirmishes opened the battle. Maurice's total strength, after deducting the losses at Leffinghem, was 10,000 infantry, 1,500 cavalry and seven guns. As his forces arrived on the east side of the estuary, Maurice drew them up on the firm beach left uncovered by the low tide. It was broad enough for the whole army to be drawn up on it, but at high tide it shrunk to 50–100 yards of firm sand leading up to the Dunes – undulating sandhills between 350 and 700 yards wide whose loose sand was overgrown with furze bushes and other low scrub. The country road from Ostend, a broad green track, ran on the far side of the Dunes.

It was anticipated that the Spanish would advance on this road, but soon it became evident that they were coming along the beach. Their army consisted of about ninety companies of foot (10,000 men); about 1,500 horsemen, comprising six cornets of pistoleers (cuirassiers), four of *herrueleros* (light horse) and nine much smaller cornets of 'lances' or men-at-arms; and six demi-cannons and two smaller pieces. The 'Mutineers', an assorted collection of Spaniards and Walloons, were an unruly but formidable body of men formed in two provisional foot regiments and a cavalry force of 600 horse, all under Francisco de Mendoza and forming the Spanish 'vaward'. Next came the Archduke with the 'main-battle' containing the 'flower of the army' – three old Spanish *tercios*, commanded by Alonzo di Avila. Louis de Villar and Jerónimo Monroy respectively, and one old Italian *tercio* under Gasparo Sapena. The Archduke had one cornet of the lancers of his guard as escort and five more were attached to the 'main-battle'. The two Walloon regiments of La Barlotte and Bucquoy, with Bostock's Irish regiment and six cornets of horse, formed the 'rearward'.

The first Spaniards to appear were ten cornets of cavalry, which took up the whole area between the sandhills and the sea, and soon there was some cavalry bickering between the Dutch light horse and the Spanish *herrueleros*. Then Francis Vere ordered Count Louis to fall his horse in on the left of the deployed infantry close to the water's edge as the Dutch skirmishers slowly gave way in front, harassed by cornets of the 'Mutineer' cavalry, who swerved off in disorder when they came under the fire of the Dutch guns higher up the beach.

The fires of battle flickered and died when the Archduke realised that the beach was rapidly narrowing as the tide came in. Several Dutch warships lying off the coast began to send long shots into the flank of the Spanish army, causing the Archduke to order two guns to be brought to the water's edge to reply to their fire. But the tide was coming in fast and more Dutch warships were appearing, so at 2.30 the Spaniards began laboriously to march off the beach up on to the soft shifting sands of the Dunes. It was an operation that took nearly two hours, until only five guns and some infantry companies remained on the beach facing the Dutch battery. The Spanish cavalry, except for one cornet, crossed the Dunes and formed up on the broad green road, while their infantry slowly trudged westward, keeping their formations with difficulty on the deep uneven sandhills.

The Spanish move off the beach was largely dictated by the incoming tide plus the flanking fire from the Dutch warships, but the Archduke may also have been aware of the inferiority of his cavalry, who were consistently ridden down by the Dutch cuirassiers, and decided to trust the battle to his strong veteran infantry units, which might gain the upper hand in the sand dunes. The Archduke was not unjustified in this assumption, as Maurice's motley infantry consisted of two English, one French, one Walloon, one German, one Swiss and only three native Dutch corps.

With plenty of time to manoeuvre, the Dutch deployed to conform to the Spanish dispositions. Leaving five Frisian and two English companies to protect the guns, with three cornets of horse from the

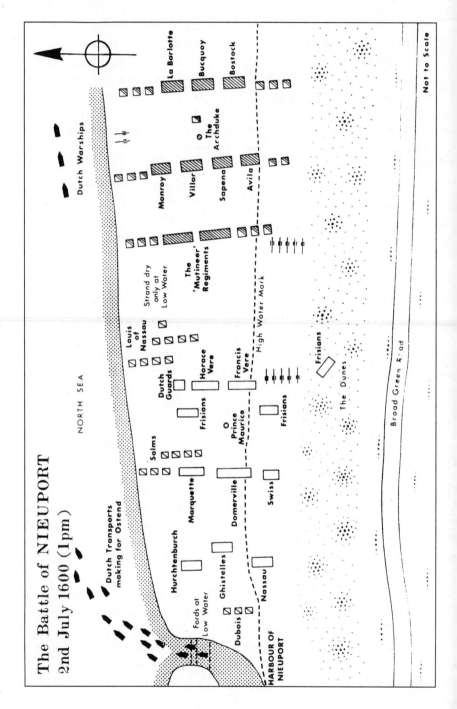

The Battle of NIEUPORT
2nd July 1600 (1pm)

'main-battle' in reserve, Vere sent the rest of his infantry up to join the six companies of Frisians already on the Dunes, arranging them behind a low sandhill, with 250 picked English infantry and Dutch Foot Guards as a 'Forlorn Hope' on a high isolated flat-topped sandhill projecting to his left front. The sailors dragged two guns from the battery on the shore on to a still higher sandhill to their right, so commanding the green road below them and on their right. On lower ground in front of these guns Vere placed 500 Frisian musketeers, whose range of fire also included any enemy approaching by the road. The rest of the English and Dutch infantry were drawn up in small supporting detachments ready to reinforce the front line. Count Louis's cavalry had gone about, to pass laboriously across the sandhills, where they continued the line of infantry by drawing up on the green road. The 'main-battle' and the 'rearward' came up and were placed behind Vere's line, with the infantry mainly on the southern side of the dunes and the cavalry supporting the 'vaward' horsemen on the green road.

The 'main-battle' consisted of the strong Huguenot/French regiment of Domerville in the centre, flanked on the right by a small Swiss battalion of 400 men and on the left by Marquette's Walloon regiment. Composed entirely of deserters from the Spanish colours, the Walloons were the only doubtful element in the Dutch army, but they fought well, probably because they knew that death would be the penalty for defeat. There was not a single Dutchman among the infantry of the 'main battle'. Also in the force were six cornets of Dutch cavalry commanded by Count Solms, and two cornets of English cavalry under Sir Edward Cecil and Captain Pembroke. The 'rearward' consisted of the German regiment of Ernest of Nassau, commanded by Lieutenant-Colonel Huysmann; the two Dutch regiments of Hurchtenburch and Ghistelles, the latter less six of its companies, which had been left in the defences outside Ostend; and two cornets of Dutch and one of English horse under Dubois.

Advancing slowly through the shifting sands of the Dunes, the Spanish infantry in three lines neared the Dutch position, and 500 arquebusiers of the 'Mutineer' regiments went forward to attack Vere's 'Forlorn Hope' on the advance sandhill. They were beaten back, as were some 500 pikemen and arquebusiers drawn from the regiments behind the 'Mutineers'. Now replacing the exhausted 'Mutineers' with the three Spanish and the Italian *tercios*, the Archduke made a general advance against the whole of Vere's front, with Monroy's and Villar's *tercios* attacking the left of the Dutch line, while Avila's and Sapena's attacked south of the two-gun battery on the high sandhill. Maurice brought up from his 'main-battle' Domerville's Huguenot regiment and the Swiss and Walloons to support his right, but sent no aid to Vere on the northern flank, although it was repeatedly requested. It might be claimed that Prince Maurice was able to keep his third line of infantry still intact when the Archduke's 'rearward' reserve had been committed by sacrificing Vere's English and Frisian 'vaward', which not only took on the Spanish 'vaward' – the 'Mutineers' – but at least two of the four *tercios* of the Spanish 'main-battle', without receiving a single reinforcement.

While the infantry attacks and counterattacks were proceeding on the undulating surface of the Dunes, the Spanish cavalry, advancing on the low ground inland, were completely routed by Louis's force, aided by crossfire from the two guns on the sandhill and by Vere's Frisian musketeers. Hotly pursued, the disordered cavalry fell back to shelter behind the infantry of its own 'rearward', though many scattered and left the battlefield; it is recorded that the 'Mutineer' horse showed up very badly. In this action Louis was only rescued from capture by a desperate cavalry charge, and it took a long time for him to re-order his squadrons and charge again on the Spanish left flank across the green road, to drive in the cavalry of the Archduke's 'main-battle'. Then Louis's depleted and exhausted squadrons were checked by crossfire from the Spanish 'rearward' infantry.

The Archduke threw in his third line, the Walloon and Irish regiments of Bucquoy, La Barlotte and Bostock, in a thrust against Vere's unreinforced section of the Dutch front line, where all the reserves had been used up. The English and Frisian infantry companies were driven off the dunes in disorder, slowly pursued by the exhausted Spanish infantry, who were mixed up in a hopeless confusion of pikemen and musketeers, so that they dissolved like the mob they were when attacked by cavalry. The retreating Dutch infantry fell back behind the battery on the shore, where a few hundred of them rallied while the guns kept up their fire on the opposing Spanish battery, although almost out of ammunition. Then Maurice threw in his reserve cavalry – the cornets of Pembroke, Balen and Sir Edward Cecil – to charge headlong into the mass of disordered Spanish infantry, and send them flying in all directions among the dunes.

Seeing their confusion, Vere's infantry rallied and pressed forward against little opposition. Count Louis's weary cavalry charged once more on the green road, and Maurice ordered his 'rearward' regiments on the dunes to make a general advance. Suddenly enemy resistance collapsed, as the thoroughly demoralised Spanish cavalry, fleeing past their flank, caused the infantry on the dunes to break up and retire in a disorderly mass of pikemen and musketeers towards the Leffinghem bridge, their natural line of retreat. Reinvigorated, the Dutch cavalry rode them down on all sides, destroying nearly half the Archduke's weary infantry, which were slaughtered wholesale, losing about 3,000 men. The four 'old' *tercios* and the 'Mutineers' were almost wiped out, and the Dutch captured 105 out of 120 standards of horse and foot on the field. The cavalry escaped more lightly, but the majority of the Spanish leaders, including the Archduke himself, were wounded, and some were killed or captured. The Dutch lost about 2,000, including the casualties at Leffinghem bridge. The two English regiments in the 'vaward' lost 600 men out of their twenty-four companies.

Nieuport was a battle where the stubbornness and endurance of the Dutch and English infantry enabled them to stand long enough for their tired cavalry to make the final attack against the similarly exhausted Spaniards. In the arduous conditions amid the sandhills, the Archduke failed to understand that by dusk his infantry, which had been under arms for twelve hours, was exhausted. Throughout military history it is a notable fact that mounted commanders and staff officers habitually failed to notice the fatigue of their infantry.

The echoes of the earlier debacle at Leffinghem bridge were still resounding when the battle ended. If Prince Maurice had not sent out the small force that was destroyed at Leffinghem earlier in the day, the Dutch army, 2,500 men stronger, would probably have seen off the Spaniards even more easily. In addition, if the Dutch garrison at Ostend had sallied out and seized Leffinghem bridge, the whole of the Spanish army would have been captured; their hesitation was perhaps due to their awareness of the disaster of the morning, when the Scottish and Zealand regiments had been wiped out.

19

The Thirty Years War 1618–48

THIS MOST SAVAGE of conflicts began as a religious war, but became increasingly a political struggle between the Catholic/Hapsburg coalition (which included Austria, the Holy Roman Empire, most of the German Catholic Princes and Spain) and the Protestant Princes of Germany and the kingdoms of Denmark, Sweden and Catholic France. There were frequent changes in these alliances, particularly by the German Princes. Fighting spread into France, Spain, Italy and the Netherlands but was concentrated mostly in Germany where savage and undisciplined mercenary armies repeatedly plundered and devastated the land. The war was divided into four main periods – the Bohemian (1618–25), the Danish (1625–29), the Swedish (1630–34) and the French-Swedish (1634–48).

The Bohemian Period
The leaders and armies in this period were those of the Catholic League commanded by Count Tilly, the Protestant Union under Christian of Anhalt, the Spanish under Spinola, and a Bohemian refugee/mercenary army under the Protestant Von Mansfeld (whose pillaging of the Rhine Valley began the depredations of the war). Then there were reinforcing Protestant armies under Duke Christian of Brunswick and Margrave George Frederick of Baden, and the Catholic Spanish army from the Netherlands under Córdoba. The principal battles were:

Pilsen	1618
Sablat	1619
White Mountain	1620
Mongolsheim	1622
Wimpfen	1622
Höchst	1622
Fleurus I	1622
Stadtlohn	1623

The Danish Period

Mercenary General Wallenstein was hired by the Hapsburgs and raised an army. King Christian IV of Denmark invaded Germany in the summer of 1625. The Danish Army marched down the Weser as he tried to gather support from the Protestant German Princes, from the Dutch and from England, with little success. To oppose the Danes, Wallenstein moved north to join Tilly. Requiring troops to cope with a Huguenot revolt, France withdrew from the war, Richelieu recalling armies from the war with Spain.

Protestant leader Mansfeld attempted to cross the Elbe *en route* for Magdeburg with 12,000 men, but was repulsed with heavy losses by Wallenstein at Dessau Bridge on 25 April 1626, being pursued into Silesia, where he died.

On 24–27 August 1626, Tilly heavily defeated Christian's Danes at Lutter am Barenberge, and again in September and October 1627, when Tilly and Wallenstein marched down the Elbe, to drive Christian over the frontiers of Holstein.

In 1628, Wallenstein spent February to July besieging Stralsund in an attempt to gain control of the Baltic coast, but a strong defence allied to Swedish threats forced his withdrawal. However, on 2 September 1628, Wallenstein heavily defeated King Christian's Danes at Wolgast, and at the Peace of Lubeck in June 1629 Denmark withdrew from the war.

In a period of complicated alliances, operations and numerous battles, the main interest lies in the decline of the Spanish as a military force, the rise of the great French armies under Turenne and Condé and the dramatic military innovations of Sweden under Gustavus Adolphus.

The Swedish Period

Undoubtedly the most significant development that arose from the Thirty Years War was the new Swedish army organised by their great warrior King Gustavus Adolphus, who revolutionised the warfare of his day in building up the first truly national army of modern times which consistently defeated the conventional armies and mercenaries of the period. Allied to John George of Saxony and later Bernard of Saxe-Weimar, the new Swedish armies fought numerous battles against Wallenstein, Tilly and Pappenheim.

The French-Swedish Period

France declared war on Spain in 1635 and battles took place in France, Switzerland, Italy and the Netherlands while a Swedish army operated in East Germany. There were a number of Spanish invasions of France culminating in the Battle of Rocroi in 1643.

Under Torstensson, the Swedes conducted operations in Bohemia and surrounding countries, but less successfully than under Gustavus Adolphus. Marshal Turenne became an outstanding French commander, as did the Duke of Enghien, fighting several battles against the Bavarians under General Mercy when, in 1646, allied French and Swedish armies invaded Bavaria in operations that continued until 1648. The War ended in October 1648, although France and Spain continued their struggle.

Of the many battles that took place during the Thirty Years War, perhaps four stand out – Lützen 1632, Nordlingen 1634, Rocroi 1643 and Breitenfeld in 1631. Breitenfeld, the first major Protestant victory, was a turning point in the Thirty Years War. It strengthened the European resistance to Catholic Hapsburg while tactically and historically it ranked as a most decisive conflict, indicating that Gustavus Adolphus had initiated a new era of warfare besides confirming that he was the best commander of the day. The Swedish victory at Breitenfeld came because their formations of cavalry, artillery, pikemen and musketeers mutually supported each other in small, self-contained combat groups with regimental guns firing three times to the once of the Imperial forces.

The tactical method which made this possible was based on the Swedish Brigade System, a formation composed of 1,000 to 1,500 men combining small battle groups of musketeers and pikemen in a wedge-shape formation. This was drawn up in three lines with three groups of pikemen (648 men) forming a protective triangle and 864 musketeers in five groups behind them, in the intervals and on the flanks. From these positions they were able to sally forth, deploy, fire and retire to reload. Another much used Swedish battle formation had the musketeers on the flanks of pikemen, with guns in the intervals between companies (each company having a total front of ninety-six feet). This formation produced maximum fire power, particularly when the musketeers fired two ranks at a time or all at the same time in a full three-rank formation. Gustavus Adolphus marked the tactics of Maurice of Nassau who ensured continuous volleys by forming his musketeers in ten-deep ranks with the front rank firing, falling back to the rear, reloading and firing when it again reached the front. The Swedes used a lighter and faster loading musket with prepared charges carried in a slung bandolier; fire discipline and training produced musketeers capable of firing thirty shots per hour. Fire power was increased by musketeers advancing in six ranks, closing up to three in the firing line; when delivering a volley, the front rank knelt and the other two fired over their heads, so that a brigade had far greater fire power than the square formations invariably adopted by the enemy. The Swedish tactic of the whole force of musketeers firing at once was intended as a preparation for the attack of either pikemen or cavalry with the musketeers either joining the charge, or reloading under cover of it. As protection against cavalry, musketeers were provided with a wooden pole six feet long with a pike head at either end, known as the Swedish Feather; it was stuck in the ground with its point about breast-high to attacking cavalry – similar to the pointed stakes used by the English archers at Agincourt.

Discarding armour, so that only pikemen and heavy cavalry continued to wear the cuirass, the Swedish army made themselves far more mobile than their opponents. Gustavus Adolphus used the pike as an offensive weapon, shortening it to eleven feet and changing the proportion of pikemen to musketeers so that they were equal in numbers, although he retained more pikemen than in other armies of the period. The Swedish leader took the best ideas of earlier successful commanders and combined them with his own theories, but there was not much information on the employment of field artillery as very little progress had been made since the days of Jan Ziska. The customary method of using artillery was to place it in front of the army in a static position where, after firing a few preliminary shots, it was often overrun as the action developed. Gustavus Adolphus made light field guns his speciality, introducing four-pounder infantry support field pieces made of leather that could be handled by four men or drawn by a single horse. Using the first ever artillery cartridge, these guns discharged eight times while the musketeers fired six volleys; initially, each infantry regiment of 1,000 men had its own gun but later this was increased to two guns per regiment. His two-pounder swivel-breech loaders were so skilfully handled that they fired three times as quickly as those of the enemy. Even the heavier brass guns and howitzers were light enough to keep up with infantry and cavalry.

At the beginning of the Thirty Years War the armoured lancer still survived, but it soon disappeared except in the armies of Poland, Spain and Scotland (Scottish lancers were light horsemen). Most European cavalry were still partially armoured, sacrificing their shock potential by riding up slowly, firing pistols and then wheeling away.

Typical horsemen of the Thirty Years War were the cuirassier and the arquebusier – the former wore three-quarter armour and carried a sword and pistol while the latter wore 'back and breast or a stout buff coat', rarely carrying an arquebus or a carbine; sword and pistol were his usual weapons. Large men on heavy horses, the Swedish cavalry formed up in two lines three ranks deep and in small, manoeuvrable squadrons so that the combination of weight and momentum in controlled shock charges made them greatly feared. There was also a trained Dragoon Corps that operated as light horse or as infantry on the defensive; they wore no armour and were armed with the carbine and sabre. They were superior to the dragoons of other armies who were said to be not quite sure whether they were cavalry or infantry, combining in equal parts the dash of cavalry and the steadiness of infantry as they advanced on foot and retreated on horseback!

At Lützen in November 1632, Gustavus Adolphus moved rapidly forward to attack Wallenstein who had weakened his army by sending Pappenheim and 8,000 men, mainly cavalry, out on a plundering expedition. Wallenstein drew up his 20,000 troops in four large infantry squares in lozenge formation behind earthworks and a shallow drainage ditch. The cavalry were split between the two wings, those on the right supported by a fifth infantry square.

Skirmishers lined the ditch and the guns were positioned along the front. Gustavus formed up his 18,000 troops with both wings composed of integrated cavalry and infantry units, taking personal command of the right, facing Count Holk, while Bernard of Saxe-Weimar led the left.

Early morning fog and smoke from the town of Lützen, burned by Wallenstein, hindered the Swedish when they attacked Holk at 11 a.m., driving his cavalry back on the guns and pushing the skirmishers out of the ditch. Capturing most of the guns, they swept on to attack the infantry squares at close quarters but lost contact with their cavalrymen who had to dismount and lead their horses across the ditch. Taking advantage of the confusion, Wallenstein's cavalry squadrons poured into the gap and pressed the Swedes so hard that Gustavus himself came galloping up from the right wing at the head of mounted reinforcements and was killed in the mêlée. Returning with his 8,000 men, Pappenheim counter-attacked and forced the Swedes back across the ditch; Pappenheim himself was fatally wounded at this moment. Bernard took command of the Swedish forces and drove Wallenstein back on Lützen, seizing the Imperial artillery and recapturing the ditch; small groups of fiercely fighting men floundered about in smoke, dust and darkness, until Bernard rallied his men for a final effort that drove Wallenstein from the field, leaving artillery and baggage behind.

The leadership of the Protestant cause was taken over by Bernard of Saxe-Weimar and the Swedish Field Marshal Horn; on the Catholic side, Wallenstein had been assassinated and the Imperial Forces were commanded by King Ferdinand of Hungary and General Gallas. At the Battle of Nordlingen in 1634, Ferdinand joined forces with a Spanish army of 20,000 highly trained infantry and cavalry – the combined force being about 35,000 strong, including 13,000 horsemen. The Swedish army consisted of about 16,000 foot and 9,000 cavalry. At dawn, Horn's veteran Swedes stormed entrenchments on commanding ground on the left flank of the Catholic position, capturing the Imperial batteries. Thrown into confusion by the explosion of a powder magazine, a heavy counter-attack flung the Swedes off the position. Then for seven hours the Swedish infantry made repeated unsuccessful attacks on the hill. It is said that the Spanish troops defending the hill were trained to kneel whenever the Swedes fired a volley so that bullets flew over their heads, rising to deliver their volley before the Swedes could reload. At midday Horn began to withdraw across the rear of the Protestant lines where Bernard's men had been battling furiously against superior numbers. Seizing their opportunity, the Spanish and the Imperialists charged Bernard's troops who buckled and broke, allowing the attackers to pour through the gap and into the flank of Horn's weary column, who were overwhelmed and almost wiped out. At Nordlingen, almost the last remnants of Gustavus's disciplined national army perished; after that the forces of the Kingdom were Swedish in name only and formed of Germans, Scottish, English, Irish, Croatian, French and Polish mercenaries.

As we shall see in more detail later, the Spanish/Imperial forces under de Mello did not fare so well when besieging Rocroi in 1643 with 18,000 infantry and 9,000 cavalry. The young Duke of Enghien, commanding a force of 15,000 infantry and 7,000 cavalry, opened the battle at dawn by personally leading a successful cavalry charge against the Spanish left. Impetuously, the French left-flank cavalry attacked the Spanish right, to be repulsed and scattered by the Spanish horse, who were checked in their turn by the French reserve. Enghien wheeled his cavalry left to swing behind the Spanish lines and then cut his way directly through their rear centre, driving a wedge between the Spanish *tercios* and the German, Italian and Walloon foot of the reserve who broke and ran. Emerging from the infantry formations, Enghien fell upon the rear of the Spanish cavalry who were facing his reserve, scattering them from the field. Completely encircled, the Spanish *tercios* fought off repeated French attacks until Enghien hammered their closely packed ranks with massed French and captured Spanish artillery. On the Spanish commanders asking for quarter, Enghien and his staff advanced between the lines to receive their surrender, but mistaking this for another charge, the Spanish infantry opened fire. This so enraged the French soldiers that they attacked and almost annihilated the Spanish infantry. Rocroi dealt the Spanish military tradtion a death blow.

Under Richelieu, France achieved a new pride and cohesion through military achievement, by organising a disciplined national army modelled on the Swedish system. Condé became an outstanding commander – the masterful way in which he handled his squadrons of horse revolutionised cavalry tactics while Turenne, learning much from Maurice and Gustavus Adolphus, was a painstaking master of small wars and his cautious manoeuvres eventually brought the Thirty Years War to a close.

THE BATTLE OF BREITENFELD 18 SEPTEMBER 1631

By 1631 the Thirty Years War, which had been devastating Europe for thirteen years, entered its third phase – the Swedish period. Opposing Gustavus Adolphus, King of Sweden, was the Imperial army commanded by the seventy-two-year-old General Count Johan Tilly ('the Monk in Armour'), a veteran Walloon who had learned his trade under Parma, trailing a pike in a Spanish *tercio* in the Netherlands. He was a good commander in the conventional Spanish tradition.

In the summer of 1631 Tilly, after laying waste the surrounding countryside, marched into unravaged Saxony, where the excesses of his army drove John George I, Elector of Saxony, to join forces with the Swedish army. The combined force of 26,000 Swedes and 16,000 Saxons hurried southward across the Elbe to intercept Tilly. The opposing armies met at Breitenfeld, six miles north of Leipzig, where, on a dusty, slightly undulating plain, bare of trees but crossed by a marshy stream, a precipitate action by Tilly's second-in-command, Count Pappenheim, committed him to battle.

On a bright hot September morning Tilly drew up his army on a two-mile front. His 35,000 infantry were positioned in two lines of *tercios* – seventeen solid squares each of 1,500 men, fifty men deep – and his cavalry stationed on either flank, the left wing comprising 5,000 Black Cuirassiers under Pappenheim, and the right 5,000 horsemen under Furstenberg and Isolani. His light guns were placed in front of the Imperial centre and his heavy between the centre and the right – twenty-six pieces of artillery in all. The Imperial army had the advantage of position on a gentle downward slope, with sun and wind at its back.

Tilly had an excellent view as Gustavus Adolphus drew up his army some 1,000 yards away in a formation that looked more and more like a chessboard as the Swedish infantry brigades and cavalry regiments took up their positions. On the far left the Saxon infantry formed a solid block, with cavalry on either flank. Next to them came the Swedish left under Horn, comprising three regiments of cavalry interspersed with detachments of musketeers, backed by two more cavalry regiments in the second line. Gustavus himself commanded the centre, whose front line was made up of four brigades of foot in their characteristic T-shaped formation, second line of two brigades of infantry and one cavalry regiment, and third line of three brigades of foot supported by two regiments of cavalry. The Swedish right comprised six cavalry regiments interspersed with musketeers in the first line, one cavalry regiment behind them, and four more forming a third line. Every regiment had its two regimental four-pounder guns to its front, and Torstensson's heavier field artillery was massed in front of the centre. In all there were 100 guns – sixty Swedish and forty Saxon.

Some reports say that Tilly began the battle by sending out 2,000 cavalry as skirmishers, to be hotly engaged and driven back by Swedish dragoons supported by Scots mercenaries. It seems quite feasible that this happened before the Swedish army, in its battle formation, advanced across the marshy stream at noon and began a cannonade that persisted for two-and-a-half hours. The numerically superior and faster-firing Swedish guns had much the best of the exchange. Eventually, galled beyond endurance by the heavy fire that was ploughing through their tightly packed ranks, the Imperialist cavalry, without orders from Tilly, spurred forward – on the right Furstenberg's Croat horsemen, and on the left the fiery Pappenheim's Black Cuirassiers.

In an avalanche of crimson cloaks and gleaming blades the Croats fell upon the 16,000 inexperienced Saxon soldiers, causing them to waver and then flee from the field in a blind rout, encouraged by their own guns, turned on them by the Imperialists. But a far sterner reception met the Black Cuirassiers as they swung out leftwards to thunder down upon the Swedish flank. Gustavus countered by swinging the five supporting cavalry regiments of Baner's wing to form a new flank at right-angles to the front line in a V-shaped defensive salient. Pappenheim, the scarred veteran of 100 charges, led his Black Cuirassiers forward at a fast trot no less than seven times, to discharge their wheel-lock pistols into the new Swedish flank, and each time the Imperialist horse were driven back, first being flayed by the Swedish regimental guns, and then by the muskets of the Swedish infantry. The latter would run out from between the

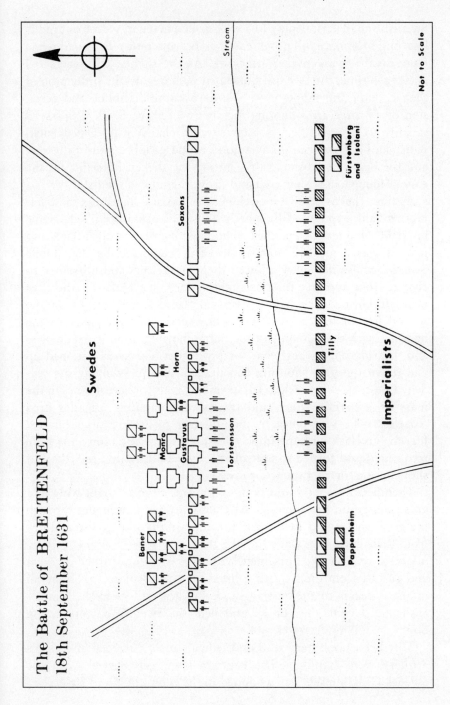

The Battle of BREITENFELD
18th September 1631

Swedes

Baner

Monro

Gustavus

Horn

Torstensson

Saxons

Stream

Not to Scale

Imperialists

Tilly

Pappenheim

Fürstenberg
and Isolani

Swedish squadrons, deploy in a well-drilled manner, with front ranks kneeling to achieve full fire-effect, then fire and return to reload while their cavalry was counter-attacking. As the shaken cuirassiers fell back each time, the Swedish horsemen withdrew to the protection of their cannon and musketeers. The devastating discipline and precision of all three arms fighting together caused the Black Cuirassiers steadily to disintegrate. As their seventh charge was turned back, Baner let his horsemen go at a good round gallop instead of a trot, and the heavy Swedish cavalry, hitting the shaken horsemen at the gallop, immediately shattered and drove them from the field.

Against the Swedish left, where the Saxons' defection had left Horn's flank exposed, Tilly marched his centre infantry blocks while his right-wing *tercios* marched obliquely towards the open flank and rear. It was a massive manoeuvre easily countered by the mobile Swedes, whose flexibility allowed their musketeers and horsemen to change front and face the onslaught as, ordering Horn to wheel his men left, Gustavus brought across two brigades of infantry from the second line of his centre. Now followed the hardest phase of the fighting, with the outcome of the battle hanging upon it. Helmetless and wearing only a buff coat for protection, Gustavus galloped up and down the line, shouting encouragement and swinging his reddened sabre in every mêlée. Torstensson's guns tore great lanes in the mass of Imperialist foot, and the Swedish infantry brigades fired ceaseless volleys of musketry before their pike formations lurched forward to clash with the Imperialist pikemen. The Saxon guns were recaptured and turned to enfilade the Imperialist flank, their hail of shot causing the vast squares to waver.

Then Gustavus led four cavalry regiments from his right wing in a great charge up the slope at the enemy artillery, sweeping through the guns and round to the left to separate the Imperialist infantry from their cavalry. Assailed to the front and left simultaneously by infantry, artillery and horsemen, with their own guns turned on them and cut off from their cavalry, the close-packed masses of Imperial infantry began to melt away, and, as dusk fell over the smoke-enshrouded field, they broke and fled, the Swedish cavalry riding down the milling fugitives.

Tilly left 13,000 men dead on the field, and 7,000 men and all his artillery were captured. The captives later took service with the Swedes. Tilly himself was wounded in the neck, chest and right arm, and only a hard-fighting rearguard action by the remains of Pappenheim's Black Cuirassiers prevented an even greater disaster. The total losses of the combined Swedish-Saxon army were about 3,000, less than a third being Swedish.

THE BATTLE OF LÜTZEN 16 NOVEMBER 1632

Wallenstein, the Imperialist leader, marching his army into Saxony pursued by Gustavus Adolphus and his Swedes, had entrenched a winter camp along the line of the Leipzig-Lützen road. His right was anchored on the village of Lützen, which fronted Windmill Hill, the only rising ground in a gently rolling plain, where most of the Imperial guns were posted. It was a position that neutralised the Swedish mobility and forced them to attack frontally, as the straight causeway road, lined with ditches deepened into trenches for the musketeers, gave no room for the type of manoeuvres that brought victory at Breitenfeld. Hearing that Pappenheim with 8,000 men, mostly cavalry, was away seeking provisions, Gustavus decided to move against the position, but the early autumn dusk prevented an immediate attack and both armies faced each other in line of battle throughout a long, damp and chilly night.

In much the same formation as at Breitenfeld the 20,000-strong Swedish army was commanded by Gustavus on the right, and Duke Bernard of Saxe-Weimar, a German Protestant with a reputation for bravery, on the left. The two lines of infantry each had four brigades of foot in their centre, commanded by General Niels Brahe and by the veteran Marshal Kniphausen. Torstensson was in charge of the artillery – twenty large pieces in the centre and forty light regimental guns divided between the wings.

Wallenstein hastily recalled Pappenheim and his 8,000 men (for whom an area was kept open on the left flank) and formed up the Imperial army of about 22,000 men along the line of the Leipzig road. Lützen was fired so that it could not be used as cover. The infantry in the centre were drawn up in four great oblong masses, solid blocks of Spanish (or Spanish-trained) pikemen in the old terciary formation, with musketeers thrust out at each corner, and other infantry formations were placed near Lützen. Cavalry were stationed on the flanks of the main body of infantry, Piccolomini commanding the Austrian and Hungarian cuirassiers opposite Gustavus. Colloredo was in command of the foot and horse supporting the fourteen guns on Windmill Hill, and the rest of the artillery (seven guns) was placed in front of the centre. Skirmishers (detached from the musketeers of the *tercios*) lined the ditch before the main body.

Forced to make a frontal attack, Gustavus planned that Duke Bernard with the cavalry of the left should attack Lützen while he, with a reinforced right wing, would crush the opposing left wing, cutting Wallenstein's line of retreat to Leipzig. Heavy fog and smoke from the burning village prevented the guns from firing until mid-morning, when, aided by their stabs of flame throwing bright orange flashes through the gloom, the two armies began groping for each other.

In the general Swedish advance along the whole line their mobile infantry in the centre reached the double-ditched road, exchanging fire with the skirmishers; then Torstensson brought up the light regimental guns and their enfilade fire soon caused the musketeers in the ditches to abandon their position. Surging across the road, the Swedish infantry over-ran the Imperial artillery positions, capturing the big immobile guns and spiking them, then pressed on to attack the massive blocks of pikemen positioned behind the guns. Deprived of their musketeers by the fighting along the road, these squares, still in formation and with their right anchored, were forced slowly back on the left. At the same time both Gustavus and Bernard were pressing forward. On the right the Swedish leader at the head of his veteran Stalhanske cavalry scattered a group of Croat light cavalry and brushed aside a solid mass of cuirassiers, who were then routed by successive waves of Swedish cavalry. On the Swedish left Duke Bernard of Saxe-Weimar, although he was overlapped and had a hill to climb, and in spite of Wallenstein taking personal command, succeeded in leading some of Brahe's men up Windmill Hill and capturing its big battery of artillery.

At this stage Gustavus, who had pulled out too far right in the restricting fog of battle, received word that Wallenstein had successfully counterattacked with pikemen and cavalry against the right flank of Brahe's infantry line, hitting them at a moment when they were disorganised by their own cavalry dismounting to lead their horses across the ditches. Hastening across to the threatened area, Gustavus outgalloped all but four of his men, and rode out of the mist straight into a party of the enemy, who shot them down, killing Gustavus and three others. As word spread that the King's riderless horse had been seen galloping from the field, the Swedish advance lost momentum. At the same time, out of the mist on to the extreme end of Brahe's line, a series of charges by Piccolomini's heavy cavalry rolled it up, recapturing the seven spiked guns and throwing the Swedes back to the road, where they lost first one ditch then the other.

After angrily rejecting advice from old Marshal Kniphausen that their second line of foot should cover a retreat, Duke Bernard took command of the Swedish army. Riding down the lines crying, 'Swedes! They have killed the King!' above the noise of gunfire, he kindled a new fury in the Swedish soldiers, so that they forgot their exhaustion and surged forward in a fresh advance.

After some hard riding, Pappenheim and his 8,000 cavalry had reached the field and moved across towards the shattered Imperialist left. Near Wallenstein's baggage park they rode out of the mist to charge the Swedish right-wing cavalry, who, lacking orders and with their leader dead, had halted indecisively. The newly arrived horse-men crashed into the much smaller stationary squadrons to send them reeling back across the causeway. Then Pappenheim was killed, and the surge of his counter-attack died with him.

About five o'clock, with the coming of dusk, Swedish fortunes began to turn when the mist cleared, so that Torstensson was able to get his guns going again; at the same time the captured Windmill Hill battery was able to enfilade the enemy and prevent them from crossing the road. The Imperialist centre battery was unable to return fire because the guns were still spiked. At this, the most desperate moment of the battle, there was little thought of tactics as desperate hand-to-hand combats took place between small groups of men. Although painfully wounded, Bernard harnessed the fury of the 'fighting-mad' Swedes to send them sweeping forward in a desperate and irresistible assault that drove the Imperialists from the field.

Wallenstein withdrew the shattered remnants of his army to Halle. With 12,000 casualties, it was not so much beaten as destroyed, some companies being reduced to two or three survivors and the whole of the artillery and baggage lost. The Swedish army had also suffered heavily, losing about 10,000 men; some of its brigades were reduced to one-sixth of their original strength.

THE BATTLE OF ROCROI 19 MAY 1643

In its twenty-sixth year, with all the old leaders dead and the major military action shifting from Germany to north-eastern France, the Thirty Years War had developed into a power struggle between the House of Bourbon and the Spanish/Austrian Hapsburgs. In spring 1643 General Francisco de Melo was besieging Rocroi, an important frontier fortress on the line of the Meuse. To its relief marched the twenty-two-year-old Duke of Enghien, with 15,000 infantry and 7,000 cavalry. After centuries of relying largely on mercenaries, the French, following their reorganisation by Richelieu, at last had what could possibly be called a French army. De Melo's army had six Spanish *tercios* (10,000 men), composed of the usual formidable veterans, and the remaining 8,000 infantry comprised Flemish, Walloon, Italian and mercenary contingents, with their own leaders but officered by Spaniards. Their well-mounted cavalry force under the Comte d'Isembourg consisted of 8,000 excellent horsemen. At this date the Spanish armies could generally be considered superior to the French.

Enghien's most trusted commander, the Comte de Gassion, reported that to attack the Spaniards the French army had to march through a narrow marsh-ridden rocky defile to reach a plateau four miles wide and surrounded by thickets and heavy undergrowth. Nevertheless, he advised battle, though L'Hopital, an older and more cautious military adviser, wished to avoid a confrontation. In the event the French marched out, and at 8 a.m. on the 18th the heads of their columns reached the fringe of the plateau, to find the approaches unguarded and their route through the woods opposed only by outposts that scattered before them. It has been said that de Melo wished to surround and take the whole French army rather than put it to flight. Pushing ahead, Enghien suddenly saw in an open space between the surrounding forests the whole Spanish array drawn up in the conventional formation of right, centre and left, with musketeers filling the gaps between cavalry squadrons, so that it looked like a single block. The Spanish *tercios* formed the centre, in front of a second line of allied foot, and the cavalry were divided equally between the two wings. In the manner of the day, the artillery was placed out in front of the infantry.

Emerging on to open ground, the French were so formed that the movements and numbers of their infantry were concealed by their advancing cavalry, in front and on both flanks. By 6 p.m. Enghien had drawn up his troops within cannon shot of the Spaniards. He personally commanded the right wing, which was formed of cavalry and faced a Spanish cavalry force under the Duke of Albuquerque, though separated from them by a thin strip of woodland occupied by Spanish musketeers. The French left wing, commanded by L'Hopital and Senneterre, opposed de Melo himself with a force of horsemen, while the Spanish infantry were commanded by the veteran Flemish general Fontaine. After a premature advance by Senneterre had almost brought disaster to the French, both armies settled down for the night.

Arising at 3 a.m., the French formed up, and in the half light of dawn Enghien's cavalry wing, comprising his own eight squadrons and seven led by Gassion, drove the Spanish musketeers out of the woodland and fell upon Albuquerque's cavalry. The Spaniards' first line was taken in flank and scattered by Enghien's 'wild and ferocious' Croat horsemen, and when the experienced Spanish cavalry leader rallied his second line, it was immediately driven back in great disorder and with heavy losses by Enghien's horse frontally and Gassion's on the flank, in a display of almost unparalleled speed of action.

With Gassion's cavalry pursuing the fugitives, Enghien surveyed the battlefield, now wreathed in billowing clouds of smoke, but he could see that his left wing was in trouble. L'Hopital and Senneterre, charging before being ordered, had been repulsed and were falling back in disorder after being attacked by d'Isembourg and his Spanish cavalry, which had spent the night close up behind their infantry and were able to jump straight into a gallop. After routing the French horse and cutting them off from the infantry in the centre, the Spanish cavalry swerved left to rout the musketeers guarding the artillery and capture the guns. A counter attack by L'Hopital won back a few pieces, but then lost them again so that the Spanish had thirty guns to bombard the French centre, which had none to answer them. The French infantry, outnumbered and outmarched, could only stand on the defensive against the Spanish infantry.

Now Gassion, who had returned from the pursuit, was ordered to remain in case Albuquerque rallied, while Enghien wheeled his eight squadrons left and, at the gallop, rode behind the enemy's centre and began cutting a path through their massed infantry formations. He passed between the first Spanish *tercio* (hotly engaged with the French infantry) and the Italian, German and Walloon formations, which were struck in flank (in that order). The surprise assault broke the allied infantry, although the Italians fought magnificently and both their leaders were killed. Without drawing rein, Enghien's cavalry circled right round the field to come up on the rear of d'Isembourg's cavalry, which, caught between two enemy forces, broke to their right and fled the field.

All that remained were the Spanish *tercios*, veterans in solid formations but hemmed in on all sides. Could they hold out until reinforcements arrived? The French infantry advanced to within fifty paces, only to be broken and sent reeling back in disorder by controlled volleys of musketry fire. His men and horses exhausted, Enghien withdrew the most fatigued and, reinforcing the infantry with some cavalry, sent them in once more – again they were repulsed and then a third time. A charge by cavalry alone was also thrown back with heavy losses, and Enghien's horse was shot from under him.

Then Gassion came up and Senneterre returned from pursuit. After a short rest while the French artillery flayed the Spanish blocks, the weary and somewhat dispirited French cavalry made a third charge. This time not a Spanish gun fired on them and there was only a splattering of musketry – seemingly the Spanish had run out of ammunition. Enghien directed the cavalry into gaps made by his artillery, disorganising the Spanish infantry, so that when their commander, Fontaine, was killed by a stray shot and the French infantry closed in the Spaniards surrendered. Unfortunately the excited French mistook a Spanish movement to be a renewal of resistance, fighting broke out again and, before Enghien and his officers could halt the massacre, the flower of the Spanish army had been cut down. The total Spanish losses were 7,000 dead and 6,000 prisoners, nearly all of them wounded. The French suffered 4,000 casualties.

Enghien's victory was won by his generalship and his calculated risk in cutting through the Spanish centre. So ended a battle that destroyed the legend of Spanish invincibility. Rocroi was a turning point in Spanish military history, for never again could Spain produce infantry the equal of those who fell here.

20

The English Civil War 1642–51

WHEN THE WAR BEGAN England possessed no standing army, so both King and Parliament had to depend on poorly armed rustics and tradesmen. The Parliamentary army was somewhat larger, better equipped and organised, although both sides lacked weapons and material. Each possessed officers with experience of Continental warfare but similarly experienced rank and file were scarce. Both armies were hampered by the reluctance of local militia bands, whose sole training amounted to one day's drill per month, to leave the area of their homes. This lack of trained soldiers did not prevent them from rushing violently at each other to seek a decision in clashes decided more by chance than skill. Inevitably, the majority of operations were notable for an amateurish clumsiness, still evident even when the war had been going on for two years. Lack of strategic planning allowed numerous minor and disconnected struggles to tie down garrisons and besiegers in different counties of England. The lack of tactical direction when they met on the field of battle often caused both sides to remain stationary for hours, neither daring to seize the initiative. Usually the battle began more by accident than design, or the 'forlorn hopes' of each force skirmished until the main body arrived and exchanged volleys, eventually causing one to falter at which point the other would charge.

As there was no national army there were no uniforms. At Edgehill the Royalists distinguished each other by their white scarves while, by tacit consent, their opponents wore orange; later blue was accepted as the King's colour with red for Parliament.

Throughout the war, the infantry were the most neglected arm. Ill-trained and poorly paid, their vulnerability to cavalry flank attacks shaped the entire course of the war, and until the New Model Army was formed, the infantry showed up badly in any situation demanding manoeuvre. Eventually tactics were influenced by Gustavus Adolphus's military innovations, with both armies following the Swedish formation of a brigade of three squadrons, each of four companies of 144 men. On the battlefield, one squadron formed the first and second lines with the musketeers drawn back behind the pikemen to form the second line. The third line was formed by the other two squadrons side-by-side with more musketeers on the outer flanks of the pikemen than on the inner. The proportion of musketeers to pikemen within the whole brigade was reduced by the detachment of groups of 'commanded musketeers' drawn up three-deep between bodies of cavalry on the flanks of the army and used to support cavalry attacks or to check victorious enemy cavalry by their fire. Drawn back behind the pikemen, as in the leading squadrons of a Swedish brigade, the musketeers were very vulnerable to cavalry attacks from the flanks; it is recorded that at Marston Moor Lindsay's and Maitland's regiments stood firm against Royalist horse, 'having interlined their musketeers with pikemen'. Prince Rupert sometimes used detached musketeers.

Borrowing their methods from the Swedes, Rupert's cavalry favoured charging home at top speed, with the front rank firing their pistols before going in with the sword, in three-rank-line close formation. For the Parliamentarians, General Monck (writing in 1644) advocated that cavalry should be drawn up three ranks deep, with troop or regiment formed in sub-divisions of ten to twenty files each, twenty-five yards between sub-divisions. In knee-to-knee close order, at fifty paces from the enemy, the flank sub-division trotted, then charged, and when they hit the enemy the centre sub-divisions charged.

Earlier in the war, particularly in the cases of the Parliamentarians, cavalry took charges at the halt, relying on the fire power of their pistols to stop the oncoming enemy. As the latter were probably attacking in reiter fashion (i.e. caracole) this was not as fatal as it sounds.

At Edgehill, Oliver Cromwell, a Huntingdon farmer in command of a troop of cavalry, noted the defects in both armies' methods of attack and devoted the winter in the Eastern Counties to recruiting and training cavalrymen; by the following spring his 400 horse were the most disciplined body in the Parliamentary ranks. Cromwell became one of the outstanding commanders of the century and was well ahead of his contemporaries during the English Civil War.

Cavalry consisted of horsemen wearing a back-and-breastplate over a buff coat, a lobster-tail helmet with high top boots, and three-quarter armoured cuirassiers whose degree of protection was probably neutralised by their lack of mobility and need for heavy horses, which were in very short supply. The usual cavalry unit consisted of a troop of sixty sabres under a captain, a cornet and a quarter master, with seven troops forming a regiment under a colonel. Then there were the Dragoons, mounted infantry who fought on foot in scattered groups as an advance or rear guard. In battle, they lined hedges or took cover in broken ground, firing their firelocks to break up attacks or support friendly cavalry charges.

Both cavalry and infantry units had several colours – each infantry regiment carried standards at least six feet square, with the coat-colour of the unit as its basic colour. The Colonel's flag was plain; the Lieutenant-Colonel's flag had a St George's Red Cross on a white background in a 'canton' at the top corner next to the staff; the Major had the same flag with a coloured streamer running from the lower right corner of the canton to the lower right corner of the flag; the Captain's flag was as the Lieutenant-Colonel's plus large coloured dots to signify his company. Dragoons had colours on the same system, but two feet square with fringes. Cavalry had fringed guidons two feet square, bearing slogans or pictures to their commander's taste.

Swedish reforms in artillery were not reflected in either army, both being encumbered with heavy and immobile guns so that only in sieges did artillery play any decisive part. Disorganised and employing civilian drivers, the artillery train had light field pieces called sakers, minions and drakes (five-pounders, three-and-a-half-pounders and three-pounders) as the most used field pieces in the Civil War. They required three to five horses to pull them and could be fired about fifteen times an hour. Also, there were leather guns and regimental pieces of one-and-a-half or three pounds. Guns were scattered along the army frontage 50–100 yards apart, with little attempt to concentrate fire. Heavy guns fired solid shot at longer ranges and were inaccurate over 300–400 yards. Smaller infantry guns fired case shot. The heaviest gun used in the field was the sixteen-pounder culverin, with a point-blank range of 400 paces and an extreme range of 2,100 paces; it took eight horses to draw it and could be fired about ten times an hour. More common was the demi-culverin, a nine-pounder with a point-blank range of about 320 paces and an extreme range of 1,800 paces; it required six horses to pull it and could be discharged about fifteen times per hour. Siege weapons (twenty-four-pounder demi-cannons, fifty-pounder cannons and mortars) were invariably transported by sea to the field of operations and then taken to join the army overland – they did *not* march with the army. The 'train' was attended by a guard of fusiliers armed with flintlocks, as the musketeers' matches would be too dangerous in proximity to open gunpowder barrels.

The New Model Army was established on 18 January 1645 by the amalgamation of the three armies of Essex, Waller and Manchester, with Sir Thomas Fairfax in command. The New Model consisted of eleven regiments of horse of 600 men each, twelve regiments of foot of 1,200 apiece and a regiment of 1,000 Dragoons, totalling 22,000. But the three armies could not supply half of the 14,400 infantry required so it was resolved to raise about 8,500 men by impressment. However, when the New Model took the field in May 1645, it was still 3,000 or 4,000 below its proper number.

In the proportion of one cavalry to two foot, the eleven regiments of horse in the New Model consisted of 600 men each exclusive of officers, and were divided into six troops of 100 men each. The field officers were a Colonel and a Major; there were four commissioned officers in each troop. Two of the troops in each regiment were without captains, the Colonel and Major commanding one each in person.

The regular cavalry wore a buff coat, 'back and breast' and a 'pot' helmet with bars to protect the face and were armed with a long sword and a pair of pistols (wheel or flintlock). Carbines were issued only to officers (although by 1660 they had been issued to every other man). The Regiment of Dragoons consisted of ten 100-men companies. It had the commissioned officers of a horse regiment, and it is probable that dragoons wore the hat and red coat of the infantry

– not the 'pot' and buff coat of the horse. There were three cornets to each troop and two drummers to each cavalry or dragoon company. The twelve regiments of foot consisted of 1,200 men divided into ten companies: the Colonel's company numbered 200 men, the Lieutenant-Colonel's 160, the Major's 140. The remaining seven companies were each 100 strong. There were three commissioned officers – a captain, a lieutenant and an ensign. Infantry wore a scarlet coat with their Colonel's colours as facings. The proportion of pikemen to musketeers was approximately one pike to every two muskets. A pikeman normally wore an iron helmet, 'back and breast', a gorget to protect his throat and tassets to cover his thighs (gorget and tassets were often abandoned) and was armed with a sword and a sixteen-foot pike. A musketeer wore no defensive armour and was armed with a matchlock musket, sword, musket-rest and a bandolier of ammunition. Each company had its own musicians and each troop or company had a flag. The New Army possessed a regular siege-train of fifty-six guns, some sixty-pounders, thirty-two-pounders and twelve-inch mortars. At the end of the second Civil War in 1647, Fairfax's artillery train consisted of sixteen demi-culverins, ten sakers, fifteen drakes and fifteen smaller pieces.

The men who formed the New Model Army were governed by strict discipline and good training that produced a well equipped, professional fighting force. Too newly formed to have any effect at Naseby, the battle that virtually ended the first Civil War, the New Model Army gave a good account of itself in the second Civil War against Parliament's former Scots allies. At the Battle of Preston in 1648, 8,500 of them administered a crushing defeat to 20,000 Scots invaders.

Among the best known battles of the English Civil War were Edgehill, Marston Moor and Naseby. At Edgehill in 1642, King Charles with 13,000 men clashed with Essex who led about 12,000. Rupert's cavalry drove the Parliamentary cavalry off the field and pursued them. Essex was forced to withdraw when Rupert returned to the field at nightfall. In 1644 at Marston Moor, Parliament had 20,000 infantry and 7,000 cavalry against the Royalists' 11,000 infantry and 7,000 cavalry. Manchester, Fairfax and Leven jointly commanded the Parliamentary/Scottish army. Cromwell's Ironsides and a Scottish force defeated part of Rupert's cavalry on the Royalist right while Lord George Goring's Horse turned back Fairfax on the left and scattered the Scottish infantry. Swinging his disciplined Ironsides to the right, Cromwell routed the disorganised Goring and then aided the Parliamentary infantry in crushing the Royalist centre. At Naseby in 1645, Charles commanded about 8,500 men against a Parliamentary force of 13,500. Rupert's cavalry chased the Parliamentary left off the field while Cromwell's horsemen defeated the cavalry on the Royalist left and, exploiting Rupert's pursuit, smashed the Royalist infantry. On returning to the field, Rupert's cavalry refused to engage the Ironsides.

When the Civil War ended in England, the Marquis of Montrose led a small and ill-equipped army in Scotland against the Covenanters. With only a single round of ammunition available per man for the few matchlocks they possessed, Montrose's force destroyed six armies in a year and mastered all Scotland. A tactical genius, Montrose skilfully employed surprise and concealment while using traditional Scottish fierce and headlong charges. Typical of Montrose's tactical brilliance was his defeat of Hurry, a competent professional soldier, at Auldearn in 1645. Montrose, with 2,000 foot and 250 horse against a force twice this size, posted his weakest troops in the village with orders to fire repeatedly and create a diversion; he stationed 500 Highlanders to fight a desperate holding battle behind a bog on his right while his cavalry and the rest of his infantry lay concealed behind a slope. When Hurry's Covenanters were fully involved with the Highlanders, Montrose led his concealed force in a flank attack to transform Hurry's army into a mob of routed fugitives.

After the Restoration in 1660, the first true English Standing Army was formed from units of both Royalist and Parliamentary troops.

Cavalry have often been a source of worry to the commanders of armies, being noted for their inclination to take off into the blue at the first sight of the enemy. Wellington recorded his disapproval of the tactics of his own cavalry on many occasions and the Light Brigade at Balaclava displayed incredible gallantry coupled with equally incredible foolishness.

THE BATTLE OF CHERITON 29 MARCH 1644

This battle was fought during the English Civil War between a Royalist army under Lord Hopton and a Parliamentary force commanded by General Sir William Waller.

On 28 March 1644 the Royalist army camped on a horseshoe shaped ridge, their guns placed to cover Cheriton Wood on their left. Forward in a little wood on a parallel ridge to the south was a detachment of 1,000 musketeers and 500 horse under Sir George Lisle. Next morning, two hours after sunrise, when the thick mist lifted, masses of Roundhead cavalry were seen deploying on the southern slopes of the ridge where Lisle was posted. Dangerously exposed, his force, covered by cavalry, had to retire. Parliamentary forces then moved forward and occupied Lisle's former position. Waller sent a force of cavalry down into the valley in front of his guns and nine regiments of infantry, each drawn up six deep, with five regiments forward and four behind, lined the ridge behind hedgerows from Cheriton Wood towards the village of Cheriton.

Commanded by Lords Hopton on the left and Forth on the right, the Royalist army of 3,500 infantry, 2,500 cavalry and ten guns was formed up with infantry in the centre and cavalry on the wings. Facing Cheriton Wood, Hopton's infantry were drawn up on reverse slopes. The Royalist army included the Queen's Regiment of cavalry, which had many Frenchmen in its ranks, and some redcoated Irish infantry regiments. The Parliamentary army consisted of 6,000 infantry, 4,000 cavalry and fifteen guns; the infantry included White and Yellow Regiments of the London Brigade and Horse and Foot from Kent, and the large cavalry force under Sir William Balfour included Hazlerig's cuirassiers, known as the 'Lobsters' because of their iron armour. A useful addition was Colonel Norton and his troop of Hambledon Boys, who knew the countryside around Cheriton.

About 1,000 men of the London Brigade went forward to capture Cheriton Wood, where hand-to-hand fighting took place with Sir George Lisle's men. Hopton had foreseen this attack and planted some drakes (field-pieces) on the high ground north-east of the wood; when the London Brigade surged out from the trees, they ran into the point-blank fire of these guns, which forced them to retreat to the shelter of the wood. Royalist musketeers who followed them were repulsed, but Royalist infantry outflanked the Roundheads on the east of the wood and threw the London Brigade back in disorder. The Royalists then reoccupied the wood.

Waller had posted his Horse in such a position that if the Royalist cavalry approached they had to come down a lane and could only deploy one regiment at a time. But Hopton, in such a strong position that it was best to stand fast and make Waller decide whether to attack him or withdraw from the field, did not intend to take any cavalry action.

However, Sir Henry Bard, a young and impetuous cavalry commander, could not resist attacking the Roundhead cavalry whom he saw drawn up in front of him. His regiment charged down the lane towards them, taking fire from musketeers posted behind hedges and in coppices. Bard was killed and his horsemen overwhelmed, but troop after troop of Royalist cavalry poured down the lane after him, to be defeated in detail by the Parliamentary horse and musketeers as they emerged on to the open ground. Before long all the Royalist cavalry on the right had been defeated and Hopton's flank was open to attack; so, to retrieve the situation, the infantry were sent down and, meeting the Parliamentary foot soldiers, they came to 'push of pike', with both sides fighting stoutly. Eventually Hazlerig's Lobsters swept round behind the Royalist cavalry and into the infantry, driving them back in disorder. Before that, a force of Parliamentary musketeers came out from their cover and fell upon the flank of the Royalist cavalry, so putting the final touch to their discomfiture.

Another Parliamentary infantry attack on Cheriton Woods drove out the Royalist infantry, so that the whole Royalist line fell back on its original position while the last of Hopton's cavalry sealed off the end of the lane. The Royalist force withdrew during the night to Basing. Casualties were 900 killed and wounded in the Parliamentary army and 1,400 Royalists.

THE BATTLE OF CROPREDY BRIDGE 29 JUNE 1644

In early summer 1644 Charles I and his army, watched by Waller's Parliamentary army, was engaged in a series of marches and manoeuvres in Oxfordshire. On 29 June, after a small skirmish at Crouch near Banbury, the two armies were marching on parallel lines on either side of the River Cherwell, in sight of one another, although out of musket shot. The Royalist army was in three divisions: the van led by Lord Wilmot; the main body, with the King and Prince of Wales; and the rearguard comprising Colonel Thelwell and 1,000 foot, and the Lords Northampton and Cleveland, each with a brigade of horse. The Parliamentary army reached Cropredy Bridge, where the river bent sharply north-east and was crossed two miles further on at Hays Bridge by the Banbury/Daventry road. The distance between the two armies led the Royalists to believe that they would not be attacked; nevertheless a party of Royalist dragoons are said to have been sent to hold Cropredy Bridge until the army had passed beyond it.

The vanguard had crossed Hays Bridge when they heard that some 300 enemy horsemen were less than two miles ahead. The Royal Horse were sent after them, followed by the infantry of the vanguard, who proceeded without orders, and the main body crossed the bridge and joined the pursuit. But the rearguard maintained its original pace and a considerable gap developed between it and the main body – by the time the rearguard neared Cropredy Bridge the interval had lengthened to one-and-a-half miles. Waller saw his chance of cutting off the Royalist rear and rushed Cropredy Bridge with two columns consisting of eight troops of Hazlerig's regiment of horse ('the Lobsters') and six troops of Vandruske's regiment, totalling some 1,500 troopers, supported by nine companies of infantry under Colonel Baines, four companies of Greencoats and five companies of Waller's own regiment. Eleven guns under James Wemyss, who had previously commanded Charles's guns but had defected to the Parliamentarians, were set up about 300 yards north of the bridge, just clear of the river bank. Lieutenant-General Middleton, with 1,000 horse, crossed the river about a mile below the bridge at Slat Mill ford.

Once across the Cherwell, Hazlerig's horse galloped wildly in pursuit of the Royalist foot regiments of the rearguard, now approaching Hays Bridge, who saw them coming and drew up facing them, lining the bridge with musketeers and overthrowing a carriage as a barricade. Seeing this, and with no supporting infantry nearer than half a mile, the Parliamentary cavalry decided discretion to be the better part of valour and retired in the direction of Cropredy Bridge. Vandruske's regiment, although charged by Cleveland with some of the rearguard Royalist cavalry, was able to rally after being supported by infantry, but Cleveland's sweeping charge had cut off from Cropredy Bridge about 1,000 Parliamentary infantry, who were in disorderly retreat when overtaken and escorted by Hazlerig's retiring troopers. Further south, Northampton and his horse boldly charged Middleton's cavalry and, although not inflicting heavy losses, forced them back to Slat Mill, where they remained for the rest of the engagement, evidently not fancying their chances of taking a second charge.

The van, now well beyond Hays Bridge, halted, and the King sent Lord Bernard Stuart with 100 Gentlemen of the King's Troop to aid the rearguard, now facing a second attack from the rallied Round-heads. Stuart came up to Cleveland and his cavalry, who were making a stand near a great ash tree (where the King had halted for refreshments some half an hour earlier), and the joint cavalry forces, in spite of considerable musketry and artillery fire, drove both Parliamentary foot and horse back over Cropredy Bridge in an untidy rabble. James Wemyss and his guns could not get away, and he was captured with five sakers, one twelve-pound piece, one demi-culverin, two minions and two three-pound pieces, besides other artillery equipment.

Waller retreated westward beyond the River Cherwell to take up a position on high ground near Bourton, leaving some foot and dra-goons at Cropredy Bridge, as the Royalists did not pursue beyond that point, and at Slat Mill ford. But the King, apparently piqued by Waller's militancy, decided to capture Cropredy Bridge and Slat Mill, and a hot engagement took place on and around the bridge. Waller's men not only held off the Royalists but also recovered three pieces of their lost artillery, after managing to advance Birch, with the Kentish Regiment and Tower Hamlet regiments and two drakes, to the bridge. The Royalists had little trouble in crossing at the ford and taking Slat Mill.

Both armies faced each other from the opposite heights, the river and the watermeadows lying between them. As night approached, the Royalist foot and horse were drawn down to the river below the ford, and cannon were fired upon the enemy horse drawn up on Bourton Hill, causing them to retire in disorder. Then the two armies fell silent and the engagement was broken off.

In this small but lively engagement the Roundheads appear to have misjudged their attack. Instead of cutting off the King's rearguard, they found themselves caught between two fires, and it seemed that the King, more by accident than design, had drawn the enemy over Cropredy Bridge and inflicted a sharp reverse upon them.

THE SECOND BATTLE OF NEWBURY 27 OCTOBER 1644

This further conflict at the Berkshire town of Newbury, fought just over a year after the earlier battle on 20 September 1643, was a similarly indecisive affair with neither side able to claim victory. It occurred because Charles, no doubt encouraged by his recent successful campaign in the West Country, resolved to relieve three small isolated Royalist forces – the besieged garrisons of Banbury Castle, Basing House near Basingstoke, and Donnington Castle, a mile north of Newbury. His march from the West alarmed the widely dispersed Parliamentary armies – Manchester at Reading, Waller at Shaftesbury, and Essex at Portsmouth – who made a rapid concentration in the area of Basingstoke by 20 October. Their combined strength of 19,000 men presented a formidable challege to Charles's 10,000-strong Royal army, although their superiority was affected by a command structure consisting of Manchester, Waller and Essex (to be absent through illness) plus some other officers and civilians. A certain element of parity existed through Charles's army being a veteran force, with Lord Astley commanding the Foot, Lord Goring the Horse, plus detachments of both horse and foot from Maurice's Western Army, with Lord Hopton's strong artillery train of twenty-nine guns.

For various reasons Charles was unable, at that stage, to relieve Basing House but took advantage of a move of the Parliamentary armies to Swallowfield, between Basingstoke and Reading, to slip into Newbury and relieve the gallant garrison commander at Donnington, Colonel Boys. This occurred on 22 October, and by the 25th of the month patrols of both armies were in contact in an area between Newbury and the village of Thatcham, about four miles east of Newbury. Leaving a garrison in that town, Charles took up a strong position to the north of the town, with his right flank covered by the River Kennet and his left by the River Lambourn and Donnington Castle; the Royalist centre rested upon Speen and Shaw House. Into Speen village Charles put Maurice's Horse and his

Cornish Foot, and a breastwork was built mounting five guns; Shaw House was garrisoned by Astley and Lisle's Foot, who positioned themselves behind massive ancient earth-banks, built years before this Civil War battle.

Manchester's Parliamentary army had marched from Reading and reached Clay Hill, about a mile east of the Royalist position; from there, they were able to see into the garden/defences of Shaw House and overlook the entire Royalist line. After a day or so of patrol activity and a desultory artillery duel, coupled with Manchester not liking what he could see of the Royalist position, the Parliamentary Council decided that the Royalist defences were too strong to be taken from the east by direct assault. Subsequently, it was decided to launch a divided attack simultaneously from east and west, to strike the Royalists in front and rear; so, orders were issued for a great flank march by Waller, with 12,000 men, of about thirteen miles via Hermitage, Chievely, North Heath, Winterbourne, Boxford and Wickham Heath, which would take about fifteen hours. Two-thirds of the Parliamentary Army would form this force, Manchester remaining on Clay Hill with most of the Parliamentary artillery train to occupy the attention of the Royalists while the outflanking march took place. He was to attack the Royalists with his 7,000 men when he heard Waller's guns open on the Royalist position in Speen.

Waller's force included Balfour's and Cromwell's horse, Essex's army and a brigade of the London Trained Bands. They set out on their march after dark on 26 October, marching northwards and resting briefly at North Heath in the early hours of 27 October. They clashed with a royalist patrol at Boxford and were spotted by the garrison of Donnington Castle, but there are conflicting accounts of whether or not Charles was kept informed or even knew about the outflanking march of the Parliamentarians. However, it is claimed that Colonel Hurry, or a similar Parliamentary 'turncoat', had given information beforehand and Charles subsequently detached a portion of his force, under Prince Maurice, to take position at Speen to resist the rear attack, and Colonel Boys' guns at Donnington Castle were trained on the Parliamentary approach-route.

The outflanking force reached the Royalist position at Speen at about three o'clock in the afternoon of 27 October and, despite fatigue, mounted an immediate attack, with Skippon's infantry in the centre, Balfour's Horse on the right and Cromwell's Horse on the left. Fending-off the first attack, Maurice's men were driven out of Speen village, their breastwork captured and guns abandoned, recognised by survivors as the guns they had taken from them at the Parliamentary defeat at Lostwithiel in the previous August. Balfour's Horse charged Maurice's supporting cavalry and dispersed them, but were themselves halted by the Earl of Cleveland's reserve brigade of 800 men, sent to the scene by Charles. On the Parliamentary left wing, Cromwell was uncharacteristically subdued and unaccountably did little. His belated attempt at intervention was driven off – it was later claimed that he was harassed from long-range by the guns of recently relieved Donnington Castle. Skippon withdrew his men as darkness made recognition difficult.

The defeat at Speen left the Royalist army in a difficult position, pushed in from the west and with an obvious threat from Clay Hill on the east, had Manchester moved on them at the same time as the Speen attack went in – as intended – then Charles would have been routed. But the signal guns from Speen were either not heard or ignored and it was not until about 4 p.m. that Manchester ordered forward 4,000 men in two converging columns. One advanced against the north-east side of Shaw House, the other and larger of the two wound through Shaw village on the north side of the Lambourne. Against them, the Royalists could muster some 1,400 men, with 800 holding Shaw House, the earthworks, and the two flanks; the remainder of the force held an outpost out in front, behind a thick hedge.

Advancing in good order, singing psalms, the Parliamentarians took casualties as they cleared the hedge and some outhouses, being briefly halted by a flank charge from Royalist Horse, and then again moving forward as the defenders, noting their superior numbers, withdrew into Shaw House garden. The attackers, coming under close range fire from the walls of the house and from guns in the earthworks, became embroiled in a fierce fire-fight and some hand-to-hand fighting around the house and in the garden. Darkness made recognition difficult and, in the village, Sir George Lisle stripped down to his white shirt to be better seen as he attacked the Parliamentary columns with both foot and horse. Five hundred men were said to have fallen in one area as the right-hand column were thrown out of the garden, while the left-hand column, moving parallel with the river, was driven back with heavy loss by a counter-attack. It is possible that the darkness saved the Royalists from further attacks on both flanks, when the superior numbers would have told, but in the end the attackers fled back up the slopes of Clay Hill.

Charles realised that, despite his troop's spirited resistance, he was outnumbered and that the renewal of attacks on him next day could bring defeat. He also had the safety of the young Prince of Wales, who was with him, to consider. So he decided to withdraw, leaving his guns, baggage and wounded in the care of Sir John Boys and the garrison of Donnington Castle. With the moon in its first quarter, his army silently marched out through a 1,500-yard gap between Shaw House and Donnington Castle, slipping away to Wallingford, to reach Oxford next day. The King himself, with an escort of 500 horsemen, rode to Bath, to confer with Prince Rupert. Back on Clay Hill and in Speen, the Parliamentarians, exhausted by the march and the fighting, lay down and slept in blissful ignorance that next morning would find them in possession of the battlefield.

At Second Newbury, each side lost about 500 men and, predictably, both claimed the victory; although the Parliamentarians remained on the field, ambitious plans they might have had to assert their numerical superiority and gain success had completely gone by the board. A week later, Prince Rupert took 1,500 men to relieve Boys at Donnington and recover their guns, while a party under Colonel Gage relieved Basing House.

THE BATTLE OF AULDEARN 9 MAY 1645

Many authorities consider the Battle of Auldearn, although it only involved small forces, to be the most brilliant battle of the English Civil War. It was a classic victory for the Marquis of Montrose, an outstanding commander of that period.

Under Colonel Sir John Hurry (later to turn his coat and serve under Montrose – both were executed in Edinburgh after the Carbisdale defeat in 1650) an English force was withdrawing to entice Montrose out of friendly hills and into Covenanter country. On the evening of 8 May, at the little village of Auldearn on a ridge of high treeless ground between the valleys of the Findhorn and the Nairn, Montrose posted his pickets carefully, pitched his camp and settled down for the night. His army, less than half the size of the English force, consisted of 250 horsemen under Louis Gordon and Lord James Aboyne, about 800 Irish under Alastair Colkitto MacDonald, and some 600 Highlanders.

Stealthily advancing towards Auldearn, Hurry lost the essential element of surprise when some of his men fired their muskets to clear out loaded charges, and Montrose's men heard the reports. In the little time remaining Montrose made hasty plans and dispositions. Alastair MacDonald, a physically strong man and a born leader with little time for tactics, was placed in command of a defensive flank with 250 men of an Irish regiment posted amid the gardens and enclosures of houses south of the church and 300 of the Gordon foot placed on the more easily defensible Castle Hill. Macdonald's line was about 400 yards long. His men were instructed, by maintaining a continuous fire, to delude the enemy into thinking that the entire force was defending the village. Montrose wished to give the impression that he was personally in command in the centre of the position, at the south end of the Gordon foot in the angled line, so he planted the Royal Standard there. He concealed the rest of his infantry and the cavalry in a dip behind the crown of the ridge on his left wing. This force consisted of 800 infantry (two Irish divisions and 100 Gordons) on the right, and on the left two bodies of horse, the right under Aboyne and the left under Lord Louis Gordon. The Royal force had no guns because its rapid marches of the past eight months had precluded recovery of the guns buried after the Battle of Aberdeen.

Montrose's dispositions, though hurried, were brilliant, for once the English were committed, he was free to swing his horse round from their cover and take the English in their right flank. Furthermore, the English cavalry would have decreased mobility among the village gardens if it attacked MacDonald, thinking his force to be the entire Royal army.

Hurry deployed his force to advance in some depth on a narrow front – a good disposition for attacking a weaker force in a relatively unknown position – and left his artillery and waggon-train on the road. On the right was Lawer's regiment (directed against that part of the position held by MacDonald's Irish regiment); on the left was Loudon's, its left flank hampered by the bog, advancing against the Gordons on Castle Hill. These two regiments were supported by

Lothian on the right and Buchanan on the left, and on the right of the Lothian regiment was the Moray horse (150 troopers under Drummond). In reserve from left to right were Seaforth's 600-strong Mackenzie contingent, the 500 Northern Levies and Sutherland's contingent of 500. Hurry's cavalry reserve of 250 remained in the rear, ready for pursuit or exploitation. The force totalled 2,000 regular and 1,600 local foot, with 400 horse and nine guns.

The battle began with the impatient MacDonald, temperamentally unsuited to stand on the defensive, leaving the shelter of the enclosures to hurl his Irish at Lawer's regiment, which, with the help of Lothian's regiment, was able to force the Irish infantry back into the enclosures. Unable to take advantage of their superior numbers on this narrow front, however, the Covenanters could make no further headway against the outnumbered Irish who fought desperately among the pigsties and gardens of the village. Having observed these events from the crest of Castle Hill, Montrose ran across to the hollow on his left from where Gordon's unseasoned horse could see nothing of the fight in the village. It was essential that they be sent into the action with dash and spirit, so Montrose cried out: 'MacDonald drives all before him! Is his Clan to have all the honours this day?'

It was enough to send Gordon's horse charging from cover, screaming a war cry as they flung themselves down the slope and into the flank of Hurry's advancing troops. The Moray horse, still disordered after negotiating a bog, was so shocked by this sudden and unexpected attack that their commander, Drummond, gave the wrong word of command and, instead of wheeling round to present a front to the new attack, the horsemen wheeled left to override some of their own infantry while offering their backs to the hotly pursuing Gordons, who emptied many a saddle in the chase. Aboyne, with the rest of the cavalry, had swung in against the flank and rear of the infantry attacking MacDonald and was making great inroads through their closely packed ranks. The Gordon foot broke from their left flank cover on Castle Hill and, in a steady disciplined mass, swept down upon Hurry's four infantry regiments, as, among the enclosures and pigsties, Alastair rallied his Irishmen and charged into the enemy's reeling centre.

Ferociously assailed in front, flank and rear, the four regiments fought gallantly, but with the Northern Levies on their left rear, the

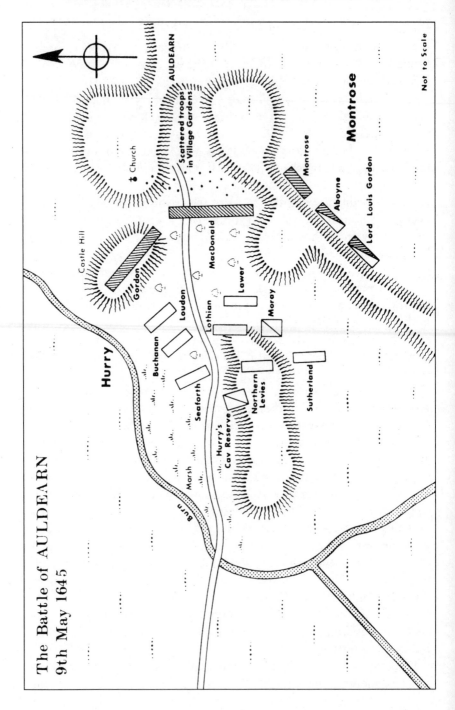

The Battle of AULDEARN
9th May 1645

Not to Scale

AULDEARN

Church

Castle Hill

Scattered troops
in Village Gardens

Montrose

Aboyne

Lord Louis Gordon

Montrose

Gordon

MacDonald

Lawer

Moray

Loudon

Lothian

Sutherland

Buchanan

Hurry

Seaforth

Northern
Levies

Hurry's
Cav Reserve

Marsh

Burn

cavalry reserve, and Sutherland's and Seaforth's men fleeing without striking a blow, the Covenanter army degenerated into a mob and fled the field. They were hotly pursued for fourteen miles, leaving behind 2,000 dead on the field as Hurry made his escape with less than 100 horsemen.

21

The Dutch Wars and the War of the Grand Alliance 1672–79 and 1689–97

Now the set-piece battles of the pike era, with both armies remaining for days in battle array even when moving, no longer existed. The greater mobility of infantry coupled with increased fire-power (due to more and better muskets as musketeers replaced pikemen) meant that a properly handled weaker force could pin down a stronger·one, giving increased opportunities for strategic and tactical manoeuvre so that generalship became important.

The seventeenth century saw a marked increase in the scale of warfare and the size of armies. Louis XIV maintained a military establishment of 400,000 and kept more than 100,000 in the field. Adopted from the Swedes, the basic French infantry formation of the mid-seventeenth century was a battalion or regiment of 600 to 800 men, on a front of about 100 yards, organised in one line six deep with the pikes in the centre and the muskets on the flanks. The battalions formed in checker-board fashion with a proportion of the musketeers in separate detachments to support the cavalry. At the same period, French cavalry consisted of the Gendarmerie; the Carabiniers, numbering about 3,000 and armed with rifled carbine; light cavalry, and by 1690 there were forty-three Dragoon regiments who used the newly developed musket and bayonet.

The Marquis François Louvois, called the Father of Modern War, created a new French army when he and Turenne realised that there was no need to manoeuvre soldiers in masses since pikemen no longer had to combine with musketeers – the day of the line formation had dawned and the infantry of France were trained to advance in three ranks, firing volleys at the word of command. Besides reorganising and training the new French army, Louvois built a chain of well-equipped fortresses enabling an army to march with the certainty that there was everything they needed ahead, including heavy artillery, while an enemy army would find it immensely difficult to destroy or capture these Vauban-built fortresses. Under Louvois, the French army became the first force on the Continent to be completely uniformed, as they simulated warfare in tactical war games on the plains of Chalons.

In 1672 France invaded Holland. At the same time, Turenne, Condé and Luxembourg crossed the Rhine with 100,000 troops in three columns. It was a triumphant procession until William of Orange, the new Dutch leader, halted them by flooding hundreds of square miles of his country. Fearing Louis's ambitions, Brandenburg and Spain formed a coalition against France, and in the autumn of 1672 Louis XIV dispersed his army into small packets: Turenne to Westphalia, Condé to Alsace and others to Spanish Netherlands. The remainder awaited the freezing of the flood-waters in Holland, and during the winter Louis (aided by de Vauban) led an army of 40,000 to capture Maastricht. But Condé and Luxembourg were less successful.

Turenne on the Middle Rhine, with a force that never exceeded 20,000, engaged in a dual of tactical manoeuvring with the veteran Montecuccoli's Imperial Army. At first Montecuccoli, without fighting a battle, gained his objectives by manoeuvre; but in the Rhineland during 1674–75, although Turenne was outnumbered by 20,000 men, he outwitted Montecuccoli by throwing his forces astride the Rhine, controlling both banks by a pontoon bridge. Turenne finally manoeuvred Montecuccoli into a bad position near Sasbach, only to be killed by a cannon-ball while drawing up his forces. Before that, in June 1674, Turenne defeated Imperial forces at Sinsheim, and in October fought the inconclusive Battle of Enzheim; John Churchill, late Duke of Marlborough, led the single English regiment at this battle. In November-December 1674, Turenne marched southward over snow-covered mountains to invade Alsace, winning the Battle of Turckheim in January 1675 to complete a brilliant campaign. Meanwhile, Frederick William of Brandenburg formed an Alliance with Lorraine, Spain and the Holy Roman Empire and refused the terms hastily offered by the French; the English signed a separate peace and remained neutral for the rest of the war. The French monarch withdrew the last of his army from Dutch soil just twenty-two months after launching the invasion.

With an army of Dutch, Danish, Spanish and German troops, William marched into the French-occupied Spanish Netherlands. During May to August 1674, Condé held the Meuse with 45,000 against William's 65,000. On 11 August, seeking a tactical advantage, Condé attacked at Senef with only half his army and no artillery and gained a victory that forced William to withdraw and drop his invasion plans. This bloody encounter cost the Allies 10,000 killed and 20,000 wounded and captured; French losses were 10,000. It taught Europe's soldiers many professional lessons – that with soldiers shoulder-to-shoulder exchanging volleys at a few yards' range, and with only iron discipline keeping them firm and able to close up their tattered ranks, the resulting heavy casualties meant that battles had to be infrequent and then only by mutual consent. They learned that infantry lines were vulnerable to cavalry attack and that they had to be protected at all times by their own cavalry; infantry lines only worked successfully on level, unbroken ground and could be completely thrown out of gear by a ditch or a hillock. So the late seventeenth century became a period of sieges – contests for fortified river and canal towns with the French usually successful because de Vauban was the master of siege-craft and fortifications. From 1675 to 1678, the French conducted operations in Germany, Lorraine, Sicily, Flanders and in the Rhineland before treaties divided the towns of that region between France and Spain.

The War of the Grand Alliance (or the War of the League of Augsburg) was fought from 1689 to 1697 because arrogant and ambitious France, seeking to dominate Europe, caused the Protestant Princes of Germany to align themselves with William of Orange's Dutch forces in an anti-French coalition (the League of Augsburg, 1688). In 1689 France declared war on Spain and a few weeks later England, Spain, Savoy, Brandenburg, Saxony, Hanover and Bavaria formed the Grand Alliance. Fought mostly in the Netherlands, the war contained numerous sieges and both sides won victories on land. At Walcourt in 1689, an allied army of 35,000 under Prince George Frederick of Waldeck and including an English contingent of

8,000 under Marlborough, defeated the French under the Duke of Humiand de Villars. In 1690 at Fleures, Luxembourg of France with 45,000 men defeated Prince George Frederick's English, Spanish and German force of 36,000 by means of a bold double cavalry envelopment. In Italy, the French gained Savoy at Staffarda when de Catinat defeated Victor Amadeus. Luxembourg stormed Mons and Hal in 1691 as William failed to intervene, and at Leuze, after a rapid night march, routed William's army as they prepared to go into winter quarters.

While de Catinat progressed in Piedmont, de Noailles gained successes in Spain; and in 1692 de Vauban, supported by Luxembourg, took Namur with William's relieving force held up by rain and floods. In the same year, William unsuccessfully attacked the French entrenchments at Steenkerke and had to withdraw, covered by the British Guards. In 1693 William's army was routed at Neerwinden by Luxembourg, who could have ended the war had he pursued. The undefeated Luxembourg died in 1695 and was succeeded by the incompetent de Villeroi. From June to September William's luck turned, and he conducted a successful campaign to recapture Namur. In 1696, a British landing near Brest failed completely and throughout that summer William was immobilised in Flanders by the French, reinforced from Savoy. Discouraged, he began secret negotiations which resulted in the Treaty of Ryswick in 1697.

War had now reached the point where armies of anything from 40,000 to 100,000 men formed in lines on a front of several miles, with the commander handling the battle from the rear. By the end of the century the French armies were past their peak and handicapped by endless directions from Versailles which reduced their mobility by maintaining armies on many widely separated fronts. During the seventeenth and eighteenth centuries a relatively new weapon was developed on the Continent: called the hand-grenade, it was a hollow, cast-iron globe a few inches in diameter containing gunpowder and a short fuse, lit before throwing. The grenadier who threw it was a strong, tall man capable of hurling the missile the greatest possible distance. By 1667 four or five grenadiers were attached to each company of French infantry and a separate company of Grenadiers was formed three years later. Their equipment included a fusil or light flintlock musket and a pouch of grenades with a slow match. The British followed suit and the Grenadiers wore buff crossbelts over redcoats and a fur cap with a baggy crown which hung down the back; later it was stiffened upright to form the mitre cap of the eighteenth-century Grenadier and Fusilier.

THE MAJOR BATTLES OF THE DUTCH WARS 1672–78

During his seventy-two-year reign Louis XIV of France (1643–1715) fought four major wars. The War of Devolution (1667–68) arose from his claim to succession of the Spanish throne in 1665, when he claimed the entire Spanish Netherlands. In this 'war', without fighting a battle, France occupied and retained twelve fortified towns on the border of the Spanish Netherlands (modern Belgium), including among them Lille, Tournay and Oudenarde.

Angered by the opposition of the Dutch during this war, Louis marched against them, declaring war in March 1672, to begin a war exclusively of battles against the Dutch and allies, ending with the Treaty of Nijmegen in August 1678. In chronological order, those battles were:

Maastricht II	1673
Sinsheim	1674
Seneffe	1674
Enzheim	1674
Turckheim	1675
Sasbach	1675

Turenne's Rhineland Campaign of 1674–75 arose from his mission of protecting Alsace against the Elector of Brandenburg and those German princes who had declared war on France, some of whom were hastily assembling armies north and south of Heidelberg. On 14 June 1674 Turenne, in an effort to get his blow in first, suddenly pushed his army across the Rhine at Philippsburg. Imperial Generals Enea Sylvio Caprara and Duke Charles Leopold of Lorraine moved 9,000 men – 7,000 were cavalry – to block the French Generals' advance, with Caprara in what he considered to be an unbreakable position behind the river Elsenz. It failed to halt Turenne, who crossed the river and fell on the Imperial force at Sinsheim, twenty miles to the east, on 16 June, driving through their outposts to vigorously attack 10,000 men of surprised Duke Charles and Caprara in a position on a plateau above rugged heights.

The battle that followed was hard and costly to both sides, with the French winning a complete victory, routing the Imperialists who had 2,000 killed and 600 captured; Turenne lost 1,200 killed. On orders from Paris, Turenne retired back across the Rhine, but recrossed at Philippsburg on 3 July with 16,000 men and set about devastating the Palatinate throughout July, August and September.

Now under Prince Alexandre-Hippolyte of Bournonville, the Imperial forces seized neutral Strasbourg on 24 September, after bridging the Rhine while Turenne was occupied to the north-west. The French commander at once moved into the area, seeking an opportunity to attack his numerically superior opponents – Bournonville having 38,000 men and fifty guns against Turenne's 22,000 and thirty guns. On 4 October 1674, although the Imperialists were strongly entrenched in a defensive position, Turenne deliberately attacked and for most of the day held the initiative without being able to drive Bournonville's army from their positions. At the end of the day, the French gave up their attempts and withdrew from the inconclusive battle, losing about 3,500 men against the 3,000 of the Allies, who also withdrew.

During the Autumn of 1674 Turenne withdrew to Dettweiler in Middle Alsace, seemingly going into winter quarters; the Allied forces were reinforced by the arrival of an army of 57,000 men under Frederick William, the 'Great' Elector of Brandenburg, who made their quarters in towns stretching from Belfort to Strasbourg. Turenne now planned one of the boldest ventures of his distinguished career, misleading the enemy by ostentatiously placing the fortresses of Middle Alsace in a state of defence, whilst moving his army elsewhere. In very cold weather, Turenne marched secretly southwards, circling behind the Vosges Mountains over snow-covered heights, his forces split into small bodies to mislead possible enemy spies, until reuniting near Belfort and marching rapidly into Alsace from the south. Bournonville woke up to the fact that he had been out-manoeuvred and tried unsuccessfully to halt Turenne at Mulhouse on 29 December, but his scattered forces were only able to withdraw towards Strasbourg.

Then, on 5 January 1675, Turenne fell upon the enemy at Turckheim near Colmar, where the Great Elector stood, with a slight numerical superiority, on the defensive. In a battle that resembled its predecessor, Enzheim, Turenne forced his exhausted troops to attack vigorously against what turned out to be but a token and perfunctory resistance; after taking light casualties, the Allies retreated from the field in semi-rout, pursued by the triumphant French as far as the Rhine. Thus, Turenne in what must be one of the most brilliant campaigns in military history, had won back all Alsace in a single stroke.

Sadly, within half-a-year, Turenne was dead. After Turckheim, there followed a war of manoeuvre between the French leader and his old opponent Montecuccoli east of the Rhine, between Philipps-burg and Strasbourg, which Turenne prevented the Allied leader from taking. Typically forcing Montecuccoli's numerically superior army to battle, Turenne prepared to attack them in a strong defensive position at Sasbach, where he had trapped them in a seemingly hopeless position, but was killed on 27 July by a cannonball, early in the battle. This caused his subordinates to falter and lose their advantage. Although inflicting double their own casualties on the Allies, at the end of the day the French broke and fled back across the Rhine.

Whilst history was being made in Alsace, significant military operations were taking place elsewhere. In the Spanish Netherlands, in Brabant Province in August 1674, the Great Condé was fighting his last battle against William of Orange, whose first great land battle it was. Seeing the chance of intercepting the Allied army on the march, Condé boldly attacked, but with only half his army and without artillery; this was probably stimulated by William withdraw-ing from an initial probing attack, when he realised the impenetra-bility of the French position. This movement exposed a flank of the Dutch-Spanish force which encouraged Condé to attack at Seneffe six miles south-west of Nivelles, on 11 August 1674, triggering off a fierce struggle, with the Allies rallying after their opening set-back and recovering lost ground. Both sides disengaged their forces after battling for nearly seventeen hours, with neither able to gain any tangible advantage, withdrawing during the night, when at least one-seventh of the total troops involved had been killed. Being joined next day by the remainder of his army, Condé tried to renew the battle, but the Allies had withdrawn completely and the best the French could do was to claim a tactical as well as a strategical victory. In numbers, total losses were more than 10,000 killed and 5,000 captured (mostly wounded) on the Allied side, plus another 15,000 wounded; French casualties were nearly 10,000.

MAJOR BATTLES OF THE WAR OF THE GRAND ALLIANCE 1689–97

Walcourt	1689
Fleurus	1690
Staffarda	1690
Leuze	1691
Steenkerke	1692
Neerwinden (Landen)	1693
Marsaglia	1693
Namur I	1695

The outstanding aspect of this war was that the principle antagonist – the French – had an incalculable advantage in that they had one command-source, as opposed to the Allies, beset by bickering and disagreements both political and strategical. More than that, their armies had the great boon of interior lines against these divided enemies, holding the hub of a strategic wheel and sallying-forth along its spokes, while their divided opponents had to traverse the lengthier rim.

As late as 1690, armies had a few pikemen remaining in their ranks, although that ancient and historical weapon had, in all armies, been generally replaced by the bayonet.

In 1688 William of Orange became King of England, his accession being denied recognition by the French king, who dispatched troops to aid the rebel Irish against the English. Subsequently, it was decided to send ten battalions of British troops, under command of General John Churchill, who had recently been created Duke of Marlborough, to join the Dutch and their allies – this force of 3,000 men became part of the 35,000-strong army of Prince George Frederick of Waldeck in Flanders. On 25 August 1689 this Allied force came into contact with a French force, under the Duke d'Humieres and the Duke of Villars at Walcourt. During the course of the battle, British infantry under Colonel Hodges of the 16th Foot beat off French attacks. The French were then charged by Marlborough at the head of the Household Cavalry, who gave them a severe beating. Although a relatively minor action, it is important because it was the first occasion for many years that the British had found themselves up against the French, besides being the first instance in which Marlborough shone when confronted by a Marshal of France.

The defeated French commander at Walcourt – Duke d'Humieres – was soon replaced by Marshal Francois de Luxembourg, an outstanding French General who rapidly became the supreme French commander. Although he was not a popular leader with the King, it is said that he never lost a battle. In the Fleurus Campaign that followed in 1690 his troops faithfully adhered to his marching-order, which was followed by armies up to the time of Napoleon: 'March always in the order in which you encamp, or propose to encamp, or fight'. Subsequently before and leading up to the Battle of Fleurus on 1 July 1690, the French army under his command advanced for four days in close order, with front flank and rear-guards, besides being covered on all sides by a cavalry screen.

At the outset of the war, both the Grand Alliance nations and their French enemies poured troops into the Spanish Netherlands and, in Summer 1690, Prince George Frederick of Waldeck, commanding an army of 40,000, occupied a strong position in the rear of marshy brooks, and with both flanks anchored on villages, at Fleurus in Hainault Province. This strong position did not deter the hunchback Luxembourg, who conceived a plan of attack which, for boldness and broadness of vision, can hardly be matched during that century. Pressing forward in the orderly manner described earlier, the 45,000-strong French army reached Fleurus on 30 June 1690, and on the next day, 1 July, Luxembourg launched a frontal assault while sending his cavalry out in a double envelopment of Waldeck's position. His left-wing cavalry drove through the woods to envelop the Allied right, then he personally led the cavalry of the French right, supported by infantry and artillery, in a wide sweep round Waldeck's left – it was all done with such perfect timing that the three attacks struck the enemy lines in rapid succession. Waldeck's frantic efforts to save the situation added nothing but confusion;

soon he was reduced to about 25 per cent of his cavalry and about fourteen battalions of infantry, which formed square and retired to some nearby broken ground.

His great victory cost Luxembourg 2,500 casualties; the Allies lost 5/6,000 killed and 8,000 captured, plus the loss of forty-eight guns and 150 colours. The French commander wished to follow up and exploit by striking deep into Holland, but was ordered by Louis to keep abreast of the other French armies manoeuvring on the Meuse and the Moselle.

However, the war did not stay in the Netherlands, and in 1690 had spread to the Duchy of Savoy, south of Switzerland, which had joined the Grand Alliance in the previous year, and was invaded by an army under General Nicolas de Catinat, sent by Louis to Piedmont. Advancing during August and September, the French army encountered the troops of Savoy, under Duke Victor Amadeus II of Savoy, at Staffarda on the upper reaches of the Po, on 18 August 1690. Although not a particularly proficient commander, Catinat overwhelmed his opponents, and proceeded to overrun most of the duchy with very little resistance.

In 1691, back in the Netherlands, Marlborough commanded a British force of about 23,000 men as part of the army of William III; no serious fighting occurred, except for an unsuccessful attempt to relieve Mons, under siege by Louis in person. Later in the year William III of England came out to take command of the alliance armies, replacing Prince George Frederick of Waldeck who, in mid-September, had been beaten by Luxembourg for the second time. This occurred at Leuze on 20 September, when Luxembourg had pressed forward from Fleurus, taken Mons in April and, after a rapid night march by the French cavalry, had routed Waldeck's Dutch and German army as they were preparing to go into winter quarters.

The 1692 campaign in the Spanish Netherlands was opened by the French troops of Louis XIV with a thirty-six-day siege, taking Namur on 5 June, a victory which forced the Alliance armies to take the initiative as it appeared to open the road to Brussels. Unsuccessful attempts were made to bring Luxembourg to battle in June and July, then, with false information misleading the French commander, William marched all night to surprise the French encamped at Steenkerke, in Hainault Province. Subsequently, Luxembourg was caught with his forces divided when, at dawn on 3 August 1692

William's vanguard of 15,000 swept into the French position, causing heavy casualties. Now began the bloodiest battle of the war as the conflict developed into a race between the two commanders, each rushing fresh troops to the scene as William realised his mistake in not initially striking with his entire strength. The French commander displayed the cool proficiency expected of him, efficiently reorganising his regiments under fire and speedily dispatching reinforcements to wherever they were needed. It was an exacting test of generalship and his troops did not let him down, taking heavy casualties as infantry formations exchanged volleys at close range – his Swiss contingent fought fiercely against General Hugh Mackay's eight English regiments, before finally giving way. French counterattacks began to level things up as the crack Household troops of France arrived, to fight a bloody battle marked by close-range gunfire and cold steel. Luxembourg managed to bring in enough fresh troops to gradually beat back William's men and take most of their guns, and by noon the Alliance attack had collapsed and their whole army was in retreat, covered by the Guards.

Distinguishing themselves by outstanding bravery while taking heavy losses – the Grenadier Guards and the Royal Warwicks in particular – the ten British battalions lost half of the 8,000 casualties sustained by William, including two generals; the French lost slightly fewer, causing Louis to impose further restrictions on Luxembourg's movements.

The two master-engineers of the day had their theories competitively tested against each other in 1692 when, from 25 May until 5 June, Dutch Baron Menno van Coehoorn, builder of Namur's defences, defended the city against France's Marquis de Vauban, legendary military engineer, then under the direct command of Louis and supported by Luxembourg. De Vauban took the city in thirty-six days at a cost of 2,600 casualties, against double that number among the Dutch-Spanish-German garrison. William attempted to relieve the besieged city but failed, being hampered by persistent rains and the flooding of the Mehaigne, a tributary of the Meuse.

It was at Namur that de Vauban perfected his most effective method of assault, having previously employed large numbers of guns to make a main breach, then using a succession of balls to 'cut' through the defences in one spot. Now, he used reduced charges in his guns so that their missiles dropped in such a manner as to ricochet and take out men, guns and everything else encountered – it was a deadly weapon when proficiently practised and difficult to counter with any known defences of the day.

Another important military innovation spawned at the Siege of Namur was the development of the Grenadiers. As already described in this chapter, these were big, strong and brave storm troops who rapidly became acknowledged as the elite of all European armies. Selected French infantrymen were trained in the use of the grenade, a comparatively recent innovation, and it is reported that as many as 20,000 grenades were used at Namur, with results that justified the formation of special battalions in the French army.

William III, the Allied leader, despite devotion to the art of war, was never more than a gallant trier, consistently out-generalled by Luxembourg – and it was to happen again in 1693. In the fourth summer of this continental war, the King-General had taken up what could be considered an almost impregnable position at the small village of Neerwinden, north-west of Liège, its convex front harbouring 100 guns, its right wing behind the small River Geete, with a marshy stream protecting the left flank. Here William positioned 70,000 troops, after sending 20,000 to the support of Liège, threatened by de Noailles; Luxembourg, with 80,000 men, 40,000 of them veterans, marched to Neerwinden and opened the battle on 29 July 1693. The French began by attacking the village in William's centre, being repulsed at least twice with heavy losses, but causing William to withdraw troops freely from both flanks to withstand the powerful French central assaults – this was as Luxembourg had anticipated and hoped for. Now he launched a double attack on both of the Allied flanks, that on the left becoming the main assault as the defenders fell into confusion changing front; the fierce onslaught buckled the Alliance line, then the Allied cavalry on the left wing fled the field. Now followed a rout, and the bulk of William's infantry – Dutch, Spanish and Germans – were driven into the Landen and Geete streams to drown.

Before William could extricate his army, he had lost 18,000 men – killed, wounded and captured – and 104 guns; although grievous, French casualties were less than half this total. It is reported that, in the beginning of the battle, the Coldstream Guards and the Royal Fusiliers held out against repeated frontal attacks by five brigades of French infantry, and flank attacks by the French Household Cavalry.

Again, Luxembourg was refused permission to pursue; had he been able to do so, William might well have had to sue for peace. It was Luxembourg's last major battle, he died in 1693.

Meanwhile, the war continued in the Duchy of Savoy, although the Spanish Netherlands remained the main theatre of operations. In Savoy, the French General Nicolas de Catinat, victor at Staffarda three years earlier, once again came up against Duke Victor Amadeus II, who had organised a new force formed of Austrian, Spanish and English troops. On 4 October 1693 this Allied army took on de Catinat at Marsaglia, near the Po, and once again found themselves no match for the experienced and well-trained French army, who drove them across the river with the loss of several thousand men.

In 1695, the general situation had somewhat changed as bravery and determination had its reward at last, when William finally had his first successful campaign. The Alliance commander, despite a steady string of reverses, still maintained a considerable army in the field, and in June to September 1695 captured Dixmude and Huy, and then set about besieging Namur, assisted by Baron Coehoorn, the defeated commander during the previous siege. The dead Luxembourg had been replaced by the far less talented Marshal the Duke of Villeroi, and the garrison of 14,000 men at Namur were commanded by Duke Louis de Boufflers. De Vauban was not present on this occasion. Early in June the siege began and the Alliance troops steadily pressed their assault; eleven British battalions were among the besiegers and were subsequently given the battle honour 'Namur', the first won by British troops on the continent of Europe. A capitulation was finally forced on 1 September, after sixty days of fighting in which the attackers lost 18,000 men in comparison to 8,000 French losses.

By 1697 both sides had fought themselves to a standstill and the war was virtually deadlocked, so Louis XIV arranged the inconclusive treaty of Ryswich from 20 September-20 October 1697. It was not a lasting settlement and four years later the War of the Spanish Succession broke out. However, something good had come out of it, at least so far as the British were concerned. The British soldier had gained experience and firmly established his reputation in European fighting, providing a foretaste of achievements and quality when led by a commander worthy of him.

Epilogue

The End of the Road

EXCEPT POSSIBLY IN a great clan battle in 1688, when Macintosh fought Macdonald, the last occasion on which the longbow was used for war in Britain is said to have been at Tippermuir in 1644. Here the Marquis of Montrose, upholding the cause of Charles I, routed the Covenanters; his army, having little ammunition for their few muskets, used hails of stones and ancient bows to bring them victory. Since there were so many more battles during the next few years of that unhappy period, it is quite likely that the bow was used to good effect on other occasions – it seems unlikely that it should have been completely abandoned in the middle of a civil war. In 1622 the longbow was no longer mentioned in the list of weapons with which the military forces were to be armed.

One of the great puzzles of military history is why artillery and fire-arms replaced the longbow so rapidly when the latter, right up to the time of Waterloo and beyond, was capable of far greater range, rate of fire and accuracy. In 1625, in his pamphlet *Double-armed Man*, W. Neade gave the effective range of the bow as sixteen to twenty score yards and claimed that the archer could discharge six arrows while the musketeer loaded and fired but once. In 1792 Lieutenant-Colonel Lee, of the 44th Regiment, strongly advocated the use of the longbow in preference to the flint-lock musket. To support his case he gave the following reasons:

1. Because a man may shoot as truly with the bow as with the common musket.

2. He can discharge four arrows in the time of charging and discharging one bullet.

3. His object is not taken from his view by the smoke of his own side.

4. A flight of arrows coming upon them terrifies and disturbs the enemy's attention to his business.

5. An arrow sticking in any part of a man puts him hors de combat until it is extracted.

6. Bows and arrows are more easily made anywhere than muskets and ammunition.

As late as 1846 the effective range of the musket in common use in the British army was, for all practical purposes, only 100 to 150 yards – the common dictum being not to fire until you could see the whites of the enemy's eyes! Why then was the bow abandoned so early in favour of the crude fire-arms of the period?

On the battlefield, archery has certain unavoidable drawbacks affecting both the man and his weapon. To use his longbow effectively, the archer needed space around him – he had to stand to deliver his shaft. Not only did this make him vulnerable to the elements, it also turned him into a good target; the whole course of warfare was altered when the breech-loading rifle enabled the soldier to re-load his arm whilst lying down. Although rain had an adverse effect upon the rate of fire of a musket, it rendered the longbow useless; wind could also severely compromise the archer. However, the crucial factor was that the archer had to be an athlete in the best physical condition, whereas the man behind the gun could function even in the state of weary debility produced by the cold, wet and hunger of extended active service. Mediaeval commanders were well aware of the importance of maintaining both the health and the stature of their archers – they mounted them on horses whenever possible, recruited them from the fixed heraldic rank of yeoman (the highest held by men of low degree) and even encouraged practice at the butts.

Although the longbow won Crécy, Poitiers and Agincourt, together with a host of smaller engagements, the Hundred Years War was won by the French. By better adapting themselves to the newly invented and primitive artillery and by using them with a superior technique, the French were able to recapture the towns and provinces lost to the English, eventually nullifying the effects of all the English victories throughout the Hundred Years War.

Perhaps regrettably, today it is only the incurable romanticist who will claim special virtues for the longbow as against fire-arms. But, in the end, he will have grudgingly to admit that the fire-arm has proved to be what the bow could not become – a perfectible weapon. Any good shot in an average modern small-bore rifle club can get a 'possible' out of every ten shots aimed at a two-inch circle 100 yards away; he will be able to do this consistently and without hesitation. The 'gold' of an archery target is as big as a saucer, yet Horace A. Ford held for years the record of twenty-eight hits in seventy-five shots at sixty yards. No archer, however skilful, can be absolutely certain within several inches where a single shaft will land. This uncertainty contrasts with the accuracy achieved by Queen Victoria when, at the inauguration of the National Rifle Association at Wimbledon on 2 July 1860, she pulled a silken cord which fired a Whitworth rifle on a fixed rest, placing a round only one-and-a-quarter inches from the centre of the target!

BIBLIOGRAPHY

Sources consulted when writing this Book

GENERAL

Adair, R. and Young, P., *Hastings to Culloden* (1964)
Ashdown, Charles, *Armour and Weapons in the Middle Ages* (1925)
Birnie, A., *The Art of War* (1942)
Boudet, J. (ed.), *The Ancient Art of Warfare* (1969)
Bowood, R., *Soldiers, Soldiers* (1965)
Brodie, B. & Brodie, F., *From Crossbow to H. Bomb* (New York, 1962)
Burne, A. H., *The Battlefields of England* (1951)
   More Battlefields of England (1952)
   The Art of War on Land (1944)
Canby, Courtland, *A History of Weaponry* (1963)
Chandler, D., *Battlefields of Europe* (1965)
Clephan R. C., *The Defensive Armour, and the Weapons, and Engines of War of Medieval Times and the Renaissance* (1900)
Coggins, J., The Fighting Men (1966)
Creasy, E. S., *The 15 Decisive Battles of the World* (1908)
Cruickshank C. G., *Army Royal* (1963)
   Elizabeth's Army (1966)
Denison, G. T., *A History of Cavalry* (1913)
Dupuy, R. E. and T. N., *The Encyclopaedia of Military History from 3500 BC to the Present* (1970)

BIBLIOGRAPHY

Eggenberger, D., *A Dictionary of Battles* (1967)
Ellecott, S. E., *Spearman to Minuteman* (1965)
  Conscripts on the March (1965)
Falls, C., *The Art of War* (1961)
  Great Military Battles (1964)
Featherstone, D. F., *The Bowmen of England* (1967)
  The History of the English Longbow (USA, 1995)
  Warriors and Warfare in Ancient & Medieval Times (1997)
Fortescue, J., *History of the British Army* (1899–1927)
Fuller, J. F. C., *Decisive Battles of the Western World* (1956)
Geyl, P., *Revolt of the Netherlands* (1966)
Halevy, D., *Armies and Their Arms* (1962)
Hargreaves, R., *The Enemy at the Gate* (1945)
Hogg, Brig. O. F. G., *English Artillery 1326–1716* (1963)
Hughes, B. P., *British Smoothbore Artillery* (1969)
Keen, M. H., *The Laws of War in the Middle Ages* (1965)
Kinross, J., *Walking and Exploring the Battlefields of Britain* (1933 &
  1988)
  The Battlefields of Britain (1979)
Laffin, J., *Links of Leadership* (1966)
Liddell-Hart, B. H., *The Decisive Wars of History* (1929)
Manucy. A., *Artillery Through the Ages* (Washington, 1949)
Martin, W. C., *History of the Crossbow* (1936)
Montgomery of Alamein, *A History of Warfare* (1968)
Montross, L., *War Through the Ages* (1944)
Oakshott, R. E., *The Archeology of Weapons* (1960)
Oman, C. W. C., *The History of the Art of War in the XIV Century*
  (1924)
  The Art of War in the Middle Ages 1278–1515 (1953)
  Warwick (1954)
O'Neil, B. H. S. and J., *Castles and Cannons* (1966)
Palmer, M., *Warfare* (1972)
Pearson, H. L., *A History of Firearms* (New York, 1961)
  Book of the Gun (1962)
Pope, D., *Guns* (1965)
Preston, R. A. and Wise, S. F., and Werner, H. O., *Men in Arms* (1956)
Roy, Ian (ed.), *The Hapsburg-Valois Wars and the French Wars of
  Religion* (1972)
Sellman, J., *Medieval English Warfare* (1960)
Smurthwaite, D., *Battlefields of Britain* (Ordnance Survey Guide) (1984)
Taylor, F. L., *The Art of War 1494–1529* (1921)
Thompson, J. W., *Wars of Religion in France 1559–1576* (1958)

[211]

Treece, H. and Oakshott, E., *Fighting Men* (1963)
Webb. H. J., *Elizabethan Military Science* (1965)
Wedeck, H. E., *Concise Dictionary of Medieval History* (1963)
Wedgewood, C. V., *Battlefields in Britain* (1944)
Weller, J., *Weapons and Tactics* (1966)
Whitman, J. E. A., *How Wars are Fought* (1944)

AGINCOURT

Burne, A., *The Agincourt War: A Military History of the Latter Part of the Hundred Years War* (1956)
Hibbert, Christopher, *Agincourt* (1964)
Nicholas, Sir H., *History of the Battle of Agincourt* (1971)

THE WARS OF THE ROSES

Lander, J. R., *The Wars of the Roses* (1965)
Ramsay, Sir James, *Lancaster and York* (1892)
Rowse, A. L., *Bosworth Field* (1966)

THE THIRTY YEARS WAR

Maland, D. & Hooper, J., *The Thirty Years War* (1971)
Polisensky, J. V., *The Thirty Years War* (1972)
Wedgwood, C. V., *The Thirty Years War* (1957)

COMMANDERS

Dupuy, T. N., *Gustavus Adolphus* (1970)
Hatton, R. M., *Charles XII of Sweden* (1968)
McMunn, Sir G., *Gustavus Adolphus* (1931)
Watson, F., *Wallenstein* (1938)
Weygand, M., *Turenne* (1929)

THE ENGLISH CIVIL WAR

Adair, J., *Roundhead General William Waller* (1969)
  Cheriton 1644 (1973)
Ashley, M., *Cromwell's Generals* (1967)
Atkyns, R. & Young, P. (eds), *The Civil War* (1967)
Buchan, J., *Montrose* (1928)
  Oliver Cromwell (1941)
Burne, A. H. & Young, P., *The Great Civil War* (1959)
Edgar, F. T. R., *Sir Ralph Hopton* (1968)
Emberton, W., *Love Loyalty: The Close and Perilous Siege of Basing House 1643–45* (1972)
Firth, P., *Cromwell's Army.* (repr., 1969)
Godwin, G. N., *The Civil War in Hampshire* (1903 repr. 1973)
Rogers, H. C. B., *Battles and Generals of the Civil War* (1968)
Tucker, J. & Winstock, L. S. (ed.), *The English Civil War: A Military Handbook* (1972)
Tucker, N. (ed.), *The Civil War* (1967)
Toynbee, M. & Young, P., *Cropredy Bridge* (1970)
Wedgwood, C. V., *The King's Peace* (1955)
  The King's War (1959)
Wenham, P., *The Great and Close Siege of York 1644* (1971)
Woolrych, A., *The Battles of the English Civil War* (1961)
Young, P., *Edgehill* (1967)
  Marston Moor (1971)
  English Civil War Armies (1973)
  Oliver Cromwell (1962)
Young, P. & Holmes, R., *The English Civil War: A Military History of the Three Civil Wars 1642–1661* (1974)

Index